DOING GENDER,
DOING DIFFERENCE

DOING GENDER,
DOING DIFFERENCE
INEQUALITY, POWER, AND INSTITUTIONAL CHANGE

Edited by

SARAH FENSTERMAKER
CANDACE WEST

ROUTLEDGE
NEW YORK • LONDON

Published in 2002 by
Routledge
29 West 35th Street
New York, NY 10001

Published in Great Britain by
Routledge
11 New Fetter Lane
London EC4P 4EE

Routledge is an imprint of the Taylor & Francis Group.

Printed on acid-free, 250-year-life paper.
Manufactured in the United States of America.

10 9 8 7 6 5 4 3 2 1

Library of Congress Cataloging-in-Publication Data

Doing Gender, Doing Difference : inequality, power, and institutional change / edited by Sarah Fenstermaker, Candace West
    p. cm.
    Includes bibliographical references and index.
    ISBN 0-415-93178-9 (hb.) — ISBN 0-415-93179-7 (pb.)
    1. Sex role. 2. Sex discrimination against women. 3. Equality. 4. Feminist theory. I. Fenstermaker, Sarah, 1949– II. West, Candace.

HQ1075 .D65 2002
305.3—dc21

2001056893

CONTENTS

ACKNOWLEDGMENTS

The work within this book represents two full careers in sociology. Sarah's analysis of the household division of labor was first conceived in her dissertation, completed at Northwestern University in 1976. Candace's original work on the accomplishment of gender emerged from her research on interruption in conversation, first conceived in her dissertation, completed at the University of California Santa Barbara in 1977. To us, this volume represents changes that have shaped our lives, as well as our careers, since "Doing Gender" was first published more than a decade ago: We have gained and lost members of our families, gained and lost relationships, friendships, and colleagues. Predictably, we have likewise lost and regained health, sometimes reshaped and sometimes reclaimed our sense of ourselves as feminists and as sociologists.

The accumulated debt to others that is represented here is staggering. In preparing this manuscript, we were struck by the presence of so many: Family, teachers, colleagues, students, personal friends, and helpers outside the discipline all convinced us that our ideas were interesting and important enough to pursue. In particular, when the work was new and seemed a little intellectually dangerous, we received unwavering support from Don Zimmerman, Bettina Aptheker, Spencer Cahill, Erving Goffman, Nancy Henley, Val Jenness, Nancy Jurik, Judith Lorber, Doni Loseke, Beth Schneider, Dorothy Smith, and Barrie Thorne. Later, as the ideas developed, accumulated, and gained some currency (as well as notoriety), there were additional colleagues who were steadfast and encouraging: Maggie Anderson, Renee Anspach, Maxine Baca Zinn, Bob Connell, Reg Daniel, Carol Brooks Gardner, Evi Glenn, Hazel Hull, Neal King, Molly Moloney,

Laury Oaks, Denise Segura, Judy Stacey, Dana Takagi, and Howard Winant. Over the course of the last decade, our seminar students have been enormously influential in shaping our ideas and in teaching us to think of those ideas as both important *and* always provisional. We thank our students for all their lessons. We also acknowledge the scores of social scientists who have used our formulations to try to make sense of their own data or who attempt to extend their own theoretical contributions by engaging with ours. There can be no more satisfying intellectual experience than influencing the work of others, and we are grateful for it.

This volume also represents the gifts of our collaborators, who coauthored particular papers in their original publication or contributed to the dialogue begun in the *Gender & Society* symposium on our 1995 publication, "Doing Difference" (reprinted here in chapter 6): Don Zimmerman, Diana Dull, Susan Dalton, Molly Moloney, Patricia Hill Collins, Lionel Maldonado, Dana Takagi, Barrie Thorne, Lynn Weber, and Howie Winant. Each of them is deserving of our thanks for showing us new aspects to our thinking.

Last in a long line of esteemed colleagues but singularly crucial to the success of this project is Mitch Duneier. His generosity, offered at the right time, was a gift we will always appreciate. Respect and thanks also go to Ilene Kalish, our editor at Routledge. Our thanks also to Sarah's research assistant, Tonya Lindsey, for her care and construction of the manuscript, and to Kimberly Guinta at Routledge. We also want to recognize, with gratitude, those who don't do what we do but who inexplicably care about it just the same: Rachel, Frank, Anita, Charles, Kate, Leigh, Ray, Robyn, Siu, Stan, and Yonie. What a group.

Finally, this collection symbolizes the most enduring feminist partnership of our careers: twenty-five years of friendship and a decade of collaboration. Each of us greatly admires the other's remarkable intellectual gifts, and over the years we have felt lucky to witness each other's growth. Only a few times did we feel like those other longtime partners Thelma and Louise, riding in the green convertible, the wind blowing in their hair, happily hurtling toward the precipice. We are grateful to have taken the trip together.

Sarah Fenstermaker
Candace West
September 2001

FOREWORD

DOROTHY E. SMITH

It's time that this developing line of thought and research in the sociology of gender was made visible in a volume of this kind. Published articles are dispersed all over the place. The continuities of dialogue aren't apparent for readers who may hold only a fragment here and there. For quite a while now sociologists like me, aware of the work done by feminist sociologists on gender as an accomplishment or the social construction of gender, have watched as postmodernist feminist theorists reinvented the wheel. I don't reject their contributions as such. On the contrary, I've learned a great deal. But it is tiresome to read contemporary feminist philosophers and literary theorists presenting as radically new discoveries ideas that are old hat to sociologists familiar with work of the kind presented in this book. It's not a matter of getting credit for inventing the original wheel. It's more a matter of bringing into view thinking which, unlike feminist philosophy and literary theory, is subject to the discipline of research.

The chapters have been written over a period of some 20 years. The two authors were among the earliest to develop specifically feminist research in sociology, and this volume builds on those early studies. The interest that organizes the collection arises out of the political and theoretical discoveries made in the women's movement. The significance of differentiating sex and gender was first of all a political move. Biological sex is a given (or so it seemed then). Yet we had to believe that change was possible, that the repressions to which women were subjected were not the simple effects of biological determinants. The notion of gender was invented or adapted from its grammatical usage to hold in place a conception of historically specific sociocultural forms of being women and men. The distinction between sex and gender performs a ruthless but invaluable surgery that has opened the way to gains in knowledge and theory that would have been unthinkable earlier. When I was in graduate school (late 1950s–early 1960s), I was taught that anything that smelled of politics tainted the (tenuous) purity of sociology's objectivity with bias. We have, of course, learned since then that the political and historical are necessary presences in the social sciences. The social sciences are all always of the society they explore. Critical investigations such as Edward Said's study of orientalism, demonstrating the imperial foundations of Western European "oriental" scholarship, have undermined sociology's dream of an archimedean point. It doesn't follow, however, that everything is up for postmodernist grabs. Rather the possibility emerges of discovering the social from the multiple sites it generates, a move that is essential to sociology's ability to escape from its own presuppositions (a struggle without conclusion). Feminist sociology has been specially productive of research that takes advantage of this discursive opening.

Sarah Fenstermaker's and Candace West's collection draws on a body of thinking and research that originated with Harold Garfinkel's invention in the 1960s of a radically new approach to sociological investigation which he called "ethnomethodology." Ethnomethodology opens up investigation into people's methods for accomplishing the recognizable facticity of a world in common. Its research practices are anchored in an ontology that commits to people's doings and sayings as they can be observed and recorded. In contrast to the abstract nominalization of much sociology, ethnomethodology, in all its variants, is oriented to discovering how people produce what we can recognize as just this or just that everyday event, occasion, setting, act, or person.

In contrast, therefore, to the tendency of sociology to generate master theories, West and Fenstermaker, in company with their collaborators, Don Zimmerman, Diana Dull, Susan Dalton, and Molly Moloney, have worked their way forward exploring the potentialities of ethnomethodology for the feminist problematic of gender. Their focus has been on how people themselves accomplish and recognize gender in their everyday practices. They have not sought determinants external to gender, and they have not displaced people's everyday knowledge with the claimed superiority of sociological interpretation. They have, however, brought to light dimensions of gender of which we had been unaware.

The theory developed in this collection is similar in some respects to the contemporary theories of feminist philosophers and literary theorists, notably to Judith Butler's thinking. A thoughtful essay in the collection by Molly Moloney and Sarah Fenstermaker examines the commonalities and divergences of theirs and Butler's theoretical frameworks. There are, however, additional differences to those addressed in that chapter. Unlike feminist philosophy and literary theory, the inquiry evolving in this collection is disciplined by research. Dialogue is not only with theoretical traditions or with contemporary feminist thought, but also with a social world to be discovered as people themselves bring it into being.

Like the novel as theorized by Mikhail Bakhtin, sociology is essentially dialogic. No matter how far it goes in attempting to bury the interchange between sociologists and other members of our society, that interchange is necessarily implicated in anything sociology can claim as knowledge. Sociological research is a specialized dialogue in which sociologists bring what sociology "knows" into dialogue with other members of the society. This double dialogic is wonderfully represented here. The chapters engage with sociology, draw on sociology, and respond to a broad spectrum of critics, particularly to anti-racist and feminist critics such as Patricia Hill Collins, as well as expose the theories and debates to research.

I'm not in entire agreement with the authors' reasoning. I'm not convinced that they have successfully drawn whatever it is we are talking about when we talk about power fully into the circumference of their theory and hence that the issues raised by Patricia Hill Collins are resolved. This reservation, however, is an indicator of the authors' success. In reading, I have been drawn into the dialogue they are developing in which research, sociological or ethnomethodological formulations, and political critique are in productive tension.

Here is a special merit of this work. It is a model for how sociology should proceed. Those who have written these papers did not know that they were going to make a book. Its coherence has arisen out of step-by-step advances. In assembling the studies and theories, the book makes visible the developing character of a body of theory and research. It is not only a fascinating and unusually coherent collection of papers, but also the record of an actively developing area of investigation. In contrast to the tendency in post–Second World War sociology to construct comprehensive theories with positively bureaucratic capacities to subsume practically anything, the inquiry you, the reader, have before you in this book is built carefully from formulations that aim to bring their object into researchable view and from researches that extend what can be known. Revisions, clarifications, reformulations are made as the line of inquiry goes forward. I have taken much pleasure in the unfolding of the work from chapter to chapter, each adding a different aspect, resolving problems, taking advantage of criticism to refine, and, in its conclusion, arriving at a direction for further studies. This, I began to realize as I read, is just how it should be done. There is good research; there is thinking extending an established area of work into an exploration of a region that was largely unknown at the outset of the work recorded here; there is dialogue with critics and appraisals of related bodies of thought; and there is a conclusion which, in reviewing the status of the research and in reaffirming and refining its major concepts, provides a base from which further studies can be launched.

Vancouver, British Columbia
August 2001

INTRODUCTION

SARAH FENSTERMAKER AND CANDACE WEST

Rather than as a property of individuals, we conceive of gender as an emergent feature of social situations: both as an outcome of and a rationale for various social arrangements, and as a means of legitimating one of the most fundamental divisions of society. ("Doing Gender," 126)

Candace West and Don Zimmerman wrote the words above in 1977. As they make clear in the introduction of the article, at that time the most sophisticated theoretical move made was drawing the clear distinction between the *ascribed* characteristics of sex ("male"/"female") and the *achieved* characteristics of gender ("boy"/"girl" or "man"/"woman"). Symbolic interaction's notion of the provisional, ever-changing, constructed nature of social life and ethnomethodology's fascination with the constitutive character of social arrangements had yet to decenter the seemingly permanent or biologically decreed nature of gender. Indeed, that is where "Doing Gender" begins, as it asserts that things sexed and things gendered are not at all what they seem.

In manuscript form, "Doing Gender" stirred great interest each time it was presented, and it circulated among a private, enthusiastic public. Yet, it faced defeat in journal reviews repeatedly. Read as a microinteractional replacement for conventional role theory (and thus trivial) or as a fundamental challenge to the existence of consequential biological differences between the sexes (and thus blasphemous), the paper was rejected and the authors retreated, shelving the manuscript. As sometimes happens with innovative theory whose time appears not to have come, other scholars began to borrow the theory and use it to make sense of their own data. Most notably, "Doing Gender" first saw the light of day in Fenstermaker's analysis of the division of household labor. The publication of *The Gender Factory* and the renewed exposure of the framework (and Fenstermaker's repeated urgings) prompted West and Zimmerman to try again. Happily, the world had changed a little. In 1987, the new journal of Sociologists for Women in Society, *Gender & Society*, edited by feminist sociologist Judith Lorber, provided a home for "Doing Gender." In the decade that followed, West and Fenstermaker published five additional papers on the formulation that first clarified and then extended the initial statement by West and Zimmerman. This volume republishes those early articles along with far newer extensions of the framework, both theoretical and empirical.[1]

As Dorothy Smith points out in the foreword, this collection did not develop by design, but by iteration: Each research problem, each exchange with other scholars, or an experience in our graduate seminars prompted another attempt to explore and problematize our ideas. Indeed, until recently, we had no intention whatever to subject readers to our work not only *once* in its original published form, but *twice*, in this newer incarnation. When graduate students told us that it would be "nice" to have all the pieces published in one place, we thought reasons of convenience (or vanity) did not justify such an undertaking. Later on, however, as we became aware of the large number of scholars who were reading, teaching, and adapting the formulation to their empirical work, *and* when we knew that we would have a number of new pieces to offer, we changed our minds and decided to go forward with publication. Our hope is that only two years from prospectus to publication means that this collection will assume a constructive role in the dialogue about gender and difference that motivated the work in the first place.

We have taken some pains to address the editorial problem posed by a collection of this sort—half old, half new. While we understood from those who encouraged the project that it was important to retain the character of the previously published pieces, we also knew that reading the rationale for our formulation again and again would be a dreary business indeed. Thus, we have done our best to retain the flavor and intention of each reprinted article while at the same time deleting the passages that seem repetitious. Sometimes, however, we allowed for repetition if we thought it important to the character of the piece as it was originally published. To indicate minor deletions of text, we employed ellipses; when larger sections are deleted, the reader will see three asterisks to denote deleted paragraphs or sections.

This introduction, then, to provide some brief context, is an exercise in hindsight. If the chapters are read in order, the reader will notice a kind of linear progression in the ideas. The obvious change in our ideas is the reflection of our own growth, the effect others' criticism and perspective had on that development, and the slow unfolding of our own discovery of the implications of our theoretical formulations. The obviously consistent thread is a result of the theoretical staying power of the ideas first published by West and Zimmerman more than a decade ago.

THEORETICAL FORMULATION, CRITICISM, AND RESPONSE

When we view gender as an accomplishment, an achieved property of situated conduct, our attention shifts from matters internal to the individual and focuses on interactional, and ultimately, institutional arenas. ("Doing Gender," 126)

"Gender Inequality: New Conceptual Terrain" (chapter 3 in this volume) amplifies the argument made by West and Zimmerman a few years before. In addition, we were trying to respond to what we regarded as a misreading—then as now—of our formulation as one best confined to microinteractional exchanges. Puzzled at first by this sort of reading, we now understand it to be a reflection of the deep-seated devotion to the bifurcation of the social world into "micro" and "macro" phenomena, as if they are not only separable but governed by different forces. Chapter 3 addresses our argument about how "doing" gender involves both the interpersonal *and* the institutional. It was the beginning of a theme that would find a place in each subsequent effort to explain the mechanisms behind the practice of inequality.

In this light, the institutional arrangements of a society can be seen as responsive to the differences—the social order being merely an accommodation to the natural order. ("Doing Gender," 146)

Chapters 4, 5, and 6 represent a new line of argument and a substantial expansion of our concerns from the "doing" of gender to the more general accomplishment of social inequality. Chapter 4 appeared in a volume edited by Paula England, which was intended to highlight the theoretical foundations of various formulations about gender, and is thus by design a statement of how the ethnomethodological viewpoint lies at the core of our thinking about gender. But we took that opportunity to tentatively suggest that more than gender can be "done" and that our more dearly felt and ubiquitously practiced social categories—categories around which we allocate social goods and social opportunities—could be productively viewed as "accomplished."

Chapters 5 and 6 return us to the debate surrounding our movement from a focus on "doing gender" to one on "doing difference." In chapter 5, our goal was to open a dialogue and a line of research inquiry into *how* sys-

tems of domination operated to produce the outcomes of inequality chron-
icled so often. We chose "difference" as the word to describe what was being
accomplished when relations of power are at work to produce the accountably weak, unworthy, or denigrated, and the justified practices surrounding
them. When writing that paper, we searched for a word that would convey
what was being created: distinctions construed to be consequential for the
organization of social life and to which social groups held themselves
"accountable." We needed a word that would accommodate the categorical
distinctions of race, class, and gender. Perhaps "difference" was not the best
choice. In using it, perhaps we inadvertently conveyed the notion that our
intention was to diminish the impact, or trivialize the exercise, of power. In
short, "difference" was taken to wash away power and domination—the very
thing we wished the formulation to illuminate. Thus, subsequently we tried
to make plain—ad nauseum, some would argue—that not each "difference"
equaled every other, that we were not interested in denying history or in dis-
regarding the suffering unique to particular groups and experiences.
Chapter 6 contains the symposium that followed the publication of "Doing
Difference," including our brief response to that exchange.

EMPIRICAL APPLICATIONS

*We contend that the "doing" of gender is undertaken by women and men
whose competence as members of society is hostage to its production.*
("Doing Gender," 126)

In her foreword to this volume, Dorothy Smith wrote, "Unlike feminist philosophy and literary theory, the inquiry evolving in this collection is disciplined by research." We are pleased that this quality may come through for
the reader, for that was our intention. Section 3 represents the empirical
complement to our largely theoretical effort. From Fenstermaker's initial
effort to apply the accomplishment of gender to the household, to Dull and
West's application of the theory to their study of cosmetic surgery, we
hoped to convey the importance we place on the productive tension
between our theories of gender and the empirical realities of gender.

The two newer chapters in this section are intended to address specifically what have been thought to be two problematic aspects of the theory,
namely, the character of accountability and the relationship between the
interpersonal and the institutional in the creation of change. Our analysis of
the public presentations at a meeting of the University of California Regents
attempts to demonstrate how a presumption of accountability operates even
in formal discourse to make present the accomplishment of class, race, and
gender. Dalton and Fenstermaker analyze Dalton's data on social workers
and their role in second-parent adoptions. The paper is intended to illus-

trate the ways in which institutional change often comes packaged as "only" interpersonal interactions, as well as how the accomplishment of gender does not preclude change in its content; indeed, that change is inherent in such accomplishment.

THEORETICAL ELABORATIONS

Gender is fundamental, institutionalized, and enduring: yet because members of social groups must constantly (whether they realize it or not) "do" gender to maintain their proper status, the seeds of change are ever present. (Judith Lorber, editor's introduction to "Doing Gender," 124)

Chapters 11 and 12 are attempts to reflect upon some underdeveloped features of our formulation. Moloney and Fenstermaker's chapter responds to the perplexing lack of dialogue but apparent similarities between the work of Judith Butler—especially her concept of gender performativity—and our formulations about difference. Born of a seminar discussion, the chapter is a close reading of text to clarify what the divide across the disciplines might mean to feminist scholars interested in gender. Chapter 12, "Doing Difference Revisited," is just that: a revisiting. Originally an invited paper for a special issue of *Kolner Zeitschrift fur Soziologie und Sozialpsychologie*, the well-known German sociology journal, this chapter tries to address directly the concern raised by our colleagues in the symposium of 1995 and in subsequent exchanges. This was our chance to more fully consider the thoughtful criticisms the formulation had received. There, we give some much-needed attention to the question of our formulation and the possibility of social change—apparently something our colleague Judith Lorber has understood for a long, long time.

CONCLUSION

An understanding of how gender is produced in social situations will afford clarification of the interactional scaffolding of social structure and the social control processes that sustain it. ("Doing Gender," 147)

We end the volume with a consideration of what might come next. This final chapter recapitulates our goal from the beginning: to encourage an empirical focus on how inequality is done and to promote a continuing dialogue among feminists about the mechanisms by which we reproduce relations of inequality via the complex and simultaneous workings of gender, race, and class. We hope too that this chapter, and the volume itself, will encourage feminist scholars to do more than *say* that gender, or race, or class, or sexuality, or nationality, or _____ is "done." The result is often quite conventional considerations—without theoretical foundation—of what inequality might be, but not at all how it is created, sustained, or changed. Finally, we hope this collection conveys the fascinating complication that has compelled our sociological attention for so long and points the way to work left to do.

NOTE

1. The designation of this volume as "edited" is an arbitrary one, necessitated by the inclusion of the multi-authored symposium in chapter 5. Nevertheless, the reader will discover that the work of Fenstermaker or West—or both—is represented in each chapter.

Section I   **THEORETICAL FORMULATION, CRITICISM, AND RESPONSE**

CHAPTER ONE

Doing Gender

CANDACE WEST AND DON H. ZIMMERMAN

In the beginning, there was sex and there was gender.[1] Those of us who taught courses in the late 1960s and early 1970s were careful to distinguish one from the other. Sex, we told students, was what was ascribed by biology: anatomy, hormones, and physiology. Gender, we said, was an achieved status: that which is constructed through psychological, cultural, and social means. To introduce the difference between the two, we drew on singular case studies of hermaphrodites (Money 1968, 1974; Money and Ehrhardt 1972) and anthropological investigations of "strange and exotic tribes" (Mead 1963, 1968).

Inevitably (and understandably), in the ensuing weeks of each term, our students became confused. Sex hardly seemed a "given" in the context of research that illustrated the sometimes ambiguous and often conflicting criteria for its ascription. And gender seemed much less an "achievement" in the context of the anthropological, psychological, and social imperatives we studied—the division of labor, the formation of gender identities, and the social subordination of women by men. Moreover, the received doctrine of gender socialization theories conveyed the strong message that although gender may be "achieved," by about age five it is certainly fixed, unvarying, and static—much like sex.

Since about 1975, the confusion has intensified and spread far beyond our individual classrooms. For one thing, we learned that the relationship between biological and cultural processes was far more complex—and reflexive—than we previously had supposed (Rossi 1984, esp. 10–14). For another, we discovered that certain structural arrangements, for example those between work and family, actually produce or enable some capacities, such as to mother, that we formerly associated with biology (Chodorow 1978 versus Firestone 1970). In the midst of all this, the notion of gender as a recurring achievement somehow fell by the wayside.

Our purpose in this article is to propose an ethnomethodologically informed, and therefore distinctively sociological, understanding of gender as a routine, methodical, and recurring accomplishment. We contend that the "doing" of gender is undertaken by women and men whose competence as members of society is hostage to its production. Doing gender involves a complex of socially guided perceptual, interactional, and micropolitical activities that cast particular pursuits as expressions of masculine and feminine "natures."

When we view gender as an accomplishment, an achieved property of situated conduct, our attention shifts from matters internal to the individual and focuses on interactional and, ultimately, institutional arenas. In one sense, of course, it is individuals who do gender. But it is a situated doing, carried out in the virtual or real presence of others who are presumed to be oriented to its production. Rather than as a property of individuals, we conceive of gender as an emergent feature of social situations: both as an outcome of and a rationale for various social arrangements and as a means of legitimating one of the most fundamental divisions of society.

To advance our argument, we undertake a critical examination of what sociologists have meant by *gender*, including its treatment as a role enactment in the conventional sense and as a "display" in Goffman's (1976) terminology. Both *gender role* and *gender display* focus on behavioral aspects of being a woman or a man (as opposed, for example, to biological differences between the two). However, we contend that the notion of gender as a role obscures the work that is involved in producing gender in everyday activities, while the notion of gender as a display relegates it to the periphery of interaction. We argue instead that participants in interaction organize their various and manifold activities to reflect or express gender, and they are disposed to perceive the behavior of others in a similar light.

To elaborate our proposal, we suggest at the outset that important but often overlooked distinctions be observed among sex, sex category, and gender. *Sex* is a determination made through the application of socially agreed upon biological criteria for classifying persons as females or males.[2] The criteria for classification can be genitalia at birth or chromosomal typing before birth, and they do not necessarily agree with one another. Placement in a *sex category* is achieved through application of the sex criteria, but in everyday life, categorization is established and sustained by the socially required identificatory displays that proclaim one's membership in one or the other category. In this sense, one's sex category presumes one's sex and stands as proxy for it in many situations, but sex and sex category can vary independently; that is, it is possible to claim membership in a sex category even when the sex criteria are lacking. *Gender*, in contrast, is the activity of managing situated conduct in light of normative conceptions of attitudes and activities appropriate for one's sex category. Gender activities emerge from and bolster claims to membership in a sex category.

We contend that recognition of the analytical independence of sex, sex category, and gender is essential for understanding the relationships among these elements and the interactional work involved in "being" a gendered person in society. While our primary aim is theoretical, there will be occasion to discuss fruitful directions for empirical research following from the formulation of gender that we propose.

We begin with an assessment of the received meaning of gender, particularly in relation to the roots of this notion in presumed biological differences between women and men.

PERSPECTIVES ON SEX AND GENDER

In Western societies, the accepted cultural perspective on gender views women and men as naturally and unequivocally defined categories of being (Garfinkel 1967) with distinctive psychological and behavioral propensities that can be predicted from their reproductive functions. Competent adult members of these societies see differences between the two as fundamental and enduring—differences seemingly supported by the division of labor into women's and men's work and an often elaborate differentiation of feminine and masculine attitudes and behaviors that are prominent features of social organization. Things are the way they are by virtue of the fact that men are men and women are women—a division perceived to be natural and rooted in biology, producing in turn profound psychological, behavioral, and social consequences. The structural arrangements of a society are presumed to be responsive to these differences.

Analyses of sex and gender in the social sciences, though less likely to accept uncritically the naive biological determinism of the view just presented, often retain a conception of sex-linked behaviors and traits as essential properties of individuals (for good reviews, see Henley 1985; Hochschild 1973; Thorne 1980; Tresemer 1975). The "sex differences approach" (Thorne 1980) is more commonly attributed to psychologists than to sociologists, but the survey researcher who determines the "gender" of respondents on the basis of the sound of their voices over the telephone is also making trait-oriented assumptions. Reducing gender to a fixed set of psychological traits or to a unitary "variable" precludes serious consideration of the ways gender is used to structure distinct domains of social experience (Stacey and Thorne 1985).

Taking a different tack, role theory has attended to the social construction of gender categories, called "sex roles" or, more recently, "gender roles," and has analyzed how these are learned and enacted. Beginning with Linton (1936) and continuing through the works of Parsons (Parsons 1951; Parsons and Bales 1955) and Komarovsky (1946, 1950), role theory has emphasized the social and dynamic aspect of role construction and enactment (Connell 1983; Thorne 1980). But at the level of face-to-face interaction, the application of role theory to gender poses problems of its own (for good reviews and critiques, see Connell 1983, 1985; Kessler et al. 1985; Lopata and Thorne 1978; Stacey and Thorne 1985; Thorne 1980). Roles are *situated* identities—assumed and relinquished as the situation demands—rather than *master identities* (Hughes 1945), such as sex category, that cut across situations. Unlike most roles, such as "nurse," "doctor," and "patient" or "professor" and "student," gender has no specific site or organizational context.

Moreover, many roles are already gender marked, so that special qualifiers—such as "female doctor" or "male nurse"—must be added to exceptions to the rule. Thorne (1980) observes that conceptualizing gender as a role makes it difficult to assess its influence on other roles and reduces its explanatory usefulness in discussions of power and inequality. Drawing on Rubin (1975), Thorne calls for a reconceptualization of women and men as distinct social groups, constituted in "concrete, historically changing—and generally unequal—social relationships" (11).

We argue that gender is not a set of traits, nor a variable, nor a role, but the product of social doings of some sort. What then is the social doing of gender? It is more than the continuous creation of the meaning of gender through human actions (Gerson and Peiss 1985). We claim that gender itself is constituted through interaction.[3] To develop the implications of our claim, we turn to Goffman's (1976) account of "gender display." Our object here is to explore how gender might be exhibited or portrayed through interaction, and thus be seen as "natural," while it is being produced as a socially organized achievement.

GENDER DISPLAY

Goffman (1976) contends that when human beings interact with others in their environment, they assume that each possesses an "essential nature"— a nature that can be discerned through the "natural signs given off or expressed by them" (75). Femininity and masculinity are regarded as "prototypes of essential expression—something that can be conveyed fleetingly in any social situation and yet something that strikes at the most basic characterization of the individual" (75). The means through which we provide such expressions are "perfunctory, conventionalized acts" (69), which convey to others our regard for them, indicate our alignment in an encounter, and tentatively establish the terms of contact for that social situation. But they are also regarded as expressive behavior, testimony to our "essential natures."

Goffman (1976) sees *displays* as highly conventionalized behaviors structured as two-part exchanges of the statement-reply type, in which the presence or absence of symmetry can establish deference or dominance. These rituals are viewed as distinct from but articulated with more consequential activities, such as performing tasks or engaging in discourse. Hence, we have what he terms the "scheduling" of displays at junctures in activities, such as the beginning or end, to avoid interfering with the activities themselves. Goffman formulates *gender display* as follows:

> If gender be defined as the culturally established correlates of sex (whether in consequence of biology or learning), then gender display refers to conventionalized portrayals of these correlates. (69)

These gendered expressions might reveal clues to the underlying, fundamental dimensions of the female and male, but they are, in Goffman's view, optional performances. Masculine courtesies may or may not be offered and, if offered, may or may not be declined. Moreover, human beings "themselves employ the term 'expression,' and conduct themselves to fit their own notions of expressivity" (1976, 75). Gender depictions are less a consequence of our "essential sexual natures" than interactional portrayals of what we would like to convey about sexual natures, using conventionalized gestures. Our *human* nature gives us the ability to learn to produce and recognize masculine and feminine gender displays—"a capacity [we] have by virtue of being persons, not males and females" (76).

Upon first inspection, it would appear that Goffman's formulation offers an engaging sociological corrective to existing formulations of gender. In his view, gender is a socially scripted dramatization of the culture's *idealization* of feminine and masculine natures, played for an audience that is well schooled in the presentational idiom. To continue the metaphor, there are scheduled performances presented in special locations, and like plays they constitute introductions to or time out from more serious activities.

There are fundamental equivocations in this perspective. By segregating gender display from the serious business of interaction, Goffman obscures the effects of gender on a wide range of human activities. Gender is not merely something that happens in the nooks and crannies of interaction, fitted in here and there and not interfering with the serious business of life. While it is plausible to contend that gender displays—construed as conventionalized expressions—are optional, it does not seem plausible to say that we have the option of being seen by others as female or male.

It is necessary to move beyond the notion of gender display to consider what is involved in doing gender as an ongoing activity embedded in everyday interaction. Toward this end, we return to the distinctions among sex, sex category, and gender introduced earlier.

SEX, SEX CATEGORY, AND GENDER

Garfinkel's (1967) case study of Agnes, a transsexual raised as a boy who adopted a female identity at age 17 and underwent a sex-reassignment operation several years later, demonstrates how gender is created through interaction and at the same time structures interaction. Agnes, whom Garfinkel characterized as a "practical methodologist," developed a number of procedures for passing as a "normal, natural female" both prior to and after her surgery. She had the practical task of managing the fact that she possessed male genitalia and that she lacked the social resources a girl's biography would presumably provide in everyday interaction. In short, she needed to display herself as a woman, simultaneously learning what it was to be a woman. Of necessity, this full-time pursuit took place at a time when most people's gender would be well accredited and routinized. Agnes had to consciously contrive what the vast majority of women do without thinking. She was not "faking" what "real" women do naturally. She was obliged to analyze and figure out how to act within socially structured circumstances and conceptions of femininity that women born with appropriate biological credentials come to take for granted early on. As in the case of others who must "pass," such as transvestites, Kabuki actors, or Dustin Hoffman's "Tootsie," Agnes's case makes visible what culture has made invisible—the accomplishment of gender.

Garfinkel's (1967) discussion of Agnes does not explicitly separate three analytically distinct, although empirically overlapping, concepts—sex, sex category, and gender.

SEX

Agnes did not possess the socially agreed upon biological criteria for classification as a member of the female *sex*. Still, Agnes regarded herself as a female, albeit a female with a penis, which a woman ought not to possess. The penis, she insisted, was a "mistake" in need of remedy (Garfinkel 1967, 126–7, 131–2). Like other competent members of our culture, Agnes honored the notion that there *are* essential, biological criteria that unequivocally distinguish females from males. However, if we move away from the commonsense viewpoint, we discover that the reliability of these criteria is not beyond question (Money and Brennan 1968; Money and Erhardt 1972; Money and Ogunro 1974; Money and Tucker 1975). Moreover, other cultures have acknowledged the existence of "cross-genders" (Blackwood 1984;

W. Williams 1986) and the possibility of more than two sexes (Hill 1935; M. Martin and Voorhies 1975; but see also Cucchiari 1981).

More central to our argument is Kessler and McKenna's (1978) point that genitalia are conventionally hidden from public inspection in everyday life; yet we continue through our social rounds to "observe" a world of two naturally, normally sexed persons. It is the *presumption* that essential criteria exist and would or should be there if looked for that provides the basis for sex categorization. Drawing on Garfinkel, Kessler and McKenna argue that "female" and "male" are cultural events—products of what they term the "gender attribution process"—rather than some collection of traits, behaviors, or even physical attributes. Illustratively they cite the child who, viewing a picture of someone clad in a suit and a tie, contends, "It's a man, because he has a pee-pee" (154). Translation: "He must have a pee-pee [an essential characteristic] because I see the *insignia* of a suit and tie." Neither initial sex assignment (pronouncement at birth as a female or male) nor the actual existence of essential criteria for that assignment (possession of a clitoris and vagina or penis and testicles) has much—if anything—to do with the identification of sex category in everyday life. There, Kessler and McKenna note that we operate with a moral certainty of a world of two sexes. We do not think, "'Most persons with penises are men, but some may not be" or "Most persons who dress as men have penises." Rather, we take it for granted that sex and sex category are congruent—that knowing the latter, we can deduce the rest.

SEX CATEGORIZATION

Agnes's claim to the categorical status of female, which she sustained by appropriate identificatory displays and other characteristics, could be *discredited* before and after her transsexual operation (see Raymond 1979). In this regard, Agnes had to be continually alert to actual or potential threats to the security of her sex category. Her problem was not so much living up to some prototype of essential femininity but preserving her categorization as female. This task was made easy for her by a very powerful resource, namely, the process of commonsense categorization in everyday life.

The categorization of members of society into indigenous categories such as "girl" or "boy," or "woman" or "man," operates in a social way. The act of categorization does not involve a positive test, in the sense of a well-defined set of criteria that must be satisfied prior to making identification. Rather, the application of membership categories relies on an "if-can" test in everyday interaction (Sacks 1972, 332–5). This test stipulates that if people *can be seen* as members of relevant categories, *then categorize them that way*. That is, use the category that seems appropriate unless discrepant information or obvious features rule it out. This procedure is quite in keeping with the attitude of everyday life, which has us take appearances at face value unless we have special reason to doubt (Bernstein 1986; Garfinkel 1967; Schutz 1943).[4] It should be added that it is precisely when we have special reason to doubt that the issue of applying rigorous criteria arises, but it is rare, outside legal or bureaucratic contexts, to encounter insistence on positive tests (Garfinkel 1967; T. Wilson 1970).

Agnes's initial resource was the predisposition of those she encountered to take her appearance (her figure, clothing, hairstyle, and so on) as the undoubted appearance of a normal female. Her further resource was our cultural perspective on the properties of "natural, normally sexed persons." Garfinkel (1967, 122–8) notes that in everyday life, we live in a world of two—and only two—sexes. This arrangement has a moral status, in that we include ourselves and others in it as "essentially, originally, in the first place, always have been, always will be, once and for all, in the final analysis, either 'male' or 'female'" (121).

Consider the following case:

> This issue reminds me of a visit I made to a computer store a couple of years ago. The person who answered my questions was truly a *salesperson*. I could not categorize him/her as a woman or a man. What did I look for? (1) Facial hair: She/he was smooth skinned, but some men have little or no facial hair. (This varies by race, Native Americans and Blacks often have none.) (2) Breasts: She/he was wearing a loose shirt that hung from his/her shoulders. And, as many women who suffered through a 1950s adolescence know to their shame, women are often flat-chested. (3) Shoulders: His/hers were small and round for a man, broad for a woman. (4) Hands: Long and slender fingers, knuckles a bit large for a woman, small for a man. (5) Voice: Middle range, unexpressive for a woman, not at all the exaggerated tones some gay males affect. (6) His/her treatment of me: Gave off no signs that would let me know if I were of the same or different sex as this person. There were not even any signs that he/she knew his/her sex would be difficult to categorize and I wondered about that even as I did my best to hide these questions so I would not embarrass him/her while we talked of computer paper. I left still not knowing the sex of my salesperson, and was disturbed by that unanswered question (child of my culture that I am). (Diane Margolis, personal communication)

What can this case tell us about situations such as Agnes's (cf. Morris 1974; Richards 1983) or the process of sex categorization in general? First, we infer from this description that the computer salesclerk's identificatory display was ambiguous, since she or he was not dressed or adorned in an unequivocally female or male fashion. It is when such a display *fails* to provide grounds for categorization that factors such as facial hair or tone of voice are assessed to determine membership in a sex category. Second, beyond the fact that this incident could be recalled after "a couple of years," the customer was not only "disturbed" by the ambiguity of the salesclerk's category but also assumed that to acknowledge this ambiguity would be embarrassing to the salesclerk. Not only do we want to know the sex category of those around us (to see it at a glance, perhaps), but also we presume that others are displaying it for us, in as decisive a fashion as they can.

GENDER

Agnes attempted to be "120 percent female" (Garfinkel 1967, 129), that is, unquestionably in all ways and at all times feminine. She thought she could protect herself from disclosure before and after surgical intervention by comporting herself in a feminine manner, but she also could have given herself away by overdoing her performance. Sex categorization and the accomplishment of gender are not the same. Agnes's categorization could be secure or suspect, but did not depend on whether she lived up to some ideal conception of femininity. Women can be seen as unfeminine but that does not make them "unfemale." Agnes faced an ongoing task of *being* a woman—something beyond style of dress (an identificatory display) or allowing men to light her cigarette (a gender display). Her problem was to produce configurations of behavior that would be seen by others as normative gender behavior.

Agnes's strategy of "secret apprenticeship," through which she learned expected feminine decorum by carefully attending to her fiancé's criticisms of other women, was one means of masking incompetencies and simultaneously acquiring the needed skills (Garfinkel 1967, 146–7). It was through her fiancé that Agnes learned that sunbathing on the lawn in front of her apartment was "offensive" (because it put her on display to other men). She also learned from his critiques of other women that she should not insist on having things her way and that she should not offer her opinions or claim equality with men. (Like other women in our society, Agnes learned something about power in the course of her "education.")

Popular culture abounds with books and magazines that compile idealized depictions of relations between women and men. Those focused on the etiquette of dating or prevailing standards of feminine comportment are meant to be of practical help in these matters. However, the use of any such source *as a manual of procedure* requires the assumption that doing gender merely involves making use of discrete, well-defined bundles of behavior that can simply be plugged into interactional situations to produce recognizable enactments of masculinity and femininity. The man "does" being masculine by, for example, taking the woman's arm to guide her across a street, and she "does" being feminine by consenting to be guided and not initiating such behavior with a man.

Agnes could perhaps have used such sources as manuals, but we contend doing gender is not so easily regimented (Mithers 1982; Morris 1974). Such sources may list and describe the sorts of behaviors that mark or display gender, but they are necessarily incomplete (Garfinkel 1967; Wieder 1974; Zimmerman and Wieder 1970). And to be successful, marking or displaying gender must be finely fitted to situations and modified or transformed as the occasion demands. Doing gender consists of managing such occasions so that, whatever the particulars, the outcome is seen and seeable in context as gender appropriate or, as the case may be, gender inappropriate—that is, *accountable*.

GENDER AND ACCOUNTABILITY

As Heritage (1984, 136–7) notes, members of society regularly engage in "descriptive accountings of states of affairs to one another," and such accounts are both serious and consequential. These descriptions name, characterize, formulate, explain, excuse, excoriate, or merely take notice of some circumstance or activity and thus place it within some social framework (locating it relative to other activities, like and unlike).

Such descriptions are themselves accountable, and societal members orient to the fact that their activities are subject to comment. Actions are often designed with an eye to their accountability, that is, how they might look and how they might be characterized. The notion of accountability also encompasses those actions undertaken so that they are specifically unremarkable and thus not worthy of more than a passing remark, because they are seen to be in accord with culturally approved standards.

Heritage (1984) observes that the process of rendering something accountable is interactional in character.

> [This] permits actors to design their actions in relation to their circumstances so as to permit others, by methodically taking account of circumstances, to recognize the action for what it is. (179)

The key word here is *circumstances*. One circumstance that attends virtually all actions is the sex category of the actor. As Garfinkel (1967) comments,

> [T]he work and socially structured occasions of sexual passing were obstinately unyielding to [Agnes's] attempts to routinize the grounds

of daily activities. This obstinacy points to the *omnirelevance* of sexual status to affairs of daily life as an invariant but unnoticed background in the texture of relevances that compose the changing actual scenes of everyday life. (118, italics added)

If sex category is omnirelevant (or even approaches being so), then a person engaged in virtually any activity may be held accountable for performance of that activity as a *woman* or a *man,* and their incumbency in one or the other sex category can be used to legitimate or discredit their other activities (Berger, Cohen, and Zelditch 1972; Berger, Conner, and Fisek 1974; Berger et al. 1977; Humphreys and Berger 1981). Accordingly, virtually any activity can be assessed as to its womanly or manly nature. And note, to "do" gender is not always to live up to normative conceptions of femininity or masculinity; it is to engage in behavior *at the risk of gender assessment.* Though it is individuals who do gender, the enterprise is fundamentally interactional and institutional in character, for accountability is a feature of social relationships, and its idiom is drawn from the institutional arena in which those relationships are enacted. If this is the case, can we ever *not* do gender? Insofar as a society is partitioned by "essential" differences between women and men and placement in a sex category is both relevant and enforced, doing gender is unavoidable.

RESOURCES FOR DOING GENDER

Doing gender means creating differences between girls and boys and women and men, differences that are not natural, essential, or biological. Once the differences have been constructed, they are used to reinforce the "essential-ness" of gender. In a delightful account of the "arrangement between the sexes," Goffman (1977) observes the creation of a variety of institutionalized frameworks through which our "natural, normal sexedness" can be enacted. The physical features of social setting provide one obvious resource for the expression of our "essential" differences. For example, the sex segregation of North American public bathrooms distinguishes "ladies" from "gentlemen" in matters held to be fundamentally biological, even though both "are somewhat similar in the question of waste products and their elimination" (315). These settings are furnished with dimorphic equipment (such as urinals for men or elaborate grooming facilities for women), even though both sexes may achieve the same ends through the same means (and apparently do so in the privacy of their own homes). To be stressed here is the fact that

the *functioning* of sex-differentiated organs is involved, but there is nothing in this functioning that biologically recommends segregation; *that* arrangement is a totally cultural matter . . . toilet segregation is presented as a natural consequence of the difference between the sex-classes when in fact it is a means of honoring, if not producing, this difference. (Goffman 1977, 316)

Standardized social occasions also provide stages for evocations of the "essential female and male natures." Goffman cites organized sports as one such institutionalized framework for the expression of manliness. There, those qualities that ought "properly" to be associated with masculinity, such as endurance, strength, and competitive spirit, are celebrated by all parties concerned—participants, who may be seen to demonstrate such traits, and spectators, who applaud their demonstrations from the safety of the sidelines.

Assortative mating practices among heterosexual couples afford still further means to create and maintain differences between women and men. For example, even though size, strength, and age tend to be normally distributed among females and males (with considerable overlap between them), selective pairing ensures couples in which boys and men are visibly bigger, stronger, and older (if not "wiser") than the girls and women with whom they are paired. So, should situations emerge in which greater size, strength, or experience is called for, boys and men will be ever ready to display it and girls and women, to appreciate its display (Goffman 1977; West and Iritani 1985).

Gender may be routinely fashioned in a variety of situations that seem conventionally expressive to begin with, such as those that present "helpless" women next to heavy objects or flat tires. But, as Goffman (1977) notes, heavy, messy, and precarious concerns can be constructed from *any* social situation, "even though by standards set in other settings, this may involve something that is light, clean, and safe" (324). Given these resources, it is clear that *any* interactional situation sets the stage for depictions of "essential" sexual natures. In sum, these situations "do not so much allow for the expression of natural differences as for the production of that difference itself" (Goffman 1977, 324).

Many situations are not clearly sex categorized to begin with, nor is what transpires within them obviously gender relevant. Yet any social encounter can be pressed into service in the interests of doing gender. Thus, Fishman's (1978) research on casual conversations found an asymmetrical "division of labor" in talk between heterosexual intimates. Women had to ask more questions, fill more silences, and use more attention-getting beginnings in order to be heard. Her conclusions are particularly pertinent here:

Since interactional work is related to what constitutes being a woman, with what a woman *is,* the idea that it *is* work is obscured. The work is not seen as what women do, but as part of what they are. (405)

We would argue that it is precisely such labor that helps to constitute the essential nature of women *as* women in interactional contexts (West and Zimmerman 1983; but see also Kollock, Blumstein, and Schwartz 1985).

Individuals have many social identities that may be donned or shed, muted or made more salient, depending on the situation. One may be a friend, spouse, professional, citizen, and many other things to many different people—or, to the same person at different times. But we are always women or men—unless we shift into another sex category. What this means is that our identificatory displays will provide an ever-available resource for doing gender under an infinitely diverse set of circumstances.

Some occasions are organized to routinely display and celebrate behaviors that are conventionally linked to one or the other sex category. On such occasions, everyone knows his or her place in the interactional scheme of things. If an individual identified as a member of one sex category engages in behavior usually associated with the other category, this routinization is challenged. Hughes (1945) provides an illustration of such a dilemma:

> [A] young woman . . . became part of that virile profession, engineering. The designer of an airplane is expected to go up on the maiden flight of the first plane built according to the design. He [*sic*] then gives a dinner to the engineers and workmen who worked on the new plane. The dinner is naturally a stag party. The young woman in question designed a plane. Her co-workers urged her not to take the risk—for which, presumably, men only are fit—of the maiden voyage. They were, in effect, asking her to be a lady instead of an engineer. She chose to be an engineer. She then gave the party and paid for it like a man. After food and the first round of toasts, she left like a lady. (356)

On this occasion, parties reached an accommodation that allowed a woman to engage in presumptively masculine behaviors. However, we note that in the end, this compromise permitted demonstration of her "essential" femininity, through accountably "ladylike" behavior.

Hughes (1945) suggests that such contradictions may be countered by managing interactions on a very narrow basis, for example, "keeping the relationship formal and specific" (357). But the heart of the matter is that even—perhaps, especially—if the relationship is a formal one, gender is still something one is accountable for. Thus a woman physician (notice the special qualifier in her case) may be accorded respect for her skill and even addressed by an appropriate title. Nonetheless, she is subject to evaluation in terms of normative conceptions of appropriate attitudes and activities for her sex category and under pressure to prove that she is an "essentially" feminine being, despite appearances to the contrary (West 1984, 97–101). Her sex category is used to discredit her participation in important clinical activities (Lorber 1984), while her involvement in medicine is used to discredit her commitment to her responsibilities as a wife and mother (Bourne and Wikler 1978). Simultaneously, her exclusion from the physician colleague community is maintained and her accountability *as a woman* is ensured.

In this context, "role conflict" can be viewed as a dynamic aspect of our current "arrangement between the sexes" (Goffman 1977), an arrangement that provides for occasions on which persons of a particular sex category can "see" quite clearly that they are out of place and that if they were not there, their current troubles would not exist. What is at stake is, from the standpoint of interaction, the management of our "essential" natures, and from the standpoint of the individual, the continuing accomplishment of gender. If, as we have argued, sex category is omnirelevant, then any occasion, conflicted or not, offers the resources for doing gender.

We have sought to show that sex category and gender are managed properties of conduct that are contrived with respect to the fact that others will judge and respond to us in particular ways. We have claimed that a person's gender is not simply an aspect of what one is, but, more fundamentally, it is something that one *does*, and does recurrently, in interaction with others.

What are the consequences of this theoretical formulation? If, for example, individuals strive to achieve gender in encounters with others, how does a culture instill the need to achieve it? What is the relationship between the production of gender at the level of interaction and such institutional arrangements as the division of labor in society? And, perhaps most important, how does doing gender contribute to the subordination of women by men?

RESEARCH AGENDAS

To bring the social production of gender under empirical scrutiny, we might begin at the beginning, with a reconsideration of the process through which societal members acquire the requisite categorical apparatus and other skills to become gendered human beings.

RECRUITMENT TO GENDER IDENTITIES

The conventional approach to the process of becoming girls and boys has been sex role socialization. In recent years, recurring problems arising from this approach have been linked to inadequacies in role theory per se—its emphasis on "consensus, stability and continuity" (Stacey and Thorne 1985, 307), its ahistorical and depoliticizing focus (Stacey and Thorne 1985; Thorne 1980), and the fact that its "social" dimension relies on "a general assumption that people choose to maintain existing customs" (Connell 1985, 263).

In contrast, Cahill (1982, 1986a, 1986b) analyzes the experiences of preschool children using a social model of recruitment into normally gendered identities. Cahill argues that categorization practices are fundamental to learning and displaying feminine and masculine behavior. Initially, he observes, children are primarily concerned with distinguishing between themselves and others on the basis of social competence. Categorically, their concern resolves itself into the opposition of "girl/boy" classification versus "baby" classification (the latter designating children whose social behavior is problematic and who must be closely supervised). It is children's concern with being seen as socially competent that evokes their initial claims to gender identities.

> During the exploratory stage of children's socialization . . . they learn that only two social identities are routinely available to them, the identity of "baby," or, depending on the configuration of their external genitalia, either "big boy" or "big girl." Moreover, others subtly inform them that the identity of "baby" is a discrediting one. When, for example, children engage in disapproved behavior, they are often told "You're a baby" or "Be a big boy." In effect, these typical verbal responses to young children's behavior convey to them that they must behaviorally choose between the discrediting identity of "baby" and their anatomically determined sex identity. (1986a, 175)

Subsequently, little boys appropriate the gender ideal of "efficaciousness," that is, being able to affect the physical and social environment through the exercise of physical strength or appropriate skills. In contrast, little girls learn to value "appearance," that is, managing themselves as ornamental objects. Both classes of children learn that the recognition and use of sex categorization in interaction are not optional, but mandatory (see also Bem 1983).

Being a "girl" or a "boy," then, is being not only more competent than a "baby," but also being competently female or male, that is, learning to produce behavioral displays of one's "essential" female or male identity. In this respect, the task of four- to five-year-old children is very similar to Agnes's.

> For example, the following interaction occurred on a preschool playground. A 55-month-old boy (D) was attempting to unfasten the clasp of a necklace when a preschool aide walked over to him.
>
> A: Do you want to put that on?
> D: No. It's for girls.

A: You don't have to be a girl to wear things around your neck. Kings wear things around their necks. You could pretend you're a king.

D: I'm not a king. I'm a boy. (Cahill, 1986a, 176)

As Cahill notes of this example, although D may have been unclear as to the sex status of a king's identity, he was obviously aware that necklaces are used to announce the identity "girl." Having claimed the identity "boy" and having developed a behavioral commitment to it, he was leery of any display that might furnish grounds for questioning his claim.

In this way, new members of society come to be involved in a *self-regulating process* as they begin to monitor their own and others' conduct with regard to its gender implications. The "recruitment" process involves not only the appropriation of gender ideals (by the valuation of those ideals as proper ways of being and behaving) but also *gender identities* that are important to individuals and that they strive to maintain. Thus gender differences, or the sociocultural shaping of "essential female and male natures," achieve the status of objective facts. They are rendered as normal, natural features of persons and provide the tacit rationale for differing fates of women and men within the social order.

Additional studies of children's play activities as routine occasions for the expression of gender-appropriate behavior can yield new insights into how our "essential natures" are constructed. In particular, the transition from what Cahill (1986a) terms "apprentice participation" in the sex-segregated worlds that are common among elementary school children to "bona fide participation" in the heterosocial world so frightening to adolescents is likely to be a keystone in our understanding of the recruitment process (Thorne 1986; Thorne and Luria 1986).

GENDER AND THE DIVISION OF LABOR

Whenever people face issues of *allocation*—who is to do what, get what, plan or execute action, direct or be directed—incumbency in significant social categories such as "female" and "male" seems to become pointedly relevant. How such issues are resolved conditions the exhibition, dramatization, or celebration of one's "essential nature" as a woman or man.

Fenstermaker Berk (1985) offers elegant demonstration of this point in her investigation of the allocation of household labor and the attitudes of married couples toward the division of household tasks. Fenstermaker Berk found little variation in either the actual distribution of tasks or perceptions of equity in regard to that distribution. Wives, even when employed outside the home, do the vast majority of household and child-care tasks. Moreover, both wives and husbands tend to perceive this as a "fair" arrangement.

Noting the failure of conventional sociological and economic theories to explain this seeming contradiction, Fenstermaker Berk contends that something more complex is involved than rational arrangements for the production of household goods and services.

> Hardly a question simply of who has more time, or whose time is worth more, who has more skill or more power, it is clear that a complicated relationship between the structure of work imperatives and the structure of normative expectations attached to work as *gendered* determines the ultimate allocation of members' time to work and home. (195–6)

She notes, for example, that the most important factor influencing wives' contribution of labor is the total amount of work demanded or expected by the household; such demands had no bearing on husbands' contributions. Wives reported various rationales (their own and their husbands) that justified their level of contribution and, as a general matter, underscored the presumption that wives are essentially responsible for household production.

Fenstermaker Berk contends that it is difficult to see how people "could rationally establish the arrangements that they do solely for the production of household goods and services"—much less how people could consider them fair. She argues that our current arrangements for the domestic division of labor support *two* production processes: household goods and services (meals, clean children, and so on) and, at the same time, gender. As she puts it,

> Simultaneously, members "do" gender, as they "do" housework and child care, and what (has) been called the division of labor provides for the joint production of household labor and gender; it is the mechanism by which both the material and symbolic products of the household are realized. (201)

It is not simply that household labor is designated as "women's work," but that for a woman to engage in it and a man not to engage in it is to draw on and exhibit the "essential nature" of each. What is produced and reproduced is not merely the activity and artifact of domestic life, but the material embodiment of wifely and husbandly roles, and derivatively, of womanly and manly conduct (see Beer 1983). What are also frequently produced and reproduced are the dominant and subordinate statuses of the sex categories.

How does gender get done in work settings outside the home, where dominance and subordination are themes of overarching importance? Hochschild's (1983a) analysis of the work of flight attendants offers some promising insights. She found that the occupation of flight attendant consisted of something altogether different for women than for men,

> As the company's main shock absorbers against "mishandled" passengers, their own feelings are more frequently subjected to rough treatment. In addition, a day's exposure to people who resist authority in a woman is a different experience than it is for a man. . . . In this respect, it is a disadvantage to be a woman. And in this case, they are not simply women in the biological sense. They are also a highly visible distillation of middle-class American notions of femininity. They symbolize Woman. Insofar as the category "female" is mentally associated with having less status and authority, female flight attendants are more readily classified as "really" females than other females are. (175)

In performing what Hochschild terms the "emotional labor" necessary to maintain airline profits, women flight attendants simultaneously produce enactments of their "essential" femininity.

SEX AND SEXUALITY

What is the relationship between doing gender and a culture's prescription of "obligatory heterosexuality" (Rich 1980; Rubin 1975)? As Frye (1983, 22) observes, the monitoring of sexual feelings in relation to other appropriately sexed persons requires the ready recognition of such persons "before one can allow one's heart to beat or one's blood to flow in erotic enjoyment of that person." The appearance of heterosexuality is produced through emphatic and unambiguous indicators of one's sex, layered on in ever more inclusive fashion (Frye 1983). Thus, lesbians and gay men concerned with passing as heterosexuals can rely on these indicators of camouflage; in contrast, those who would avoid the assumption of heterosexuality may foster ambiguous indicators of their categorical status through their dress, behaviors, and style. But "ambiguous" sex indicators are sex indicators nonetheless. If one wishes to be recognized as a lesbian (or as a heterosexual woman), one must first establish a categorical status as female. Even as popular images portray lesbians as "females who are not feminine" (Frye 1983, 29), the accountability of persons for their "normal, natural sexedness" is preserved.

Nor is accountability threatened by the existence of "sex-change operations"—presumably, the most radical challenge to our cultural perspective on sex and gender. Although no one coerces transsexuals into hormone

therapy, electrolysis, or surgery, the alternatives available to them are unde-
niably constrained.

> When the transsexual experts maintain that they use transsexual pro-
> cedures only with people who ask for them, and who prove that they
> can "pass," they obscure the social reality. Given patriarchy's prescrip-
> tion that one must be *either* masculine or feminine, free choice is con-
> ditioned. (Raymond 1979, 135, italics added)

The physical reconstruction of sex criteria pays ultimate tribute to the
"essentialness" of our sexual natures—as women *or* as men.

GENDER, POWER, AND SOCIAL CHANGE

Let us return to the question: Can we avoid doing gender? Earlier, we proposed that insofar as inclusion in a sex category is used as a fundamental criterion for differentiation, doing gender is unavoidable. It is unavoidable
because of the social consequences of sex category membership: the allocation of power and resources not only in the domestic, economic, and political domains but also in the broad arena of interpersonal relations. In
virtually any situation, one's sex category can be relevant, and one's performance as an incumbent of that category (i.e., gender) can be subjected to
evaluation. Maintaining such pervasive and faithful assignment of lifetime
status requires legitimation.

But doing gender also renders the social arrangements based on sex category accountable as normal and natural, that is, legitimate ways of organizing social life. Differences between women and men that are created by this
process can then be portrayed as fundamental and enduring dispositions. In
this light, the institutional arrangements of a society can be seen as responsive
to the differences—the social order being merely an accommodation to the
natural order. Thus if, in doing gender, men are also doing dominance and
women are doing deference (cf. Goffman 1967), the resultant social order,
which supposedly reflects "natural differences," is a powerful reinforcer and
legitimator of hierarchical arrangements. Frye (1983) observes,

> For efficient subordination, what's wanted is that the structure not
> appear to be a cultural artifact kept in place by human decision or cus-
> tom, but that it appear natural—that it appear to be quite a direct conse-
> quence of facts about the beast which are beyond the scope of human
> manipulation. . . . That we are trained to behave so differently as women
> and men, and to behave so differently toward women and men, itself
> contributes mightily to the appearance of extreme dimorphism, but also,
> the *ways* we act as women and men, and the *ways* we act toward women

and men, mold our bodies and our minds to the shape of subordination and dominance. We do become what we practice being. (34)

If we do gender appropriately, we simultaneously sustain, reproduce, and render legitimate the institutional arrangements that are based on sex category. If we fail to do gender appropriately, we as individuals—not the institutional arrangements—may be called to account (for our character, motives, and predispositions).

Social movements such as feminism can provide the ideology and impetus to question existing arrangements, and the social support for individuals to explore alternatives to them. Legislative changes, such as that proposed by the Equal Rights Amendment, can also weaken the accountability of conduct to sex category, thereby affording the possibility of more widespread loosening of accountability in general. To be sure, equality under the law does not guarantee equality in other arenas. As Lorber (1986) points out, assurance of "scrupulous equality of categories of people considered essentially different needs constant monitoring" (577). What such proposed changes *can* do is provide the warrant for asking why, if we wish to treat women and men as equals, there need be two sex categories at all (see Lorber 1986).

The sex category/gender relationship links the institutional and interactional levels, a coupling that legitimates social arrangements interaction. Doing gender furnishes the interactional scaffolding of social structure, along with a built-in mechanism of social control. In appreciating the institutional forces that maintain distinctions between women and men, we must not lose sight of the interactional validation of those distinctions that confers upon them their sense of "naturalness" and "rightness."

Social change, then, must be pursued both at the institutional and cultural level of sex category and at the interactional level of gender. Such a conclusion is hardly novel. Nevertheless, we suggest that it is important to recognize that the analytical distinction between institutional and interactional spheres does not pose an either/or choice when it comes to the question of effecting social change. Reconceptualizing gender not as a simple property of individuals but as an integral dynamic of social orders implies a new perspective on the entire network of gender relations, comprising

the social subordination of women, and the cultural practices which help sustain it; the politics of sexual object-choice, and particularly the oppression of homosexual people; the sexual division of labor, the formation of character and motive, so far as they are organized as femininity and masculinity; the role of the body in social relations, especially the politics of childbirth; and the nature of strategies of sexual liberation movements. (Connell 1985, 261)

Gender is a powerful ideological device that produces, reproduces, and legitimates the choices and constraints that are predicated on sex category. An understanding of how gender is produced in social situations will afford clarification of the interactional scaffolding of social structure and the social control processes that sustain it.

NOTES

1. The original version of this chapter was published in 1987 in *Gender & Society*, 1: 124–51. That article was based in part on a paper presented at the annual meeting of the American Sociological Association, Chicago, September 1977.

2. This definition understates many complexities involved in the relationship between biology and culture (Jaggar 1983). However, our point is that the determination of an individual's sex classification is a *social* process through and through.

3. This is not to say that gender is a singular "thing," omnipresent in the same form historically or in every situation. Because normative conceptions of appropriate attitudes and activities for sex categories can vary across cultures and historical moments, the management of situated conduct in light of those expectations can take many different forms.

4. Bernstein (1986) reports an unusual case of espionage in which a man passing as a woman convinced a lover that he/she had given birth to "their" child, who, the lover thought, "looked like" him.

CHAPTER TWO

Gender Inequality: New Conceptual Terrain

SARAH FENSTERMAKER, CANDACE WEST, AND DON H. ZIMMERMAN

It is now a sociological truism that the manifestations of gender inequality in the family and in the economy are related.[1] Countless studies (e.g., Amsden 1980; Beneria and Stimpson 1987; Blumberg 1978, 1984; Gates 1987; Gerstel and Gross 1987; Stacey 1983; Stromberg and Harkess 1988; Zavella 1987) demonstrate that while the "arrangement between the sexes" displays great variation across culture and time, it reveals unique stability in the connection between women's personal experience as wives and mothers and women's social status as workers. We learn, for example, of the crippling constraint on women who, by virtue of their exclusion from adequately paid employment, are bound to an economic dependence on a husband or father and, thus, to some form of servitude at home. With that familial and interpersonal expectation of servitude comes the institutional practices that further constrain the opportunities women can realize in employment. (For a review of work and family "linkages" see Blau and Ferber 1985; Chafetz 1984; Hartmann 1987; Nieva 1985.) And so the seesaw of gender inequality in its individual and institutional manifestations persists, even as historical period, particular cultural form, and social change foster variation in it.

While the persistence and ubiquity of gender inequality have been well documented, the mechanism by which related systems of inequality are maintained and intersect remains a mystery. As a result, social science has been able to empirically describe and explain gender inequality without adequately apprehending the common elements of its daily unfolding. More specifically, the lack of conceptual clarity surrounding the concept of gender as distinct from sex results in a failure to precisely articulate the relationship between forms of inequality as they are experienced and to adequately anticipate change in them.

In this chapter, we draw on our earlier research on work and gender (Fenstermaker Berk 1985; West and Zimmerman 1987) to set forth some assertions, not yet empirically tested, surrounding the concept of gender and how different forms of inequality intersect and complement one another. We argue that the conceptualization of gender as an interactional accomplishment affords a new and different understanding of the mechanism behind various manifestations of gender inequality. We suggest that members of society are motivated to "accomplish" gender along with whatever other social business they transact and that institutions as well as individuals are held "gender accountable" in their daily dealings. Through this process, gender *stratification* becomes at once both an individual and institutional practice, providing an interactional "bridge" between different spheres of human activity. The result is what sociology has already so amply documented: the *outcomes* of gender inequality, revealed in the compelling connections between work and family as everyday, meaningful, "natural" facts of modern social life. (For a broad overview of these gender-related stratification "outcomes," see Marini 1988.)

We first consider the current problematic status of gender as a sociological concept, and then recast the concept of gender as an interactional accomplishment. Using the example of women's labor market and household work, we argue that a reconceptualization of gender reveals the intersection between gender inequality at work and at home. With those examples set forth, our conclusion will suggest some potentially fruitful avenues of research on gender as a ubiquitous companion to all sorts of human interaction.

TRADITIONAL CONCEPTIONS
GENDER AS INDIVIDUAL ATTRIBUTE

Increasingly, it is acknowledged that gender is a social construction, but a concept of gender that would allow for variation by setting, the actions of individuals, and prevailing institutional and cultural expectations has yet to be developed. Much of social science still relegates the study of gender to the effects of "sex," male or female, as an individual attribute or characteristic (for discussion, see Stacey and Thorne 1985). Recently, Gerson (1986) has pointed out that this conceptual dualism, where sex (male or female) and gender (masculine or feminine) are bifurcated, effectively reduces gender to sex, leaving little conceptual advance over earlier notions. Since there is no evidence to suggest an absolute or determinant relation between biological sex and the social meanings attributed to it, Gerson notes that we are "thereby artificially truncating the conceptual apparatus for observing and understanding the possible variation in gender relations" (1). Thus the goal of articulating variability in gender relations first requires a concept that itself resides in the dynamics of human interaction and in the institutional structures that emerge from and are maintained by such interaction.

GENDER AS ROLE OR STATUS

The conceptual waters are further muddied by the treatment of gender as a status or role: that is, the social manifestation of maleness or femaleness in an uncharted configuration of social expectations. Traditionally, the notion of role has constituted a largely normative orientation that determined the ideal expectations and actions associated with those in various social locations (see also Connell 1987b; Lopata and Thorne 1978; Thorne 1980). Departing from that view, but providing no further precision, Goffman (1961) defined role as "the typical response of individuals in a particular position" (93). Thus the actual performance of a role turns on a specific social position and a situated set of social actions. One problem with this view is that no concept of role can specify such actions a priori. The potential omnirelevance of gender in human affairs means that when paired with the concept of role, the result is like "the happy drunk" Connell (1983) describes: "The more it tries to take in, the more incoherent it becomes" (198).

In the literature on women's work, social science has scarcely heeded the advice given 10 years ago by Feldberg and Glenn (1979) in their article on sociological approaches to women's work. They argued for systematic analysis of what they termed "gender stratification" on the job, with an

> [examination of the] conditions which create and maintain gender
> differences and attitudes . . . [which] would enable us to sort out the
> impacts of informal organizational hierarchies and informal gender
> hierarchies, and the interaction between the two. (78)

In the otherwise rich and revealing sociological project that followed, women's *work* was granted a prime place in the sociological agenda (e.g., Daniels 1986; Kahn-Hut, Daniels, and Colvard 1982; Kaminer 1984; Lorber 1984; Oakley 1974; K. Sacks and Remy 1984; Walshok 1981), but the *relationship* between gender and work was not made empirically problematic.

Studies of women's employment as tokens have proved particularly valuable as they provided a chronicle of what it was to be different, visible, and often less powerful (e.g., Adams 1984; C. Epstein 1981; Floge and Merrill 1985; Laws 1975; S. Martin 1980; Yoder 1984; Zimmer 1986) on the job. Yet such studies conceptualize gender as some combination of: (a) a role; (b) an individual attribute, which the token is motivated to alternately divert attention from or draw attention to; and (c) a "master" status, which can inexplicably "intrude" into otherwise untainted interactions.[2] Indeed, to date, arguably the most influential scholarship on women's work (Kanter 1977) rejects outright the unique role of gender in the experience of organizational tokens; instead, it is token status and not gender that determines women's experiences. Zimmer (1988) points out one crucial consequence of such a "gender-neutral" theory of women in organizations:

> The major limitation of this approach is its failure to acknowledge the degree to which organizational structures and the interactions that take place within them are embedded in a much broader system of social and cultural inequality between the sexes. (71)

The implicit presumption in such work is that one's gender could be *overcome* interactionally, eventually prove no longer noteworthy, nor require accommodation. And with that, the "real" business of the interaction might resume its central position. The fellows at work might well "forget" a coworker is a woman, much as they might "forget" one was born outside the United States or had a withered arm. In this sort of formulation, gender likely remains a feature of the individual rather than an accomplishment that emerges from interaction in a specific setting, and thus undermines any attempt to clearly articulate the various workings of gender *in situ*. Instead, an understanding of how gender unfolds in the course of other everyday activities must allow for the ways that social interaction can reflect and reiterate the gender inequality characteristic of society more generally. The concept should accommodate to authentic variability in its relevance to interaction, its meaning and salience to members, with content that could be endlessly and effortlessly adapted by participants to the situation at hand.

The next section will outline in detail the notion of gender as an accomplishment. As gender is achieved through ongoing interaction, the particular way in which it is accomplished in conjunction with other everyday activities (e.g., paid or unpaid work, recreation, and so forth) can only be determined as the interaction unfolds. Moreover, gender is not thought to be something that is "overcome," "gotten around," or otherwise risen above so that interaction can proceed unhampered. Instead, the accomplishment of gender is its own reward, and as a "natural" feature of everyday life, its absence is more often notable than its presence. And, from a theoretical point of view, gender is not a manipulable "variable" to safely ignore, hold constant, or examine as sociological sense dictates. Quite the contrary, to study some ongoing feature of social life such as human work is *necessarily* to explore gender in its unique and situated partnership with those activities.

GENDER AS SITUATED ACCOMPLISHMENT

Elsewhere (Fenstermaker Berk 1985; West and Zimmerman 1987), we argue that one's gender is not simply something one "is," but rather that it is something one does in interaction with others. To advance this claim, we stress the often overlooked but important distinctions among sex, sex category, and gender. We note that one's sex (male or female) is determined through the application of biological criteria that are established within a particular culture. These biological criteria may vary and even be in conflict with one another, but categorization itself is compulsory. Assignment to a sex category is initially made on the basis of biological criteria, but more pertinently, everyday categorization is established and maintained by socially necessary displays of identification as a member of one category or another. So, we note that while one's sex category "rests on" one's sex and can often serve as an emblem of it, one can sustain claims to categorical membership even if presumed biological criteria are absent. Thus, preoperative transsexuals can "pass" as members of one sex category (Garfinkel 1967), and persons on the street can "recognize" a population of two and only two sexes from the dress and the demeanor of those who inhabit the streets (Kessler and McKenna 1978). We contend that gender is an accomplishment—"the activity of managing situated conduct in light of normative conceptions, attitudes and activities appropriate for one's sex category" (West and Zimmerman 1987, 127). The key to our formulation of gender as an accomplishment is the notion of accountability; that is, the possibility of describing activities, states of affairs, and descriptions themselves in serious and consequential ways—for example, as "manly" or "womanly" behaviors.[3]

Now, to the heart of the matter. Insofar as societal members know that their conduct is accountable, they will frame their actions in relation to how they might be construed by others in the contexts in which they occur. And insofar as sex category is omnirelevant to social life (Garfinkel 1967), it serves as an ever-available resource for the design and interpretation of social conduct. What this means is that an individual involved in virtually any course of action may be held accountable for her/his execution of that action *as a woman* or *a man*. Membership in one or the other sex category can afford a means of legitimating or discrediting one's other actions. What is more, virtually *any* pursuit can be evaluated in relation to its womanly or manly nature. For example, what will people think if Marcia becomes a police officer, firefighter, or a Boy Scout troop leader? What will people think if John becomes a househusband or a preschool teacher's aide? To be a woman or a man and to engage in such extended and absorbing courses of action is to *do* gender, for involvement in them is accountable as *gendered activity*. And note, to do gender is not always to live up to normative conceptions of femininity or masculinity; it is to engage in action *at the risk of* being held accountable for it.

In this view, gender is not an invariant idealization of womanly and manly nature that is uniformly distributed in society. What is constant is the notion that women and men have different natures (Goffman 1977) as derived from incumbency in one or the other sex category. And these different natures entail accountable differences. Just *how* different women and men are thought to be, and in what particular details, is subject to local and historical variation. Doing gender involves the management of conduct by sexually categorized human beings who are accountable to local conceptions of appropriately gendered conduct.

When gender is seen as an accomplishment, "an achieved property of situated conduct" (West and Zimmerman 1987, 126), the focus of analysis shifts from the individual to the interactional and, finally, to the institutional level. We note, of course, that in the most concrete sense, individuals are the ones who "do" gender. However the process of rendering something accountable is interactional in nature, with the idiom of accountability deriving from those institutional arenas in which social relationships are enacted. Hence, the accomplishment of gender must be seen as located in *social situations*. The task of "measuring up" to one's gender is faced again and again in different situations with respect to different particulars of conduct. The problem involved is to produce configurations of behavior that can be seen by others as normative gender behavior (Fenstermaker Berk 1985).

What we have, then, is an essentially interactional and ultimately institutional undertaking. From this perspective, gender is much more than an attribute embodied within the individual, or a vaguely defined set of role expectations. Here, gender becomes as theoretically central to understanding how situated human interaction contributes to the reproduction of social structure as is its practical importance to daily affairs. . . .

The first implication of our formulation is that not only individuals but also institutions are accountable to normative conceptions of gender. For example, Hochschild (1983a) observes that the job of airline flight attendant is something quite different for women than for men. She found that women flight attendants "are also a highly visible distillation of middle-class American notions of femininity," responsible for the "emotional labor" required to sustain market advantage and company profits (175). To the extent that the women involved in such labor are required to perform it as a function of their sex category, we can observe that in the course of the work, they are held accountable to notions of "essential" femininity. And likewise, for example, Hochschild notes that male flight attendants are more often charged with disciplinary tasks, such as remonstrating the "truly unruly" passenger or settling disputes among occupants of the flight cabin.

But beyond the issue of the flight attendants' individual accountability, we can observe that the airline industry is *itself* accountable to normative conceptions of gender. Advertisements that promise to "move our tails for you," those that invite the public to "catch our smile," and more recently, those that feature the "Singapore Girl—she's a great way to fly" cast the work of the airlines as the expression of essential femininity. Thus, not only the flight attendant, but the airline, too, presents itself and can be assessed in relation to gender.[4]

Second, even though sex category is potentially omnirelevant, the salience of gender cannot be determined apart from the context in which it is "done." Members of society inhabit many different social identities, and these may be stressed or muted, according to the situation. Some occasions (e.g., organized sporting events, bachelor parties, baby showers) are expressly designed to provide for the routine display of behaviors that are normatively associated with one or the other sex category (Goffman 1977). Other occasions (e.g., those involving the lifting of heavy objects or the changing of flat tires) seem conventionally expressive to begin with, their sheer typicality overwhelming the fact of their design. . . . The mother who, as a matter of course, may carry her 40-pound child into a grocery store will find herself the recipient of offers from men who bag her groceries to "help" her carry a 10-pound bag to the car. In short, any social situation can be *made* to suffice for the accomplishment of gender, and it is in that making that gender is granted its salience in human conduct.

A third and related feature of this conceptual recasting is that the doing of gender does not require heterosocial groups. Indeed, as Gerson (1985) points out, the most exaggerated expressions of womanly and manly behaviors may be as readily observed in settings inhabited by members of a single sex category (e.g., Army boot camp, fraternity initiations) as they are in heterosocial contexts (e.g., a wedding reception). What heterosocial contexts do is highlight categorical difference in gender displays, and thus make the fact of gender accomplishment more noticeable. A Tupperware party attended only by wives can set the stage as well as a bridge game attended with spouses. The point is that such situations "do not so much allow for the expression of natural differences as for the production of that difference itself" (Goffman 1977, 324).

Fourth, doing gender is so fundamental to our ways of being and behaving in the company of others that it ought not be conceptualized as an intrusion or intervention in interaction. To be sure, its variable salience means that in some situations its accomplishment will be more obvious than in others. For example, the entry of a member of one sex category (e.g., a woman) into a setting usually reserved for members of the other category (e.g., a military academy) may well elicit challenges to routinized ways of doing things. In response to such challenges, the celebration of the virtues of categorical solidarity can be lavish indeed. But in attending primarily to them, we run the risk of overlooking less ostentatious ones, for example, those that constitute membership in that setting in the first place (e.g., a men's club). Those activities may be no less constitutive of, for example, "essential" masculinity than the bonding that occurs in response to a woman's potential contamination of the setting through her presence in it.

Given this possibility, a final implication of our formulation is that in some situations, the accomplishment of gender may be the primary work that is being done. For example, Goffman (1977) notes that while size, strength, and age are generally normally distributed between members of two sex classes (females and males), selective pairing among heterosexual couples guarantees that boys and men will be clearly bigger, stronger, and older than the girls and women with whom they are paired. That such assortive mating practices are necessary or desirable in our society is, of course, debatable (especially on grounds of the differential in women's and men's mortality rates and the incidence of men's violence against women). What these practices ensure is that if situations arise in which greater size, strength, or age can be made relevant, boys and men will be the ones to display it, and girls and women will be the ones to appreciate their display.

In short, the reformulation of gender as an achievement provides for an understanding of how the significance of our essential natures as women and men might vary, depending upon the setting, prevailing institutional and cultural expectations, and ultimately, on the actions of individuals. Below, we offer some examples of how gender works to maintain relations between various forms of inequality at work and at home.

INEQUALITY AT HOME AND WORK: OLD WINE, HIDDEN ADDITIVES

The distinctly American version of gender inequality finds the last 50 years marked by extraordinary change in the participation of women in public life (for discussion, see Blau and Ferber 1985). Since the turn of the century the profile of the American women's workforce has changed from a homogeneous one of primarily young, single, American-born white women to a workforce virtually indistinguishable from the general population of women. This has meant change, of course, in not only who sought employment, but also for how long. Once only poor women sought employment after marriage; in the post-1950s period, women with older children joined the ranks. A generation ago, mothers did not seek employment until their children reached school age. Today the pattern of labor force participation has become nearly a continuous one, in which women work from the time they enter the job market until they retire.

We find mass-media interpretations of this remarkable story everywhere; indeed we are inundated with this tale of white middle-class married women going to work: from television talk shows, where housewives and employed women are pitted against each other; to news programs that argue that everything from teenage pregnancy to increasing childhood obesity is linked to increased women's employment; to the countless magazine articles and self-help books on women *at* work, and on what they have done (or can do) to the office environment.

The parallel concerns about managing the impossible workloads of employment and middle-class home life are no less telling in employed women's reluctant and somewhat shell-shocked admission that the "thirty-something" husband appears little evolved from his "fifty-something" father, whose housework and child care were largely supplemental and severely constrained by concerns about what was appropriate "men's work." A model of social change is always presumed in which, subject to the demands of the marketplace, husbands' and wives' domestic labor was orchestrated in tandem; one might do a little more, and the other a little less, but it all "evened out" in the end.

After years of anticipating significant change in the division of household labor, social science is still searching for the "symmetrical family" heralded by M. Young and Wilmott (1973) nearly 20 years ago. In explaining the apportionment of work, researchers consistently find that work imperatives—the demands of the job, of children, of home—make a difference only to the household contributions of wives. Thus, while the presence of children and the nature of women's employment outside the home determine how much time wives devote to household labor, these factors do not significantly influence men's contributions to such labor (e.g., Bahr 1974; Berk and Berk 1979; Farkas 1976; Fenstermaker Berk 1985; Meissner et al. 1975; Pleck 1977).

Although this is one of the most consistent findings in all of sociological research, it is tempting to fall back on our belief in transformative social change and simply ignore the data and their implications. Researchers either hopefully conclude that change is "on the way" (Fenstermaker Berk 1985) as some small suggestions of it is overinterpreted, or worse, through a sort of sociological sleight of hand, eager observers conclude that change *has* arrived, and with it hope for the new egalitarian family (e.g., Hertz 1986; Pleck 1985).

A preoccupation with changes in the sheer participation of women in the labor force (and the presumed increased participation of men in household labor) neglects a more subtle but growing sense of disjuncture between what changes in women's labor force participation were expected to bring and what sort of climate they have in fact wrought. In the case of the "dual linkages" between family and market work, the social change that has occurred has been described with little appreciation for the dynamics by which that social change stakes a claim in daily interaction or becomes thwarted by traditional expectations and practices. But the dislocations we sense—both as social observers and as family members—between our expectations of change and the change we actually *experience* may well be explained by this neglected dimension of gender inequality as it joins the worlds of labor market and private household. We suggest that our concept of gender can be employed to point toward the apparent but inexplicable resistance to the sorts of transformations expected in the "new" household, office, and factory.

GENDER AT WORK

The social science literature on women and work is now blessed with numerous descriptions of women's lives on the job. Most are meticulously crafted accounts of the direct experience of women in all kinds of work, in various degrees of isolation from other women. Regardless of position, the *practice* of gender and its complex relation to the practice of work will support inequality on the job.

Howe (1977) offers a description of a waitress' least favorite customer—the "one man sitting alone." It is reminiscent of Hochschild's (1983a) description of flight attendants who were expected to bring gender accountability to bear on the work itself.

> They often want you to entertain them. But I'm not there to keep them company if they're lonely. . . . The worst thing a customer can say to me when I'm pouring water with one hand, and putting bread on the table with the other, is "Honey why aren't you smiling?" (113)

Far from the New York waitress, Fernandez-Kelly's (1983) compelling portrait of her field experience working at a sewing machine in a maquiladora, a plant on the Mexican side of the U.S.-Mexican border, suggests the intimate and "natural" relation between the subordination of the worker and the domination of women.

> But this time my inquiry was less than welcome. Despite my over-shy approach to the personnel manager, his reaction was hostile. And then to me. "I told you already we do piecework here; if you do your job you get a wage, otherwise you don't. That's clear isn't it? What else do you want? You should be grateful! This plant is giving you a chance to work! What else do you want? Come back tomorrow and be punctual." (115)

Fernandez-Kelly (1983) also reports that in the early years of the maquiladora program,

> there were ingenieros [engineers] who insisted on having only the prettiest workers under their command. A sort of factory harem mentality had been at work. [Sandra] had known a man . . . who wanted as much female diversity as possible. He had a crew formed of women all of whom had—upon his own request—eyes and hair of a different color. Another one took pride in boasting that every woman in his line had borne him a child. . . . Sandra knew how to take care of herself, but she still thought it was better to have only female fellow workers. The factory was not a good place to meet men. (129)

Accounts of women's work in the trades strike a similar chord, regardless of the work or the degree of tokenism represented at the job site. From Walshok's (1981) study of female craft apprentices:

> I just kind of let them know it's my job and I didn't want guys hanging around waiting to help me do something. It was important to let them see I could handle the job. Sometimes you wish they would treat you a little more equal and not so helpless sometimes. (217)

Similar reflections come from two of Schroedel's (1985) respondents, a steel hauler and a shipscaler. The woman working as a steel hauler said,

> But I found, like for me, you have to walk on a fence, you have to be willing to put up with a certain amount of teasing and carrying on, and joking. You can't just be straight-arrow rigid. You gotta be willing to be teased, to flirt back. You gotta be willing to just get along. (11)

The shipscaler reported,

> In some ways, I still overlook a lot. I figure it's better than making a big deal out of it. You learn to be grateful to the men that are glad to have you there. . . . When a man found out I did my share and sometimes helped him on his job, he would begin to accept me and find another woman to be rude to. (113)

Finally, a more subdued but nevertheless recognizable reprise on the gender accomplishment theme comes from women within the academy (Aisenberg and Harrington 1988):

I am very aware of it now trying to chair the department, that people expect you to be an authority figure. They expect you to sort of stand above the rest. And there is a certain amount of that that comes with the role. . . . And yet I think this is a style that I am not comfortable with. . . . I don't like competition that requires that in order for one person to win others have to lose. . . . There are times that I think. . . . that it would be better for me if I weren't so sensitive to losers. (60)

The foregoing illustrates that when "gender-relevant" occasions transpire or are sought out at the work site, they are met by the structured status distinctions that surround all social relations; considerations of class, age, seniority, race, and organizational station enter in. Yet these quotations suggest that insofar as the accomplishment of gender remains omnirelevant and ubiquitous, it provides a ready resource for the demonstration of inequality. Finally, these data suggest that the demands of gender do not *compete* for attention on the job; together they form one of the dimensions of the job that is daily enacted by participants.[5]

GENDER AT HOME
Elsewhere (Fenstermaker Berk 1985) we argue that the relatively uniform and lopsided patterns of household labor apportionment, while appearing irrational and unfair, nevertheless are elected by most households. The "rationality" of such a system, and an account for its unchanging quality, is made explicable only through the conception of the household production process as comprising two crucial components: the production of household goods and services and the production of gender. In concert, and through their daily doing, the "natural" accomplishment of each is defined by the other, and the seeming asymmetry of who does what in the household assumes a status difficult to question or change. From this emerges the variety of individual members' adaptations to household arrangements and perceptions of choices made and contemplated. Thus, child care (or laundry, or household repair, and so on) can become occasions for producing commodities such as clean children (or clean laundry, or new light switches), but it can also serve to reaffirm one's *gendered* relation to the work and to the world. . . .

The specific content of interactions around which work and gender are done together may vary, and the outcomes of gender inequality may look very different from one social location to another, but the contours of their *practice* are similar. Indeed, they are similar enough to conclude that the structural intersection of inequality as it is experienced in the family and in the economy is made possible by the mechanism of gender's interactional achievement.

There are thus countless occasions where gender becomes relevant to either who accomplishes the work or the ways in which it is accomplished. And this is true regardless of the particular situations examined, the content of those interactions, the actors involved, or the extent to which other categorical-relevant concerns (i.e., race, class, age) are also introduced (see, for example, Cahill 1986b; Hurtado 1989). Thus, we are drawn back to the actual practice of gender inequality as women and men experience it, and we suggest that it is at this level that economy and family combine to produce both change and continued inequities. Deep-seated, authentic social change will require a profoundly different organization of interactional practices around gender in *everyday* affairs. In conclusion, we suggest some ways in which such change may occur, and we identify the empirical questions that are implied by our formulation.

SUMMARY AND CONCLUSIONS

Our aim in this chapter has been to respecify the concept of gender to better understand the mechanisms of inequality and subordination. We have proposed that gender be viewed, first, as an interactional accomplishment oriented to normative accountability. In this view, members design their conduct in anticipation of how others will construe (and evaluate) its gendered character. From this it follows that gender as a property of interaction will vary situationally. Women and men, then, *do* gender, but the work of gender is not an intrusion on otherwise neutral activity. Instead, it is a coextensive feature of everyday business, a seen but often unnoticed feature of the "natural" and "normal" social environment involving both work and play, and it is done in same-sex and heterosocial groupings. As we have suggested above, a heterosexual context is not required for doing gender, and indeed, same-sex contexts may provide the most intense (and explicit) arenas for gender accomplishment. And although the production of gendered conduct may not be the primary *focus* of activity in these or other settings, it nevertheless is the nearly inevitable outcome.

It will be useful here to recall the discussion of household labor, and in particular the idea that work of a specific variety can produce not only the outcome or product targeted by that activity, but also gender. From this, it is a small step to the idea that a large range of activities, including occupational pursuits of all sorts, can be implicated in the production of gender. The workplace is, after all, a setting of activity and an arena of interaction. And, just as individuals hold themselves accountable to gender ideals, occupations also can hold themselves accountable to normative conceptions of gender.

The gendering of occupations is an institutional phenomenon, but it has intimate connections to the doing of gender in individual interaction. The socially evaluated properties of activities such as work may be appropriated as, and understood as, reflecting the innate characteristics of individuals. Such characteristics form the framework of accountability for evaluating the conduct exhibited in interaction. We might say (to put the case starkly) that, historically, it is men who go to war not so much because war demands the qualities and virtues commonly associated with manhood (warfare being quintessentially men's work); rather, in going to war, men appropriate the occasion and its resources to demonstrate and establish manliness.

The importance of such an understanding is underscored by the following reflections. First, while social scientists have tended to view gender as socially constructed, there is no satisfactory account available of the persistence of the fundamental notion that women and men are differently constituted with respect to their behavioral and emotional potentials (whatever these might be in a given situation). Second, as we have argued, conduct in accord with one's "nature" appears to be treated as an accountable matter. As discussed previously (see also Fenstermaker Berk 1985), the persistence of an unequal distribution of household labor and the belief that the distribution of these tasks is fair and equitable suggest that in doing housework, men and women also do gender.

In short, doing gender and doing work, while analytically separable, appear to be empirically intertwined. If we are to entertain the vision that one day inequality based on sex will be substantially overcome, we will need to understand the mechanisms by which it is sustained in institutional social arrangements. Those social arrangements daily provide for the reproduction of a framework of accountability that casts gender as an essential feature of the individual's very being. It is thus a potent force, which in turn tends to ensure that even significantly altered social arrangements preserve the relevance of gender to conduct.

This is not a counsel of despair, but rather a recognition that finding the means to social change rests on a fuller understanding of how inequality is rooted in gender and understood as an accomplishment and how interaction facilitates that accomplishment. That mechanism cannot be stipulated; it must be discovered.

NOTES

1. The original version of this chapter appears in a 1991 volume edited by Rae Lesser Blumberg, *Gender, Family, and the Economy: The Triple Overlap*, Sage: 289–307. It was drawn in part from a paper by Sarah Fenstermaker presented at the annual meeting of the American Sociological Associaton, Washington, D.C., 1985.

2. This is reminiscent, of course, of the term "diffuse status characteristic" in the tradition of research on expectation states and its treatment of sex and gender. (For discussion, see Webster and Driskell 1985.)

3. We draw on Heritage's (1984) observation that members of society routinely produce descriptions that take notice of some activity (e.g., naming, characterizing, explaining, excusing,

excoriating, or merely recognizing it) and locate it in a social framework (situating it in relation to other like and unlike activities). The fact that activities can be described in this way means that they may be undertaken with reference to their accountability, that is, how they might appear to be and are characterized by others.

4. More impressionistic examples abound in a culture steeped in images of individual determination and morbid nation-state competitiveness. We have, for instance, apparently survived the transition from a "cowboy" chief executive to a presidential "wimp" who later redeemed himself as a "tough guy" in Middle East showdowns.

5. Some caution on this issue is in order, however. An empirically adequate description of the accomplishment of gender at work should distinguish between those truly situated activities that participants orient to as part of their work and *merely* situated activities that happen to occur in the workplace and involve participants who happen to be workers. Such distinctions would permit attention to the specifically gendered character of work, in contradistinction to the gendering of casual interaction as such. However, even as we call for such distinctions we fear the attendant distortions brought on by making gross categorical divisions between "work" and "nonwork" interactions.

CHAPTER THREE

Power, Inequality, and the Accomplishment of Gender:
An Ethnomethodological View

CANDACE WEST AND SARAH FENSTERMAKER

As Connell (1985) has observed, "We are in the middle of the most important change in the social sciences, and Western social thought generally, since the impact of socialist class analysis in the mid-nineteenth century" (260). What is involved is a thoroughgoing rethinking of gender relations: the division of labor, the formation of gender identities, and the social subordination of women by men.[1] The impact of such thinking has been profound, resulting in new conceptualizations of the very foundations of gender inequality (for example, women's relationship to the means of production, the relationship between work and family, and the politics of sexual object choices). Despite these advances, we have yet to see a feminist revolution in our field (Stacey and Thorne 1985). In sociology, as in psychology and economics, new conceptualizations of the foundations of gender inequality have relied on old conceptualizations of gender. . . .

In this chapter, we extend our analysis to an explicit consideration of questions of power and inequality. . . . We review empirical evidence that indicates the utility of our perspective to address widely acknowledged aspects of gender inequality. Here, we cast a broad net over a number of diverse problems, ranging from the subordination of women in the family and in the economy to the domination of women in face-to-face interaction. Through these examples, we attempt to show that a wide variety of activities may be implicated in the accomplishment of gender. And, just as individuals are accountable to normative conceptions of their womanly or manly natures, so may institutional arrangements be accountable to normative conceptions of gender (cf. Goffman 1977). Perhaps most important, we suggest that an ethnomethodological perspective on gender can advance our understanding of less widely acknowledged—but increasingly significant—areas of sociological concern, such as those that lie in the interstices of gender, race, and class.

BASIC ASSUMPTIONS OF ETHNOMETHODOLOGY

Zimmerman (1978) offers a succinct description of ethnomethodology that is useful to our purposes here. As he notes, "Ethnomethodology proposes that the properties of social life which seem objective, factual and transsituational, are actually managed accomplishments or achievements of local processes" (11). In other words, "objective" and "factual" properties of social life acquire their status as such through the situated conduct of societal members. The aim of ethnomethodological inquiry is to analyze the situated conduct of societal members in order to see how "objective" properties of social life are achieved.

For example, within Western societies, people in everyday life take for granted that there are two and only two sexes (Garfinkel 1967). This state of affairs is perceived as "only natural" insofar as persons are seen to be "essentially, originally [and] in the final analysis, either 'male' or 'female'" (Garfinkel 1967, 122–8). When persons interact with one another, they take for granted that each has an essential manly or womanly nature—one that derives from their sex and one that can be detected from the "natural signs" they give off (Goffman 1977).

These then are the *normative conceptions* of our culture regarding the properties of normally sexed persons. Such conceptions underlie the seemingly "objective," "factual," and "transsituational" character of gender in social life and, in this sense, are experienced as exogenous—outside the particular situation and particular individual. However, at the same time, the "meaning" of these conceptions is dependent on the context in which they are invoked rather than being transsituational, as suggested by the popular notion of "cognitive consensus" (Zimmerman 1978). Moreover, because these conceptions are held to be only natural, to question them is tantamount to calling oneself into question as a competent cultural member. Thus, it is not surprising that traditional perspectives of gender have also relied on these conceptions.

* * *

"DOING" GENDER

What are the implications of this ethnomethodological perspective? First, and perhaps most important, conceiving of gender as an ongoing accomplishment, accountable to interaction, implies that we must locate its emergence in *social situations*, rather than within the individual or some ill-defined set of role expectations. The task of rendering actions accountable arises recurrently across different situations and different particulars of conduct. What it involves is crafting conduct that can be evaluated in relation to normative conceptions of manly and womanly natures (Fenstermaker Berk 1985) and assessing conduct in light of those conceptions—given the situation at hand (West and Zimmerman 1987).

A second and related implication of our perspective is that we cannot determine the relevance of gender to social action apart from the context in which it is accomplished (Fenstermaker, West, and Zimmerman 1991). While sex category is potentially omnirelevant to social life, individuals inhabit many different social identities that may be stressed or muted, depending on the situation. To be sure, some standardized social occasions (e.g., organized sporting events) seem specifically designed to pay homage to "essential" and "natural" differences between women and men (Goffman 1977). Other occasions (e.g., those involving the manipulation of heavy objects or the changing of flat tires) seem conventionally expressive in themselves—virtual prototypes of situations in which masculine and feminine virtues can be compared. . . .

A third implication of this view is that doing gender does not require heterosocial situations (Fenstermaker et al. 1991). Social situations "do not so much allow for the expression of natural differences as for the production of that difference itself" (Goffman 1977, 324). Hence, we may find some of the most extreme versions of essential womanly and manly natures in those settings that are reserved for members of a single sex category, for example, locker rooms or beauty salons (Gerson 1985). Heterosocial situations may highlight categorical membership and make gender's accomplishment more noticeable, but they are not necessary for doing gender in the first instance. This point bears emphasizing, particularly insofar as role theory's assumptions of complementary role relations might lead one to believe that members of both sex categories must be present for gender to get done.

A fourth implication of our reconceptualization is that institutions as well as individuals may be held accountable to normative conceptions of gender. For example, here in the United States, when the activities of children or teenagers have become foci of public concern, both motherhood and the family have been held accountable to normative conceptions of essential femininity (including virtues such as nurturance, protectiveness, and caring). In such cases, gender is clearly much more than an individual attribute or role: It is central to our understanding of how situated social action contributes to the reproduction of social structure.

Fifth and finally, we suggest that doing gender is so central to the organization of human conduct that it should not be conceptualized as an intrusion on nor an "intervening variable" in such conduct (as approaches predicated on sex differences often imply). Indeed, in the case of some social arrangements, gender's achievement may be the central work accomplished (Fenstermaker et al. 1991). . . .

In summary, doing gender consists of creating differences between girls and boys and between women and men—differences that are neither natural nor biological (West and Zimmerman 1987). Once created, these differences are used to maintain the essential distinctiveness of feminine and masculine natures. From this perspective, femininity and masculinity are not invariant idealizations of our human natures that are uniformly distributed in society. Nor are normative conceptions of attitudes and activities appropriate for one's sex category templates for manly or womanly behaviors. Rather, what is invariant is the notion that women and men *possess* essentially different natures, for which they will be held accountable in human affairs.

Below, we consider empirical evidence that illustrates the utility of this perspective in addressing many diverse aspects of gender inequality.

POWER, INEQUALITY, AND THE ACCOMPLISHMENT OF GENDER

To evaluate the empirical evidence that might be relevant to our ethnomethodological view, we begin by considering the conditions under which concerns for *accountably* gendered conduct are likely to emerge. In Western societies, whenever people confront issues of *allocation* (e.g., who will do what, get what, plan or execute some activity, give directions or take them), sex category becomes especially salient (West and Zimmerman 1987). Because our existing institutional arrangements are predicated on the belief that women are not only essentially different from—but essentially inferior to—men, the resolution of such issues shapes the exercise of power and manifestation of inequality between women and men through the enactment of our essential natures.

CONVERSATIONAL SHIFT WORK

Questions of allocation can arise even in something so mundane as casual conversation. There, the activities that must be coordinated include opening and closing a state of talk, maintaining an orderly exchange of turns at talk, and providing for a steady stream of conversational topics. Empirical research on the allocation of work involved (e.g., Fishman 1978; West and Garcia 1988; West and Zimmerman 1983) indicates that such activities afford the resources for doing gender. For example, in a recent study of conversations between white, middle-class women and men (West and Garcia 1988), we examined the allocation of "shift work"— the procedures speakers use to effect topical transitions.

Our examination of exchanges among unacquainted persons showed that most topic transitions were the products of speakers' collaborative activities, or a means of coping with topics that had "died." But some transitions were the result of unilateral topic changes—and all of these were initiated by men. Detailed analysis of these changes showed how sex category membership became relevant to particular conversational trajectories and thereby provided for men's control over topics in progress.

Below are three examples of a man's unilateral topic changes in the vicinity of a woman's potential "tellables," that is, things about which more might have been said if only they had been pursued. (Here, verbatim transcripts have been simplified for ease of presentation. The brackets are used to indicate portions of speakers' utterances that are simultaneous; capital letters are used to designate stressed utterances or portions of utterances.)

(1) (West and Garcia 1988, 569–70)
> *Beth:* If I didn't live in VenTURa I'd really like it on the beach. It's just so close, my Mom comes up to see me all the time ya' know. My sister comes up to see me all the time.
> *Andy:* (softly) Ah. (inhales, then exhales) Have you ever participated in something like this before?

(2) (West and Garcia 1988, 563)
> *Andy:* I'm in Soc. Soc One, but I find it's so much Be[e ES] that-[I'm]
> *Beth:* Oh Well, this is my major
> *Andy:* (softly) Oh!
> *Beth:* (laughter, [more laughter)]
> *Andy:* My goodness! (intake of breath)
> *Beth:* But I'm gonna do it, like I wanna go to law school.
> *Andy:* Oh I follow.
> *Beth:* So it's a good [major for that]
> *Andy:* Did ju take this for—did you sign up for this test to impress?

(3) (West and Garcia 1988, 570)
> *Beth:* Yeah, I'd like to take uh-[something like] history
> *Andy:* (breathing)
> *Beth:* of philosophy or something where you don't have to do any of that kind of—I don't thINK that way, I'm not that logical. Yuh know they go step by step. An' I Just—I'm REally an irRAtional person sometimes. So.
> *Andy:* Where do you live in IV?

Here, Beth's turns at talk *prior* to Andy's topic changes offer strong evidence that she had something more to say. For example, her complaints about family members' visits, her statement of her future plans, and her successive self-deprecations suggest that there were additional tellables that might have been told. But note further the *nature* of the tellables that were curtailed by Andy's unilateral shifts: In the first excerpt, Beth's feelings about being too close to her home and family; in the second, her hopes for law school; and in the third, any grounds for disagreeing with her negative self-assessment.

The point here is not merely that Beth pursued certain conversational activities (such as description of her personal feelings) that Andy wanted to avoid. Rather, we argue that Beth's pursuit of these activities—and Andy's curtailment of them—both drew on and demonstrated what it was *to be a woman—or a man*—in these contexts (West and Garcia 1988). Thus, explanation of the relationship between Beth's major and her plans for law school (arguably, an unwomanly aspiration) was aborted midstream; exploration of her feelings about being too close to family members (perhaps an unmanly course of topical talk) never took place; and her assessment of herself as "REally an irRAtional person sometimes" received no disagreement. Simultaneously, Andy demonstrated his essential nature as a man through his exercise of control over topics in progress.

The conclusion we draw from such findings is not that men always (or even usually) change topics unilaterally (West and Garcia 1988). Instead, it is that *when* unilateral changes occurred, they were initiated by men—in ways that curtailed the development of women's activities and tellables. Hence, the enactment of women's and men's essential natures conditions what gets talked about (and by whom).

* * *

PARENTING

Consider now the issues of allocation involved in parenting. As Coltrane (1989, 473) observes, mothering is often seen as "the quintessence of womanhood." The tasks it involves, especially those associated with caring, offer countless occasions for the expression of essential femininity. By contrast, fathering is generally regarded as a more limited vehicle for the expression of manhood, restricted as it is to the tasks of "begetting, protecting and providing" (473). To assess the nature of relations between sex category and the allocation of caring tasks, Coltrane conducted intensive interviews with white, dual-earner couples in which fathers assumed significant responsibility for child care.

Like participants in our own studies of household labor (Berk and Berk 1979; Fenstermaker Berk 1985), Coltrane's (1989) dual-earner couples perceived their parenting arrangements as fair. Moreover, these couples also cited work imperatives (such as outside employment schedules) as central to their allocation of tasks. But in this case (admittedly, an atypical sample), more than half the couples reported that they took *equal* responsibility for child care. And among all the couples, the allocation of parenting tasks varied with perceptions of the essentially gendered character of the work involved.

For example, mothers and fathers who shared tasks most successfully also believed that men could nurture children as well as women could. One mother explained,

> I don't necessarily think that skill comes with a sex-type. Some women nurture better than others, some men nurture better than other men. I think that those skills can come when either person is willing to have *the* confidence and commitment to prioritize them. (Coltrane 1989, 485)

Parents who shared equally in child care also reported that their children were emotionally "close" to both of them, and that they often called their mothers "Daddy" or fathers "Mommy," when turning to someone for comfort.

Conversely, parents who shared parenting tasks less equally (i.e., those with "manager-helper" arrangements) legitimated their arrangements by citing essential differences between women and men. For example,

> Anybody can slap together a cream cheese and cucumber sandwich and a glass of milk and a few chips and call it lunch, but the ability to see your child is troubled about something or to be able to help them work through a conflict with a friend, that is really much different. (Coltrane 1989, 484)

Another mother claimed that "the woman has it more in her genes to be more equipped for nurturing" (Coltrane 1989, 485).

But no matter how mothers and fathers legitimated their arrangements to themselves and to their interviewer, they were still held accountable for those arrangements by others with whom they interacted. One mother observed,

> I think I get less praise because people automatically assume that, you know, the mother's *supposed* to do the child care. . . .. I can bust my butt at that school and all he has to do is show up at the parking lot and everybody's all *gah gah* over him. (Coltrane 1989, 486)

And one father complained of

> constantly going shopping and having women stop me and say "Oh it's so good to see you fathers." I was no longer an individual; I was

this generic father who was now a liberated father who could take care of his child. (Coltrane 1989, 486)

Another father spoke of being "in the closet" with respect to his execution of child-care tasks, lest his business associates interpret his commitment to parenting as fundamentally equivalent to a *lack* of commitment to his job (cf. Bourne and Wikler 1978). Thus, their own arrangements and their own perceptions of those arrangements notwithstanding, these couples were accountable to normative conceptions regarding the essential womanly nature of child care.

PAID LABOR

Finally, we turn to questions of allocation that arise in the paid labor force. Here, as in our earlier work (Fenstermaker et al. 1991; West and Zimmerman 1987), we draw on Hochschild's (1983a, 1983b) study of airline flight attendants—some of the most detailed evidence we have seen of what it means to do gender on the job. Hochschild's interviews and observations indicate that the job of flight attendant is something quite different for a woman than it is for a man. She found that women flight attendants served as airline "shock absorbers," placating and soothing mishandled passengers in ways that insulated the company from potential complaints. By contrast, men flight attendants were used as authority figures, charged with tasks such as managing "uncontrolled" passengers or settling differences between them.

Hochschild's (1983b) observations at a training center for flight attendants show that preparation for the job drew explicitly on white, middle-class ideals of essential femininity and masculinity. For example, women trainees were told to treat their passengers as they would treat guests in their living room—thus invoking the duties of hostess as an essentially feminine set of activities. Through such instructions, the job of flight attendant was portrayed to them as a natural extension of women's nature, and doing gender was fused with doing the work itself.

[I]n this case, they are not simply women in the biological sense. They are also a highly visible distillation of middle-class American notions of femininity. They symbolize Woman. Insofar as the category "female" is mentally associated with having less status and authority, female flight attendants are more readily classified as "really" females than other females are. (Hochschild 1983a, 175)

Thus, while performing the emotional labor needed to generate profits for the airline, Hochschild's women flight attendants simultaneously produced enactments of their essential feminine natures.

Here, we can see accountability operating not only at the interactional level, but also at the level of corporate doings. For example, consider the advertising campaigns, waged by competing airline companies, that invite customers to "catch our smile," offer to "move our tails for you," or feature "The Singapore Girl—she's a great way to fly." That such campaigns are sexist and racist is indisputable (Hochschild 1983a), but beyond that, they reformulate the *business* of this business as, in part, the production of essential femininity (Fenstermaker et al. 1991). They invite customers to select an airline and evaluate its performance in relation to idealized notions of feminine nature; in fact, they imply that living up to such notions is the primary work of the airlines.

GENDER, RACE, AND CLASS

To this point, we have focused on white, middle-class enactments of womanly and manly natures because these have dominated scholarly discourse on sex differences and sex roles. Indeed, to the extent that existing theories of gender relations are predicated on femininity and masculinity as individual attributes—or on white, middle-class prototypes of the female role and the male role—they are incapable of accounting for the considerable diversity of human conduct across class and color lines. We suggest that by reconceptualizing gender as a situated accomplishment, further theoretical and empirical gains can be made.

FEEDING THE FAMILY

DeVault (1991) employs our perspective in an effort to understand what is involved in "feeding the family." Her interviews and observations in poor, working-class, and middle-class households reveal remarkable diversity in the content and experience of the work itself. As she observes, both middle-class and poor women may see feeding the family as a way of showing love and caring to family members, but poor women are also conscious of the work as a matter of survival. Middle-class women may see provisioning, cooking, and serving food as restrictions on their personal autonomy, but less affluent women are more likely to see these activities as essential contributions to group survival—contributions that they are not always able to provide. And while some women see the work of feeding as a fundamental aspect of their identity and family relations, others simply get it done as best they can.

In light of this diversity, DeVault (1991) argues that women's responsibility for feeding the family involves something far more complex than the reflection of sex differences or execution of sex roles. It is not only that women *do* more of the work, but that the work affords the resources for doing gender. For example, in one working-class household,

[Teresa] talks quite straightforwardly about the fact that she does not enjoy cooking, but she does not complain about doing it; instead she cooks simple meals so that she can "get it over with." Her husband does the shopping for meats, and Teresa explains that he does so *because* he knows more about meat and can negotiate more success-fully with the neighborhood butcher . . . he also helps more with the shopping when she is pregnant. (99, emphasis added)

Here, a woman's cooking is described as something she simply does (with-out complaint and despite her obvious dislike for it), while a man's small contribution to provisioning is something that must be explained (citing his knowledge and ability to negotiate with the butcher). Through these means, the tasks involved in feeding the family are constituted as activities that are *only* natural for a woman (her departure from their full expression must be accounted for), and *not* natural for a man. In this context, it is interesting to note that Teresa's husband "also helps more with the shopping when she is pregnant." Insofar as being pregnant can be seen as the ultimate expression of essential womanliness, perhaps it serves to rationalize the reorganization of a previously established gendered division of labor.

Certainly, pregnancy itself is invoked as the basis for women's "natural" responsibility for feeding. As one woman put it,

Now that I'm pregnant I'm trying to have a pretty decent lunch. Before, if I felt like peanut butter and jelly I would have it, not worry-ing about getting enough vitamins and stuff. Now I'm more conscious about it. (DeVault 1991, 112)

Of course, females are, by virtue of their *sex,* the ones who nourish fetuses. However, subsequent to birth, this biological fact is put forward to explain a variety of social practices. As DeVault (1991) observes, women are held accountable as women for the nutrition of infants and children, and they "learn from public sources all around them about their responsibility for another life" (113–4). On these grounds, poor women's inability to fulfill such responsibility may mark them as "unfit mothers" (even before child-birth), and it can be used to legitimize a variety of interventions in their lives by medical and social welfare workers.

Thus, DeVault's (1991) analysis shows how normative conceptions of essential womanliness

are easily brought to bear on the activities of women in vastly differ-ent material circumstances. The category "woman" obscures these dif-ferences, however, by calling for a particular kind of activity . . . that assumes particular features of material settings—not just money, but also time, space, equipment, the security of an adequate home and safe neighborhood, and so on. Discourses of "family life," instructions for being a "wife" and especially for "mothering," suggest that those for whom the models are often inappropriate should be held to the same standards as others, and if they do not measure up, should be blamed, *as inadequate women*, for their families' difficulties. (230, emphasis added)

RELATING TO PRIVILEGE

Hurtado (1989) also draws on our notion of gender as an accomplishment in her analysis of relationships of white women and women of color to white men. In launching this analysis, she characterizes much of what passes for feminist theory as "white feminist theory," noting its inability to account for the experiences of women of color. The primary problem, she suggests, is uncritical reliance on *women* and *men* as self-evident categories (cf. Connell 1987b):

When Sojourner Truth, baring her muscular arm asked "ain't I a woman," the reply might not have been obvious, even though she had borne thirteen children. The answer to her question involves defining *woman*. The white Women in the room [when she posed the question] did not have to plough the fields, side by side with Black men, and see their offspring sold into slavery, yet they were clearly "women." Sojourner Truth had worked the fields, and she had borne children, but she was not a woman in the sense of having the same experiences as the white women at the meeting. (844–5)

Hurtado (1989) argues that white men's subordination of white women and women of color involves holding them accountable to normative conceptions of essential womanly nature in different ways. By virtue of the fact that white men need white women to produce racially pure offspring, they are subordinated through *seduction:* wooed into joining white men with the expectation of sharing privilege with them. Hence, for white women, received notions of essential femininity include qualities of docility, passivity, and subservience. In the daily doing of gender between white women and white men, the distinction between public and private spheres of activity looms large, enactments of essential femininity that serves to legitimate white women's proper place as a sheltered one. Thus, white women's concerns for liberation from their subordination involve recasting the personal as political (e.g., their domination by white men in conversation, their exploitation by white men in household labor, and their use as emotional shock absorbers by white men on the job)—freedom from the continuing consequences of seduction.

By contrast, Hurtado (1989) argues, women of color cannot meet white men's need for racially pure offspring. As a result of this difference in their circumstances, women of color are subordinated through *rejection:* denied the patriarchal invitation to privilege, and seen primarily as workers and objects of sexual aggression. Hurtado notes that white men's sexual objectification of women of color allows them to display power and aggression sexually, minus the intimate rituals and emotional involvements that are requisite to their relations with white women,

> In many ways the dual conception of woman based on race—"white goddess/black she-devil, chaste virgin/nigger whore, the blond blue-eyed doll/the exotic 'mulatto' object of sexual craving"—has freed women of color from the distraction of the rewards of seduction. Women of color "do not receive the respect and treatment—molly-coddling and condescending as it sometimes is—afforded to white women." (Hurtado 1989, 846, including the quote from Joseph 1981, 27)

And here, the distinction between public and private dissolves as normative conceptions of essential femininity are employed to legitimate welfare programs that militate against family life and for sterilization programs that have restricted reproductive rights. Thus, the concerns of women of color for liberation involve acute recognition of the ways in which the public is *personally* political (Hurtado 1989).

Hurtado's analysis is a compelling one. It shows how gender is accomplished differently for white women and women of color because of differences in their circumstances. In relation to white men, white women are held accountable as subservients—dependent, fragile, and somewhat child-like. But women of color are held accountable as drones and as sexual objects—willful, resilient, and bawdy. Hence, the doing of gender may involve something very different for white women and women of color, given the difference in their *relational position* to white men (Hurtado 1989).

CONCLUSIONS

Of course, this is only the tip of the iceberg. We have indicated the utility of our ethnomethodological perspective to address widely recognized aspects of social inequality, but we have not yet tested it empirically. And while works such as DeVault's (1991) and Hurtado's (1989) further our understanding of specific aspects of the relations among gender, race, and class, full-fledged integration of these concerns remains to be achieved. For example, how might the notion of gender as a situated accomplishment contribute to our understanding of relationships between women of color and men of color in everyday life (cf. Hurtado 1992)? If the ways gender is accomplished may vary with relational positions between groups, what are the mechanisms that distinguish the subordination of, for example, African American women by African American men from the subordination of Chicanas by Chicanos? And, how may the doing of gender be affected by differing material circumstances? These are but a few of the questions that are stimulated—rather than stifled—by a shift from conventional conceptions of gender to an ethnomethodological view.

In closing, we wish to address one question that often arises in conjunction with theories of gender relations, namely, the question of *why* these relations demonstrate such persistence and ubiquity. For theories predicated on sex differences, the why question is a moot one: Insofar as gender is conflated with sex, the answer is biological determinism (albeit usually dressed up in more lavish attire). But for theories based on some notion of sex roles, the why question is a serious and troubling one: Why would people persist in socialization practices that restrict the activities of their children, and why would girls and women internalize expectations that disadvantage them in relation to power, freedom, and other resources? And given that, what explains obvious variation among women in their preferences, demands for opportunity, and ultimate life choices? As Connell (1987b) observes, these questions do not admit to answers within the formal parameters of role theory—unless we track them through some variant of infinite regress (e.g., parents socialize their children in accord with their own internalized expectations, because they were socialized as children in accord with their parents' internalized expectations, etc.).

With respect to our reconceptualization of gender, the same why question is often posed as follows: Why would people attempt to render actions accountable in terms of normative conceptions of manly and womanly natures? By this point, we hope the answer will be obvious: because they cannot avoid it. Since sex category and the demonstration of essential difference are potentially omnirelevant to social life, and since gender is an *interactional* accomplishment, we can be held accountable for our essential nature as women or men even when we wish it otherwise. This is not to say that individual resistance and collective social change are impossible. Indeed, the accomplishment of gender is what gives existing social arrangements that are predicated on sex category their legitimacy (i.e., as "only natural" ways of organizing social life). So, even as we as individuals may be held accountable (in relation to our character and motives) for our failure to live up to normative conceptions of gender, the accountability of *particular* conduct to sex category may thereby be weakened. What is more, collective social movements may, by calling into question *particular* institutional practices based on sex category, promote alternatives to those practices. Thus, while accountability is invariant and hence doing gender is unavoidable (West and Zimmerman 1987), there is no necessary or inherent link between particular classes of behaviors or specific institutional practices and "essential" manly or womanly natures.

NOTE

1. The original version of this chapter appears in a 1993 volume edited by Paula England, *Theory on Gender/Feminism on Theory*, Aldine Press: 151–74.

CHAPTER FOUR

Doing Difference

CANDACE WEST AND SARAH FENSTERMAKER

Few persons think of math as a particularly feminine pursuit.[1] Girls are not supposed to be good at it, and women are not supposed to enjoy it. It is interesting, then, that we who do feminist scholarship have relied so heavily on mathematical metaphors to describe the relationships among gender, race, and class.[2] For example, some of us have drawn on basic arithmetic, adding, subtracting, and dividing what we know about race and class to what we already know about gender. Some have relied on multiplication, seeming to calculate the effects of the whole from the combination of different parts. And others have employed geometry, drawing on images of interlocking or intersecting planes and axes.

To be sure, the sophistication of our mathematical metaphors often varies with the apparent complexity of our own experiences. Those of us who, at one point, were able to "forget" race and class in our analyses of gender relations may be more likely to "add" these at a later point. By contrast, those of us who could never forget these dimensions of social life may be more likely to draw on complex geometrical imagery all along; nonetheless, the existence of so many different approaches to the topic seems indicative of the difficulties all of us have experienced in coming to terms with it.

Not surprisingly, proliferation of these approaches has caused considerable confusion in the existing literature. In the same book or article, we may find references to gender, race, and class as "intersecting systems," as "interlocking categories," and as "multiple bases" for oppression. In the same anthology we may find some chapters that conceive of gender, race, and class as distinct axes and others that conceive of them as concentric ones. The problem is that these alternative formulations have very distinctive, yet unarticulated, theoretical implications. For instance, if we think about gender, race, and class as additive categories, the whole will never be greater (or less) than the sum of its parts. By contrast, if we conceive of these as multiples, the result could be larger or smaller than their added sum, depending on where we place the signs.[3] Geometric metaphors further complicate things, since we still need to know where those planes and axes go after they cross the point of intersection (and if they are parallel planes and axes, they will never intersect at all).

Our purpose in this article is not to advance yet another new math but to propose a new way of thinking about the workings of these relations. . . . Our earlier formulation neglected race and class; thus, it is an incomplete framework for understanding social inequality. In this article we extend our analysis to consider explicitly the relationships among gender, race, and class and to reconceptualize "difference" as an ongoing interactional accomplishment. We start by summarizing the prevailing critique of much feminist thought as severely constrained by its white, middle-class character and preoccupation. Here, we consider how feminist scholarship ends up borrowing from mathematics in the first place. Next, we consider how existing conceptualizations of gender have contributed to the problem, rendering mathematical metaphors the only alternatives. Then, calling on our earlier ethnomethodological conceptualization of gender, we develop the further implications of this perspective for our understanding of race and class. We assert that, while gender, race, and class—what people come to experience as organizing categories of social difference—exhibit vastly different descriptive characteristics and outcomes, they are, nonetheless, comparable as mechanisms for producing social inequality.

WHITE, MIDDLE-CLASS BIAS IN FEMINIST THOUGHT

What is it about feminist thinking that makes race and class such difficult concepts to articulate within its own parameters? The most widely agreed upon and disturbing answer to this question is that feminist thought suffers from a white, middle-class bias. The privileging of white and middle-class sensibilities in feminist thought results from both who did the theorizing and how they did it. White, middle-class women's advantaged viewpoint in a racist and class-bound culture, coupled with the Western tendency to construct the self as distinct from "other," distorts their depictions of reality in predictable directions (Young 1990). The consequences of these distortions have been identified in a variety of places, and analyses of them have enlivened every aspect of feminist scholarship (see, for example, Aptheker 1989; Collins 1990; A. Davis 1981; Hurtado 1989; Zinn 1990).

For example, bell hooks (1984) points out that feminism within the United States has never originated among the women who are most oppressed by sexism, "women who are daily beaten down, mentally, physically, and spiritually—women who are powerless to change their condition in life" (1). The fact that those most victimized are least likely to question or protest is, according to hooks, a consequence of their victimization. From this perspective, the white, middle-class character of most feminist thought stems directly from the identities of those who produce it.

Aida Hurtado (1989) notes further the requisite time and resources that are involved in the production of feminist writing: "Without financial assistance, few low-income and racial/ethnic students can attend universities; without higher education, few working-class and ethnic/racial intellectuals can become professors" (838). Given that academics dominate the production of published feminist scholarship, it is not surprising that feminist theory is dominated by white, highly educated women (see also hooks 1981; Joseph and Lewis 1981).

Still others (Collins 1990; A. Davis 1981; Lorde 1984; Moraga and Anzaldua 1981; Zinn et al. 1986) point to the racism and classism of feminist scholars themselves. Maxine Baca Zinn and her colleagues (1986) observe that, "despite white, middle-class feminists' frequent expressions of interest and concern over the plight of minority and working-class women, those holding the gatekeeping positions at important feminist journals are as white as are those at any mainstream social science or humanities publication" (293).

Racism and classism can take a variety of forms. Adrienne Rich (1979) contends that although white (middle-class) feminists may not consciously believe that their race is superior to any other, they are often plagued by a form of "white solipsism"—thinking, imagining, and speaking "as if whiteness described the world," resulting in "a tunnel-vision which simply does not see nonwhite experience or existence as precious or significant, unless in spasmodic, impotent guilt reflexes, which have little or no long-term, continuing usefulness" (306). White, middle-class feminists, therefore, may offer conscientious expressions of concern over "racism-and-classism," believing that they have thereby taken into consideration profound differences in women's experience; simultaneously they can fail to see those differences at all (Bhavani 1994).

There is nothing that prevents any of these dynamics from coexisting and working together. For example, Patricia Hill Collins (1990) argues that the suppression of Black feminist thought stems both from white feminists' racist and classist concerns and from Black women intellectuals' consequent lack of participation in white feminist organizations. Similarly, Cherrie Moraga (1981) argues that the "denial of difference" in feminist organizations derives not only from white, middle-class women's failure to "see" it but also from women of color's and working-class women's reluctance to challenge such blindness. Alone and in combination with one another, these sources of bias do much to explain why there has been a general failure to articulate race and class within the parameters of feminist scholarship; however, they do not explain the attraction of mathematical metaphors to right the balance. To understand this development, we must look further at the logic of feminist thought itself.

MATHEMATICAL METAPHORS AND FEMINIST THOUGHT

Following the earlier suggestion of bell hooks (1981; see also Hull, Scott, and Smith 1982), Elizabeth Spelman (1988) contends that, in practice, the term "women" actually functions as a powerful false generic in white feminists' thinking.

> The "problem of difference" for feminist theory has never been a general one about how to weigh the importance of what we have in common against the importance of our differences. To put it that way hides two crucial facts: First, the description of what we have in common "as women" has almost always been a description of white middle-class women. Second, the "difference" of this group of women—that is, their being white and middle-class—has never had to be "brought into" feminist theory. To bring in "difference" is to bring in women who aren't white and middle class. (4)

She warns that thinking about privilege merely as a characteristic of individuals—rather than as a characteristic of modes of thought—may afford us an understanding of "what privilege feeds but not what sustains it" (1988, 4).

What are the implications of a feminist mode of thought that is so severely limited? The most important one, says Spelman (1988), is the presumption that we can effectively and usefully isolate gender from race and class. To illustrate this point, she draws on many white feminists who develop their analyses of sexism by comparing and contrasting it with "other" forms of oppression. Herein she finds the basis for additive models of gender, race, and class, and "the ampersand problem."

> De Beauvoir tends to talk about comparisons between sex and race, or between sex and class, or between sex and culture. . . comparisons between sexism and racism, between sexism and classism, between sexism and anti-Semitism. In the work of Chodorow and others influenced by her, we observe a readiness to look for links between sexism and other forms of oppression as distinct from sexism. (115)

Spelman notes that in both cases, attempts to add "other" elements of identity to gender, or "other" forms of oppression to sexism, disguise the race (white) and class (middle) identities of those seen as "women" in the first place. Rich's "white solipsism" comes into play again, and it is impossible to envision how women who are not white and middle class fit into the picture. . . . Spelman's (1988) analysis highlights the following problem: If we conceive of gender as coherently isolatable from race and class, then there is every reason to assume that the effects of the three variables can be multiplied, with results dependent on the valence (positive or negative) of those multiplied variables; yet, if we grant that gender cannot be coherently isolated from race and class in the way we conceptualize it, then multiplicative metaphors make little sense.

If the effects of "multiple oppression" are neither merely additive nor simply multiplicative, what are they? Some scholars have described them as the products of "simultaneous and intersecting systems of relationship and meaning" (Andersen and Collins 1992, xiii; see also Almquist 1989; Collins 1990; Glenn 1985). This description is useful insofar as it offers an accurate characterization of persons who are simultaneously oppressed on the basis of gender, race, and class, in other words, those "at the intersection" of all three systems of domination; however, if we conceive of the basis of oppression as more than membership in a category, then the theoretical implications of this formulation are troubling. For instance, what conclusions shall we draw from potential comparisons between persons who experience oppression on the basis of their race and class (e.g., working-class men of color) and those who are oppressed on the basis of their gender and class (e.g., white, working-class women)? Would the "intersection of two systems of meaning in each case be sufficient to predict common bonds among them"? Clearly not, says June Jordan (1985): "When these factors of race, class and gender absolutely collapse is whenever you try to use them as automatic concepts of connection." She goes on to say that while these concepts may work very well as indexes of "commonly felt conflict," their predictive value when they are used as "elements of connection" is "about as reliable as precipitation probability for the day after the night before the day" (46).

What conclusions shall we draw from comparisons between persons who are said to suffer oppression "at the intersection" of all three systems and those who suffer in the nexus of only two? Presumably, we will conclude that the latter are "less oppressed" than the former (assuming that each categorical identity set amasses a specific quantity of oppression). Moraga (1981) warns, however, that, "the danger lies in ranking the oppressions. *The danger lies in failing to acknowledge the specificity of the oppression*" (29).

Spelman (1988) attempts to resolve this difficulty by characterizing sexism, racism, and classism as "interlocking" with one another. Along similar lines, Margaret Andersen and Patricia Hill Collins (1992) describe gender, race, and class as "interlocking categories of experience." The image of interlocking rings comes to mind, linked in such a way that the motion of any one of them is constrained by the others. Certainly, this image is more dynamic than those conveyed by additive, multiplicative, or geometric models: We can see where the rings are joined (and where they are not), as well as how the movement of any one of them would be restricted by the others, but note that this image still depicts the rings as separate parts.

If we try to situate particular persons within this array, the problem with it becomes clear. We can, of course, conceive of the whole as "oppressed people" and of the rings as "those oppressed by gender," "those oppressed by race," and "those oppressed by class.". . . This allows us to situate women and men of all races and classes within the areas covered by the circles, save for white, middle- and upper-class men, who fall outside of them. However, what if we conceive of the whole as "experience"[4] and of the rings as gender, race, and class. . . .

Here, we face an illuminating possibility and leave arithmetic behind: No person can experience gender without simultaneously experiencing race and class. As Andersen and Collins (1992) put it, "While race, class and gender can be seen as different axes of social structure, individual persons experience them simultaneously"(xxi).[5] It is this simultaneity that has eluded our theoretical treatments and is so difficult to build into our empirical descriptions (for an admirable effort, see Segura 1992). Capturing it compels us to focus on the actual mechanisms that produce social inequality. How do forms of inequality, which we now see are more than the periodic collision of categories, operate together? How do we see that all social exchanges, regardless of the participants or the outcome, are simultaneously "gendered," "raced," and "classed"? . . .

To address these questions, we first present some earlier attempts to conceptualize gender. Appreciation for the limitations of these efforts, we believe, affords us a way to the second task: reconceptualizing the dynamics of gender, race, and class as they figure simultaneously in human institutions and interaction.

TRADITIONAL CONCEPTUALIZATIONS OF GENDER

To begin, we turn to Arlie Russell Hochschild's "A Review of Sex Roles Research" (1973). At that time, there were at least four distinct ways of conceptualizing gender within the burgeoning literature on the topic: (1) as sex differences, (2) as sex roles, (3) in relation to the minority status of women, and (4) in relation to the caste/class status of women. Hochschild observes that each of these conceptualizations led to a different perspective on the behaviors of women and men.

What is to type 1 a feminine trait such as passivity is to type 2 a role element, to type 3 is a minority characteristic, and to type 4 is a response to powerlessness. Social change might also look somewhat different to each perspective; differences disappear, deviance becomes normal, the minority group assimilates, or power is equalized. (1013)

Nona Glazer (1977) observes a further important difference between the types Hochschild identified, namely, where they located the primary source of inequality between women and men.

The *sex difference* and [*sex*] *roles* approaches share an emphasis on understanding factors that characterize individuals. These factors may be inherent to each sex or acquired by individuals in the course of socialization. The *minority group* and *caste/class* approaches share an emphasis on factors that are external to individuals, a concern with the structure of social institutions, and with the impact of historical events. (103)

In retrospect, it is profoundly disturbing to contemplate what the minority group approach and the class/caste approach implied about feminist thinking at the time. For example, Juliet Mitchell (1966) launched "Women: The Longest Revolution" with the claim that "[t]he situation of women is different from that of any other social group . . . within the world of men, their position is comparable to that of an oppressed minority" (11). Obviously, if "women" could be compared to "an oppressed minority," they had to consist of someone other than "oppressed minorities" themselves (cf. Hacker 1951).

Perhaps because of such theoretical problems, feminist scholars have largely abandoned the effort to describe women as a caste, as a class, or as a minority group as a project in its own right (see, for example, Aptheker 1989; Hull et al. 1982). What we have been left with, however, are two prevailing conceptualizations: (1) the sex differences approach and (2) the sex roles approach. And note, while the minority group and caste/class approaches were concerned with factors external to the individual (e.g., the structure of social institutions and the impact of historical events), the approaches that remain emphasize factors that characterize the individual (Glazer 1977).

Arguably, some might call this picture oversimplified. Given the exciting new scholarship that focuses on gender as something that is socially constructed, and something that converges with other inequalities to produce difference among women, have we not moved well beyond "sex differences" and "sex roles"? A close examination of this literature suggests that we have not. For example, Collins (1990) contends that *[w]hile race and gender are both socially constructed categories, con-structions of gender rest on clearer biological criteria than do construc-tions of race. Classifying African-Americans into specious racial categories is considerably more difficult than noting the clear biological differences distinguishing females from males. . . . Women do share common experiences, but the experiences are not generally the same type as those affecting racial and ethnic groups. (27, emphasis added)*

Of course, Collins is correct in her claim that women differ considerably from one another with respect to the distinctive histories, geographic origins, and cultures they share with men of their same race and class. The problem, how-ever, is that what unites them as women are the "clear biological criteria dis-tinguishing females from males." Here, Collins reverts to treating gender as a matter of sex differences (i.e., as ultimately traceable to factors inherent to each sex), despite her contention that it is socially constructed. Gender becomes conflated with sex, as race might speciously be made equivalent to color.

Consider a further example. Spelman (1988) launches her analysis with a discussion of the theoretical necessity of distinguishing sex from gender. She praises de Beauvoir (1953) for her early recognition of the difference between the two and goes on to argue:

It is one thing to be biologically female, and quite another to be shaped by one's culture into a "woman"—a female with feminine qualities, someone who does the kinds of things "women" not "men" do, someone who has the kinds of thoughts and feelings that make doing these things seem an easy expression of one's feminine nature. (124)

How, then, does Spelman (1988) conceive of the social construction of woman? She not only invokes "sexual roles" to explain this process (121–3) but also speaks of "racial roles" (106) that affect the course that the process will take. Despite Spelman's elegant demonstration of how "woman" con-stitutes a false generic in feminist thought, her analysis takes us back to "sex roles" once again.

Our point here is not to take issue with Collins (1990) or Spelman (1988) in particular. We cite these works to highlight a more fundamental difficulty facing feminist theory in general: New conceptualizations of the bases of gender inequality still rest on old conceptualizations of gender.

* * *

Seeking a solution to these difficulties, Joan Acker (1992b) has advanced the view that gender consists of something else altogether, namely, "patterned, socially produced distinctions between female and male, feminine and masculine. . . . [that occur] in the course of participation in work organizations as well as in many other locations and relations" (250). The object here is to document the "gendered processes" that sustain "the pervasive ordering of human activities, practices and social structures in terms of differentiations between women and men" (1992a, 567).

We agree fully with the object of this view and note its usefulness in capturing the persistence and ubiquity of gender inequality. Its emphasis on organizational practices restores the concern with "the structure of social institutions and with the impact of historical events" that characterized earlier class/caste approaches and facilitates the simultaneous documentation of gender, race, and class as basic principles of social organization. We suggest, however, that the popular distinction between "macro" and "micro" levels of analysis reflected in this view makes it possible to empirically describe and explain inequality without fully apprehending the common elements of its daily unfolding. For example, "processes of interaction" are conceptualized apart from the "production of gender divisions," that is, "the overt decisions and procedures that control, segregate, exclude, and construct hierarchies based on gender and often race" (Acker 1992a, 568). The production of "images, symbols and ideologies that justify, explain, and give legitimacy to institutions" constitutes yet another "process," as do "the [mental] internal processes in which individuals engage as they construct personas that are appropriately gendered for the institutional setting" (Acker 1992a, 568). The analytic "missing link," as we see it, is the mechanism that ties these seemingly diverse processes together, one that could "take into account the constraining impact of entrenched ideas and practices on human agency, but [could] also acknowledge that the system is continually construed in everyday life and that, under certain conditions, individuals resist pressures to conform to the needs of the system" (Essed 1991, 38).

In sum, if we conceive of gender as a matter of biological differences or differential roles, we are forced to think of it as standing apart from and outside other socially relevant, organizing experiences. This prevents us from understanding how gender, race, and class operate simultaneously with one another. It prevents us from seeing how the particular salience of these experiences might vary across interactions. Most important, it gives us virtually no way of adequately addressing the mechanisms that produce power and inequality in social life. Instead, we propose a conceptual mechanism for perceiving the relations between individual and institutional practice and among forms of domination. . . .

AN ETHNOMETHODOLOGICAL PERSPECTIVE

The goal of this article is not to analyze situated conduct per se but to understand the workings of inequality. We should note that our interest here is not to separate gender, race, and class as social categories but to build a coherent argument for understanding how they work simultaneously. How might an ethnomethodological perspective help with this task? As Marilyn Frye (1983) observes,

> For efficient subordination, what's wanted is that the structure not appear to be a cultural artifact kept in place by human decision or custom, but that it appear natural—that it appear to be quite a direct consequence of facts about the beast which are beyond the scope of human manipulation. (34)

GENDER

Within Western societies, we take for granted in everyday life that there are two and only two sexes (Garfinkel 1967). We see this state of affairs as "only natural" insofar as we see persons as "essentially, originally and in the final analysis either 'male' or 'female'" (Garfinkel 1967, 122). When we interact with others, we take for granted that each of us has an "essential" manly or womanly nature—one that derives from our sex and one that can be detected from the "natural signs" we give off (Goffman 1976).

These beliefs constitute the normative conceptions of our culture regarding the properties of normally sexed persons. Such beliefs support the seemingly "objective," "factual," and "transsituational" character of gender in social affairs, and in this sense, we experience them as exogenous (i.e., as outside of us and the particular situation we find ourselves in). Simultaneously, however, the meaning of these beliefs is dependent on the context in which they are invoked—rather than transsituational, as implied by the popular concept of "cognitive consensus" (Zimmerman 1978, 8–9). What is more, because these properties of normally sexed persons are regarded as "only natural," questioning them is tantamount to calling ourselves into question as competent members of society. Consider how these beliefs operate in the process of sex assignment—the initial classification of persons as either females or males (West and Zimmerman 1987). We generally regard this process as a biological determination requiring only a straightforward examination of the "facts of the matter" (cf. the description of sex as an "ascribed status" in many introductory sociology texts). The criteria for sex assignment, however, can vary across cases (e.g., chromosome type before birth or genitalia after birth). They sometimes do and sometimes do not agree with one another (e.g., hermaphrodites), and they show considerable variation across cultures (Kessler and McKenna 1978). Our *moral conviction* that there are two and only two sexes (Garfinkel 1967) is what explains the comparative ease of achieving initial sex assignment. This conviction accords females and males the status of unequivocal and "natural" entities, whose social and psychological tendencies can be predicted from their reproductive functions (West and Zimmerman 1987). From an ethnomethodological viewpoint, sex is socially and culturally constructed rather than a straightforward statement of the biological "facts."

Now, consider the process of sex categorization—the ongoing identification of persons as girls or boys and women or men in everyday life (West and Zimmerman 1987). Sex categorization involves no well-defined set of criteria that must be satisfied to identify someone; rather, it involves treating appearances (e.g., deportment, dress, and bearing) as if they were indicative of underlying states of affairs (e.g., anatomical, hormonal, and chromosomal arrangements). The point worth stressing here is that, while sex category serves as an "indicator" of sex, it does not depend on it. Societal members will "see" a world populated by two and only two sexes, even in public situations that preclude inspection of the physiological "facts." From this perspective, it is important to distinguish sex category from sex assignment and to distinguish both from the "doing" of gender.

Gender, we argue, is a situated accomplishment of societal members, the local management of conduct in relation to normative conceptions of appropriate attitudes and activities for particular sex categories (West and Zimmerman 1987). From this perspective, gender is not merely an individual attribute but something that is accomplished in interaction with others. Here, as in our earlier work, we rely on John Heritage's (1984) formulation of accountability: the possibility of describing actions, circumstances, and even descriptions of themselves in both serious and consequential ways (e.g., as "unwomanly" or "unmanly"). Heritage points out that members of society routinely characterize activities in ways that take notice of those activities (e.g., naming, describing, blaming, excusing, or merely acknowledging them) and place them in a social framework (i.e., situating them in the context of other activities that are similar or different).

The fact that activities can be described in such ways is what leads to the possibility of conducting them with an eye to how they might be assessed (e.g., as "womanly" or "manly" behaviors). Three important but subtle points are worth emphasizing here. One is that the notion of accountability is relevant not only to activities that conform to prevailing normative conceptions (i.e., activities that are conducted "unremarkably," and, thus, do not warrant more than a passing glance) but also to those activities that deviate. The issue is not deviance or conformity; rather, it is the possible evaluation of action in relation to normative conceptions and the likely consequence of that evaluation for subsequent interaction. The second point worth emphasizing is that the process of rendering some action accountable is an interactional accomplishment. As Heritage (1984) explains, accountability permits persons to conduct their activities in relation to their circumstances—in ways that permit others to take those circumstances into account and see those activities for what they are. "[T]he intersubjectivity of actions," therefore, "ultimately rests on a symmetry between the *production* of those actions on the one hand and their *recognition* on the other" (179)—both in the context of their circumstances.[6] And the third point we must stress is that, while individuals are the ones who do gender, the process of rendering something accountable is both interactional and institutional in character: It is a feature of social relationships, and its idiom derives from the institutional arena in which those relationships come to life. In the United States, for example, when the behaviors of children or teenagers have become the focus of public concern, the Family and Motherhood (as well as individual mothers) have been held accountable to normative conceptions of "essential" femininity (including qualities like nurturance and caring). Gender is obviously much more than a role or an individual characteristic: It is a mechanism whereby situated social action contributes to the reproduction of social structure (West and Fenstermaker 1993). . . .

Through this formulation, we resituate gender, an attribute without clear social origin or referent, in social interaction. This makes it possible to study how gender takes on social import, how it varies in its salience and consequence, and how it operates to produce and maintain power and inequality in social life. Below, we extend this reformulation to race and, then, to class. Through this extension, we are not proposing an equivalence of oppressions. Race is not class, and neither is gender; nevertheless, while race, class, and gender will likely take on different import and will often carry vastly different social consequences in any given social situation, we suggest that how they operate may be productively compared. Here, our focus is on the social mechanics of gender, race, and class, for that is the way we may perceive their simultaneous workings in human affairs.

RACE

Within the United States, virtually any social activity presents the possibility of categorizing the participants on the basis of race. Attempts to establish race as a scientific concept have met with little success (Gossett 1965; Montagu 1975; Omi and Winant 1986; Stephans 1982). There are, for example, no biological criteria (e.g., hormonal, chromosomal, or anatomical) that allow physicians to pronounce race assignment at birth, thereby sorting human beings into distinctive races.[7] Since racial categories and their meanings change over time and place, they are, moreover, arbitrary.[8] In everyday life, nevertheless, people can and do sort out themselves and others on the basis of membership in racial categories.

Michael Omi and Howard Winant (1986) argue that the "seemingly obvious, 'natural' and 'common sense' qualities" of the existing racial order "themselves testify to the effectiveness of the racial formation process in constructing racial meanings and identities" (62). Take, for instance, the relatively recent emergence of the category "Asian American." Any scientific theory of race would be hard-pressed to explain this in the absence of a well-defined set of criteria for assigning individuals to the category. In relation to ethnicity, furthermore, it makes no sense to aggregate in a single category the distinctive histories, geographic origins, and cultures of Cambodian, Chinese, Filipino, Japanese, Korean, Laotian, Thai, and Vietnamese Americans. Despite important distinctions among these groups, Omi and Winant (1986) contend, "the majority of Americans cannot tell the difference" between their members (24). "Asian American," therefore, affords a means of achieving racial categorization in everyday life.

Of course, competent members of U.S. society share preconceived ideas of what members of particular categories "look like" (Omi and Winant 1986, 62). Remarks such as "Odd, you don't look Asian" testify to underlying notions of what "Asians" ought to look like. The point we wish to stress, however, is that these notions are not supported by any scientific criteria for reliably distinguishing members of different "racial" groups. What is more, even state-mandated criteria (e.g., the proportion of "mixed blood" necessary to legally classify someone as Black)[9] are distinctly different in other Western cultures and have little relevance to the way racial categorization occurs in everyday life. As in the case of sex categorization, appearances are treated as if they were indicative of some underlying state.

Beyond preconceived notions of what members of particular groups look like, Omi and Winant (1986) suggest that Americans share preconceived notions of what members of these groups are like. They note, for example, that we are likely to become disoriented "when people do not act 'Black,' 'Latino,' or indeed 'white'" (62). From our ethnomethodological perspective, what Omi and Winant are describing is the accountability of persons to race category. If we accept their contention that there are prevailing normative conceptions of appropriate attitudes and activities for particular race categories, and if we grant Heritage's (1984) claim that accountability allows persons to conduct their activities in relation to their circumstances (in ways that allow others to take those circumstances into account and see those activities for what they are), we can also see race as a situated accomplishment of societal members. From this perspective, race is not simply an individual characteristic or trait but something that is accomplished in interaction with others.

To the extent that race category is omnirelevant (or even verges on this), it follows that persons involved in virtually any action may be held accountable for their performance of that action as members of their race category. As in the case of sex category, race category can be used to justify or discredit other actions; accordingly, virtually any action can be assessed in relation to its race categorical nature. The accomplishment of race (like gender) does not necessarily mean "living up" to normative conceptions of attitudes and activities appropriate to a particular race category; rather, it means engaging in action at the risk of race assessment. . . .

The accomplishment of race renders the social arrangements based on race as normal and natural, that is, legitimate ways of organizing social life. In the United States, it can seem "only natural" for counselors charged with guiding high school students in their preparation for college admission to advise Black students against advanced courses in math, chemistry, or physics "because Blacks do not do well" in those areas (Essed 1991, 242). The students may well forgo such courses, given that they "do not need them" and "can get into college without them." However, Philomena Essed (1991) observes this ensures that students so advised will enter college at a disadvantage in comparison to classmates and creates the very situation that is believed to exist, namely, that Blacks do not do well in those areas. Small wonder, then, that the proportion of U.S. Black students receiving college degrees remains stuck at 13 percent, despite two decades of affirmative action programs (Essed 1991). Those Black students who are (for whatever reason) adequately prepared for college are held to account for themselves as "deviant" representatives of their race category and, typically, exceptionalized (Essed 1991). With that accomplishment, institutional practice and social order are reaffirmed.

Although the distinction between "macro" and "micro" levels of analysis is popular in the race relations literature, too (e.g., in distinguishing "institutional" from "individual" racism or "macro-level" analyses of racialized social structures from "micro-level" analyses of identity formation), we contend that it is ultimately a false distinction. Not only do these "levels" operate continually and reciprocally in "our lived experience, in politics, in culture [and] in economic life" (Omi and Winant 1986, 67), but distinguishing between them "places the individual outside the institutional, thereby severing rules, regulations and procedures from the people who make and enact them" (Essed 1991, 36). We contend that the accountability of persons to race categories is the key to understanding the maintenance of the existing racial order.

Note that there is nothing in this formulation to suggest that race is necessarily accomplished in isolation from gender. To the contrary, if we conceive of both race and gender as situated accomplishments, we can see how individual persons may experience them simultaneously. For instance, Spelman (1988) observes that

[i]nsofar as she is oppressed by racism in a sexist context and sexism in a racist context, the Black woman's struggle cannot be compart-

mentalized into two struggles—one as a Black and one as a woman. Indeed, it is difficult to imagine why a Black woman would think of her struggles this way except in the face of demands by white women or by Black men that she do so. (124)

To the extent that an individual Black woman is held accountable in one situation to her race category, and in another to her sex category, we can see these as "oppositional" demands for accountability. But note, it is a *Black woman* who is held accountable in both situations.

Contrary to Omi and Winant's (1986) use of hypothetical cases, on any particular occasion of interaction we are unlikely to become uncomfortable when "people" do not act "Black," "people" do not act "Latino," or when "people" do not act "white." Rather, we are likely to become disconcerted when particular Black *women* do not act like Black *women*, particular Latino *men* do not act like Latino *men*, or particular white *women* do not act like white *women* in the context in which we observe them. Conceiving of race and gender as ongoing accomplishments means we must locate their emergence in social situations, rather than within the individual or some vaguely defined set of role expectations.[10]

Despite many important differences in the histories, traditions, and varying impacts of racial and sexual oppression across particular situations, the mechanism underlying them is the same. To the extent that members of society know their actions are accountable, they will design their actions in relation to how they might be seen and described by others. And to the extent that race category (like sex category) is omnirelevant to social life, it provides others with an ever-available resource for interpreting those actions. In short, inasmuch as our society is divided by "essential" differences between members of different race categories and categorization by race is both relevant and mandated, the accomplishment of race is unavoidable (cf. West and Zimmerman 1987).

For example, many (if not most) Black men in the United States have, at some point in their lives, been stopped on the street or pulled over by police for no apparent reason. Many (if not most) know very well that the ultimate grounds for their being detained is their race and sex category membership. Extreme deference may yield a release with the command to "move on," but at the same time, it legitimates the categorical grounds on which the police (be they Black or white) detained them in the first place. Indignation or outrage (as might befit a white man in similar circumstances) is likely to generate hostility, if not brutality, from the officers on the scene (who may share sharply honed normative conceptions regarding "inherent" violent tendencies among Black men). Their very survival may be contingent on how they conduct themselves in relation to normative conceptions of appropriate attitudes and activities for Black men in these circumstances. Here, we see both the limited rights of citizenship accorded to Black men in U.S. society and the institutional context (in this case, the criminal justice system) in which accountability is called into play.

In sum, the accomplishment of race consists of creating differences among members of different race categories—differences that are neither natural nor biological (cf. West and Zimmerman 1987). Once created, these differences are used to maintain the "essential" distinctiveness of "racial identities" and the institutional arrangements that they support. From this perspective, racial identities are not invariant idealizations of our human natures that are uniformly distributed in society. Nor are normative conceptions of attitudes and activities for one's race category templates for "racial" behaviors. Rather, what is invariant is the notion that members of different "races" *have* essentially different natures, which explain their very unequal positions in our society.[11]

CLASS

This, too, we propose, is the case with class. Here, we know that even sympathetic readers are apt to balk: Gender, yes, is "done," and race, too, is "accomplished," but class? How can we reduce a system that "differentially structures group access to material resources, including economic, political and social resources" (Andersen and Collins 1992, 50) to "a situated accomplishment"? Do we mean to deny the material realities of poverty and privilege? We do not. There is no denying the very different material realities imposed by differing relations under capital; however, we suggest that these realities have little to do with class categorization—and ultimately, with the accountability of persons to class categories—in everyday life.

For example, consider Shellee Colen's (1986) description of the significance of maids' uniforms to white, middle-class women who employ West Indian immigrant women as child care workers and domestics in New York City. In the words of Judith Thomas, one of the West Indian women Colen interviewed,

> She [the employer] wanted me to wear the uniform. She was really prejudiced. She just wanted that the maid must be identified. . . . She used to go to the beach every day with the children. So going to the beach in the sand and the sun and she would have the kids eat ice cream and all that sort of thing. . . . I tell you one day when I look at myself, I was so dirty . . . just like I came out from a garbage can. (57)

At the end of that day, says Colen, Thomas asked her employer's permission to wear jeans to the beach the next time they went, and the employer gave her permission to do so. When she did wear jeans, and the employer's brother came to the beach for a visit, Thomas noted,

> I really believe they had a talk about it, because in the evening, driving back from the beach, she said "Well, Judith, I said you could wear something else to the beach other than the uniform [but] I think you will have to wear the uniform because they're very informal on this beach and they don't know who is guests from who isn't guests." (57)

Of the women Colen interviewed (in 1985), not one was making more than $225 a week, and Thomas was the only one whose employer was paying for medical insurance. All (including Thomas) were supporting at least two households: their own in New York and that of their kin back in the West Indies. By any objective social scientific criteria, then, all would be regarded as members of the working-class poor; yet, in the eyes of Thomas's employer (and, apparently, the eyes of others at the beach), Thomas's low wages, long hours, and miserable conditions of employment were insufficient to establish her class category. Without a uniform, she could be mistaken for one of the guests and, hence, not be held accountable as a maid.

There is more to this example, of course, than meets the eye. The employer's claim notwithstanding, it is unlikely that Thomas, tending to white, middle-class children who were clearly not her own, would be mistaken for one of the guests at the beach. The blue jeans, however, might be seen as indicating her failure to comply with normative expectations of attitudes and behaviors appropriate to a maid and, worse yet, as belying the competence of her employer (whose authority is confirmed by Thomas displaying herself as a maid). As Evelyn Nakano Glenn (1992) notes in another context, "the higher standard of living of one woman is made possible by, and also helps to perpetuate, the other's lower standard of living" (34).

Admittedly, the normative conceptions that sustain the accountability of persons to class category are somewhat different from those that sustain accountability to sex category and race category. For example, despite earlier attempts to link pauperism with heredity and thereby justify the forced sterilization of poor women in the United States (Rafter 1992), scientists today do not conceive of class in relation to the biological characteristics of a person. There is, moreover, no scientific basis for popular notions of what persons in particular class categories "look like" or "act like." But although the dominant ideology within the United States is no longer based explicitly on Social Darwinism (see, for example, Gossett 1965) and although we believe, in theory, that anyone can make it, we as a society still hold certain truths to be self-evident.

As Donna Langston (1991) observes,

> If hard work were the sole determinant of your ability to support yourself and your family, surely we'd have a different outcome for many in our society. We also, however, believe in luck and on closer examination, it certainly is quite a coincidence that the "unlucky" come from certain race, gender and class backgrounds. In order to perpetuate racist, sexist and classist outcomes, we also have to believe that the current economic distribution is unchangeable, has always existed, and probably exists in this form throughout the known universe, i.e., it's "natural." (146)

Langston pinpoints the underlying assumptions that sustain our notions about persons in relation to poverty and privilege—assumptions that compete with our contradictory declarations of a meritocratic society, with its readily invoked exemplar, Horatio Alger. For example, if someone is poor, we assume it is because of something *they* did or did not do: They lacked initiative, they were not industrious, they had no ambition, and so forth. If someone is rich or merely well-off, it must be by virtue of *their own* efforts, talents, and initiative. While these beliefs certainly *look* more mutable than our views of women's and men's "essential" natures or our deep-seated convictions regarding the characteristics of persons in particular race categories, they still rest on the assumption that a person's economic fortunes derive from qualities of the person. Initiative is thus treated as inherent among the haves, and laziness is seen as inherent among the have-nots.[12] Given that initiative is a prerequisite for employment in jobs leading to upward mobility in this society, it is hardly surprising that "the rich get richer and the poor get poorer." As in the case of gender and race, profound historical effects of entrenched institutional practice result, but they unfold one accomplishment at a time.

To be sure, there are "objective" indicators of one's position within the system of distribution that differentially structure our access to resources. It is possible to sort members of society in relation to these indicators, and it is the job of many public agencies (e.g., those administering Aid to Families with Dependent Children, health benefits, food stamps, legal aid, and disability benefits) to do such sorting. In the process, public agencies allocate further unequal opportunities with respect to health, welfare, and life chances; however, whatever the criteria employed by these agencies (and these clearly change over time and place), they can be clearly distinguished from the accountability of persons to class categories in everyday life.

As Benjamin DeMott (1990) observes, Americans operate on the basis of a most unusual assumption, namely, that we live in a classless society. On the one hand, our everyday discourse is replete with categorizations of persons by class. DeMott (1990) offers numerous examples of television shows, newspaper articles, cartoons, and movies that illustrate how class "will tell" in the most mundane of social doings. On the other hand, we believe that we in the United States are truly unique "in escaping the hierarchies that burden the rest of the developed world" (DeMott 1990, 29). We cannot see the system of distribution that structures our unequal access to resources. Because we cannot see this, the accomplishment of class in everyday life rests on the presumption that everyone is endowed with equal opportunity and, therefore, that real differences in the outcomes we observe must result from individual differences in attributes like intelligence and character.

For example, consider the media's coverage of the trial of Mary Beth Whitehead, the wife of a sanitation worker and surrogate mother of Baby M. As DeMott (1990) points out, much of this trial revolved around the question of the kind of woman who would agree to bear and sell her child to someone else. One answer to this question might be "the kind of woman" who learned early in life that poverty engenders obligations of reciprocal sacrifice among people—even sacrifice for those who are not their kin (cf. Stack 1974). Whitehead was one of eight children, raised by a single mother who worked on and off as a beautician. Living in poverty, members of her family had often relied on "poor but generous neighbors" for help and had provided reciprocal assistance when they could. When William and Betsy Stern (a biochemist and a pediatrician) came to her for help, therefore, Whitehead saw them as "seemingly desperate in their childlessness, threatened by a ruinous disease (Mrs. Stem's self-diagnosed multiple sclerosis), [and] as people in trouble, unable to cope without her" (DeMott 1990). Although she would be paid for carrying the pregnancy and although she knew that they were better off financially than she was, Whitehead saw the Sterns as "in need of help" and, hence, could not do otherwise than to provide it. DeMott (1998) explains,

> She had seen people turn to others helplessly in distress, had herself been turned to previously; in her world failure to respond was unnatural. Her class experience, together with her own individual nature, made it natural to perceive the helping side of surrogacy as primary and the commercial side as important yet secondary. (98)

Another answer to the "what kind of woman" question might be Whitehead's lack of education about the technical aspects of artificial insemination (DeMott 1990). A high school dropout, she thought that this procedure allowed clinicians to implant both a man's sperm and a woman's egg in another woman's uterus, thereby making it possible for infertile couples to have their own genetic children. Just before the birth Whitehead learned she was the one who had contributed the egg and, subsequently, would not be bearing their child but her own. Under these circumstances, it would certainly seem "natural" for her to break her contract with the Sterns at the point of learning that it required her to give them her baby.

The media coverage of Whitehead's trial focused neither on class-based understandings of altruism nor on class-associated knowledge of sexual reproduction; rather, it focused on the question of Whitehead's character.

> The answers from a team of expert psychologists were reported in detail. Mrs. Whitehead was described as "impulsive, egocentric, self-dramatic, manipulative and exploitative." One member of the team averred that she suffered from a "schizotypal personality disorder." [Another] gave it as his opinion that the defendant's ailment was a "mixed personality disorder," and that she was "immature, exhibition-istic, and histrionic." . . . [U]nder the circumstances, he did not see that "there were any 'parental rights'"; Mrs. Whitehead was "a surro-gate uterus . . . and not a surrogate mother." (DeMott 1990, 96)

Through these means, "the experts" reduced Whitehead from a woman to a womb, and, therefore, someone with no legitimate claim to the child she had helped to conceive. Simultaneously, they affirmed the right of Betsy Stern to be the mother—even of a child she did not bear. As Whitehead's attorney put it in his summation, "What we are witnessing, and what we can predict will happen, is that one class of Americans will exploit another class. And it will always be the wife of the sanitation worker who must bear the children for the pediatrician" (Whitehead and Schwartz-Nobel 1989, as cited in DeMott 1990, 97). The punch line, of course, is that our very prac-tices of invoking "essential differences" between classes support the rigid system of social relations that disparately distributes opportunities and life chances. Without these practices, the "natural" relations under capital might well seem far more malleable.

The accomplishment of class renders the unequal institutional arrange-ments based on class category accountable as normal and natural, that is, as legitimate ways of organizing social life (cf. West and Zimmerman 1987). Differences between members of particular class categories that are created by this process can then be depicted as fundamental and enduring disposi-tions.[13] In this light, the institutional arrangements of our society can be seen as responsive to the differences—the social order being merely an accommodation to the natural order.

In any given situation (whether or not that situation can be character-ized as face-to-face interaction or as the more "macro" workings of institutions), the simultaneous accomplishments of class, gender, and race will differ in content and outcome. From situation to situation, the salience of the observables relevant to categorization (e.g., dress, interpersonal style, skin color) may seem to eclipse the interactional impact of the simultaneous accomplishment of all three. We maintain, nevertheless, that, just as the mechanism for accomplishment is shared, so, too, is their simultaneous accomplishment ensured.

CONCLUSION: THE PROBLEM OF DIFFERENCE

As we have indicated, mathematical metaphors describing the relations among gender, race, and class have led to considerable confusion in feminist scholarship. As we have also indicated, the conceptualizations of gender that support mathematical metaphors (e.g., "sex differences" and "sex roles") have forced scholars to think of gender as something that stands apart from and outside of race and class in people's lives.

In putting forth this perspective, we hope to advance a new way of thinking about gender, race, and class, namely, as ongoing, methodical, and situated accomplishments. We have tried to demonstrate the usefulness of this perspective for understanding how people experience gender, race, and class simultaneously. We have also tried to illustrate the implications of this perspective for reconceptualizing "the problem of difference" in feminist theory.

What are the implications of our ethnomethodological perspective for an understanding of relations among gender, race, and class? First, and perhaps most important, conceiving of these as ongoing accomplishments means that we cannot determine their relevance to social action apart from the context in which they are accomplished (Fenstermaker, West, and Zimmerman 1991; West and Fenstermaker 1993). While sex category, race category, and class category are potentially omnirelevant to social life, individuals inhabit many different identities, and these may be stressed or muted, depending on the situation. For example, consider the following incident described in detail by Patricia Williams (1991), a law professor who, by her own admission, "loves to shop" and is known among her students for her "neat clothes."[14]

> Buzzers are big in New York City. Favored particularly by smaller stores and boutiques, merchants throughout the city have installed them as screening devices to reduce the incidence of robbery: if the face at the door looks desirable, the buzzer is pressed and the door is unlocked. If the face is that of an undesirable, the door stays pressed and the door is locked. I discovered [these buzzers] and their meaning one Saturday in 1986. I was shopping in Soho and saw in a store win-

dow a sweater that I wanted to buy for my mother. I pressed my
round brown face to the window and my finger to the buzzer, seeking
admittance. A narrow-eyed white teenager, wearing running shoes
and feasting on bubble gum glared out, evaluating me for signs that
would pit me against the limits of his social understanding. After
about five minutes, he mouthed "we're closed," and blew pink rubber
at me. It was two Saturdays before Christmas, at one o'clock in the
afternoon; there were several white people in the store who appeared
to be shopping for things for *their* mothers. (44)

In this incident, says Williams, the issue of undesirability revealed itself as
a racial determination. This is true in a comparative sense; for example, it is
unlikely that a white, woman law professor would have been treated this
way by this salesperson and likely that a Latino gang member would have.
This is also true in a legal sense; for example, in cases involving discrimination, the law requires potential plaintiffs to specify whether or not they were
discriminated against on the basis of sex *or* race or some other criterion. We
suggest, however, that sex category and class category, although muted, are
hardly irrelevant to Williams's story. Indeed, we contend that one reason
readers are apt to find this incident so disturbing is that it did not happen
to a Latino gang member but to a Black, woman law professor. Our point
is not to imply that anyone should be treated this way but to show that one
cannot isolate Williams's race category from her sex category or class category and fully understand this situation. We would argue, furthermore, that
how class and gender are accomplished in concert with race must be understood through that specific interaction.

A second implication of our perspective is that the accomplishment of
race, class, and gender does not require categorical diversity among the participants. . . . Some of the most extreme displays of "essential" womanly and
manly natures may occur in settings that are usually reserved for members
of a single sex category, such as locker rooms or beauty salons (Gerson
1985). Some of the most dramatic expressions of "definitive" class characteristics may emerge in class-specific contexts (e.g., debutante balls).
Situations that involve more than one sex category, race category, and class
category may highlight categorical membership and make the accomplishment of gender, race, and class more salient, but they are not necessary to
produce these accomplishments in the first place. This point is worth stressing, since existing formulations of relations among gender, race, and class
might lead one to conclude that "difference" must be present for categorical
membership and, thus, dominance to matter.

A third implication is that, depending on how race, gender, and class
are accomplished, what looks to be the same activity may have different

meanings for those engaged in it. Consider the long-standing debates among feminists (e.g., Collins 1990; A. Davis 1971; Dill 1988; Firestone 1970; Friedan 1963; hooks 1984; Hurtado 1989; Zavella 1987) over the significance of mothering and child care in women's lives. For white, middle-class women, these activities have often been seen as constitutive of oppression in that they are taken as expressions of their "essential" womanly natures and used to discredit their participation in other activities (e.g., Friedan 1963). For many women of color (and white working-class women), mothering and child care have had (and continue to have) very different meanings. Angela Davis (1971) points out that, in the context of slavery, African American women's efforts to tend to the needs of African American children (not necessarily their own) represented the only labor they performed that could not be directly appropriated by white slave owners. Throughout U.S. history, bell hooks (1984) observes,

> Black women have identified work in the context of the family as humanizing labor, work that affirms their identity as women, as human beings showing love and care, the very gestures of humanity [that] white supremacist ideology claimed black people were incapable of expressing. (133–4)

Looking specifically at American family life in the nineteenth century, Bonnie Thornton Dill (1988) suggests that being a poor or working-class African American woman, a Chinese American woman, or a Mexican American woman meant something very different from being a Euro-American woman. Normative, class-bound conceptions of "woman's nature" at that time included tenderness, piety, and nurturance—qualities that legitimated the confinement of middle-class, Euro-American women to the domestic sphere and that promoted such confinement as the goal of working-class and poor immigrant Euro-American families' efforts. Dill (1988) states,

> For racial-ethnic women, however, the notion of separate spheres served to reinforce their subordinate status and became, in effect, another assault. As they increased their work outside the home, they were forced into a productive sphere that was organized for men and "desperate" women who were so unfortunate or immoral that they could not confine their work to the domestic sphere. In the productive sphere, however, they were denied the opportunity to embrace the dominant ideological definition of "good" wife and mother. (429)

Fourth and finally, our perspective affords an understanding of the accomplishment of race, gender, or class as constituted in the context of the differential "doings" of the others. Consider, for example, the very dramatic case of the U.S. Senate hearings on Clarence Thomas's nomination to the Supreme Court. Wherever we turned, whether to visual images on a television screen or to the justificatory discourse of print media, we were overwhelmed by the dynamics of gender, race, and class operating in concert with one another. It made a difference to us as viewers (and certainly to his testimony) that Clarence Thomas was a Black *man* and that he was a *Black* man. It also made a difference, particularly to the African American community, that he was a Black man who had been raised in poverty. Each categorical dimension played off the others and off the comparable but quite different categorizations of Anita Hill (a "self-made" Black, woman law professor, who had grown up as one of 13 children). Most white women who watched the hearings identified gender and men's dominance as the most salient aspects of them, whether in making sense of the Judiciary Committee's handling of witnesses or understanding the relationship between Hill and Thomas. By contrast, most African American viewers saw racism as the most salient aspect of the hearings, including white men's prurient interest in Black sexuality and the exposure of troubling divisions between Black women and men (Morrison 1992). The point is that how we label such dynamics does not necessarily capture their complex quality. Foreground and background, context, salience, and center shift from interaction to interaction, but all operate interdependently.

Of course, this is only the beginning. Gender, race, and class are only three means (although certainly very powerful ones) of generating difference and dominance in social life.[15] Much more must be done to distinguish other forms of inequality and their workings. Empirical evidence must be brought to bear on the question of variation in the salience of categorical memberships, while still allowing for the simultaneous influence of these memberships on interaction. We suggest that the analysis of situated conduct affords the best prospect for understanding how these "objective" properties of social life achieve their ongoing status as such and, hence, how the most fundamental divisions of our society are legitimated and maintained.

NOTES

1. The original version of this chapter was published in February 1995 in *Gender & Society* 9 (1): 8–37.

2. In this article, we use "race" rather than "ethnicity" to capture the commonsensical beliefs of members of our society. As we will show, these beliefs are predicated on the assumption that different "races" can be reliably distinguished from one another.

3. Compare, for example, the very different implications of "Double Jeopardy: To Be Black and Female" (Beale 1970) and "Positive Effects of the Multiple Negative: Explaining the Success of Black Professional Women" (C. Epstein 1973).

4. In this context, we define "experience" as participation in social systems in which gender, race, and class affect, determine, or otherwise influence behavior.

5. Here, it is important to distinguish an individual's experience of the dynamics of gender, race, and class as they order the daily course of social interaction from that individual's sense of identity as a member of gendered, raced, and classed categories. For example, in any given interaction, a woman who is Latina and a shopkeeper may experience the simultaneous effects of gender, race, and class, yet identify her experience as only "about" race, only "about" gender, or only "about" class.

6. That persons may be held accountable does not mean that they necessarily will be held accountable in every interaction. Particular interactional outcomes are not the point here; rather, it is the possibility of accountability in any interaction.

7. To maintain vital statistics on race, California, for instance, relies on mothers' and fathers' self-identifications on birth certificates.

8. Omi and Winant (1986, 64–75) provide numerous empirical illustrations, including the first appearance of "white" as a term of self-identification (circa 1680), California's decision to categorize Chinese people as "Indian" (in 1854), and the U.S. Census's creation of the category "Hispanic" (in 1980).

9. Consider Susie Guillory Phipps's unsuccessful suit against the Louisiana Bureau of Vital Records (Omi and Winant 1986, 57). Phipps was classified as "Black" on her birth certificate, in accord with a 1970 Louisiana law stipulating that anyone with at least one-thirty-second "Negro blood" was "Black." Her attorney contended that designating a race category on a person's birth certificate was unconstitutional and that, in any case, the one-thirty-second criterion was inaccurate. Ultimately, the court upheld Louisiana's state law quantifying "racial identity" and thereby affirmed the legal principle of assigning persons to specific "racial" groups.

10. This would be true if only because outcomes bearing on power and inequality are so different in different situations. Ours is a formulation that is sensitive to variability, that can accommodate, for example, interactions where class privilege and racism seem equally salient, as well as those in which racism interactionally "eclipses" accountability to sex category.

11. As Spelman observes, "The existence of racism does not require that there are races; it requires the belief that there are races" (1988, 208).

12. A devil's advocate might argue that gender, race, and class are fundamentally different because they show different degrees of "mutability" or latitude in the violation of expectations in interaction. Although class mobility is possible, one might argue, race mobility is not; or, while sex change operations can be performed, race change operations cannot. In response, we would point out that the very notion that one cannot change one's race—but can change one's sex and manipulate displays of one's class—only throws us back to biology and its reassuring, but only apparent, immutability.

13. Although we as a society believe that some people may "pull themselves up by their bootstraps" and others may "fall from grace," we still cherish the notion that class will reveal itself in a person's fundamental social and psychological character. We commonly regard the self-made man, the welfare mother, and the middle-class housewife as distinct categories of persons, whose attitudes and activities can be predicted on categorical grounds.

14. We include these prefatory comments about shopping and clothes for those readers who, on encountering this description, asked, "What does she look like?" and "What was she wearing?" Those who seek further information will find Williams featured in a recent fashion layout for *Mirabella* magazine (As Smart as They Look 1993).

15. We cannot stress this strongly enough. Gender, race, and class are obviously very salient social accomplishments in social life, because so many features of our cultural institutions and daily discourse are organized to perpetuate the categorical distinctions on which they are based. As Spelman (1988) observes, "the more a society has invested in its members' getting the categories right, the more occasions there will be for reinforcing them, and the fewer occasions there will be for questioning them" (152). On any given occasion of interaction, however, we may also be held accountable to other categorical memberships (e.g., ethnicity, nationality, sexual orientation, place of birth), and thus "difference" may then be differentially constituted.

CHAPTER FIVE

Symposium on West and Fenstermaker's "Doing Difference"

PATRICIA HILL COLLINS

How wonderful it would be to possess the insight to see beyond the messy, contemporary politics of race, class, and gender in order to propose "a new way of thinking about the workings of these relations" (West and Fenstermaker 1995a, 9).[1] The area of race, class, and gender studies struggles with the complex question of how to think about intersections of systems of oppression of race, class, and gender. We clearly need new models that will assist us in seeing how structures of power organized around intersecting relations of race, class, and gender frame the social positions occupied by individuals, work explaining how interlocking systems of oppression produce social locations for us all, where Black men are routinely stopped by the police for no apparent reason, or African American women like Patricia Williams are denied entry to stores where they could spend their hard-earned law professor salaries.

Despite West and Fenstermaker's initial promises to retheorize the intersections of race, class, and gender in a way that transcends the limitations of existing models, a surprising thing happened on the way to the end of their article. One by one, race, gender, and even class were erased. As a result, an article that claims to retheorize the interconnections of race, class, and gender said remarkably little about racism, patriarchy, and capitalism as systems of power. How this happened was impressive. Race and class appeared as gender in drag, each arriving in analytical forms virtually unrecognizable to practitioners of these respective fields. Each made brief appearances before returning to the safe haven of social constructionist arguments about difference. In the place of race, class, and gender came a rehashing of social constructionist views of society, a technique of eth-nomethodology masquerading as new theory, and—most amazing—the concept of difference used as proxy for the interconnectedness of race, class, and gender itself. The very things the article claimed to reveal it curiously erased, all the while talking about them.

Perhaps articles like "Doing Difference" wouldn't bother me so much if the stakes weren't so high. Since I have long worked in the field of race, class, and gender studies, a quick summary of the field provides a context for evaluating the contributions of this article. For years, scholars in the sep-arate areas of race or class or gender struggled for the primacy of each as an analytical category explaining inequality. To do this, they diligently chipped away at a social science logic that constructed race, class, and gender as benign attributes that were useful for describing human subjects in research designs, but treated racism, sexism, and class exploitation as variations of other more fundamental processes. More important, race, class, and gender studies each emerged, not in the rarefied atmosphere of academia, but in conjunction with social movements populated by people who had a real stake in understanding and changing inequalities of power resulting from systems of oppression called racism, patriarchy, and class exploitation.

These links between theory and politics meant that, despite their his-torical differences, all three areas shared certain fundamentals. Each aimed to explain the links between micro-level experiences structured along axes of race, class, and gender, with the larger, overarching macro systems. Each reasoned that if individuals could link their own experiences with oppres-sion on a micro level with the larger macro forces constructing their social position, they could address some of the major social problems of our day.

This commitment to theorizing oppression via these distinctive emphases eventually encountered the limitations of privileging any one system of oppres-sion over others—of patriarchy over class, for example, or white supremacy over homophobia. The very notion of the intersections of race, class, and gen-der as an area worthy of study emerged from the recognition of practitioners of each distinctive theoretical tradition that inequality could not be explained, let alone challenged, via a race-only, class-only, or gender-only framework. No one had all the answers and no one was going to get all of the answers with-out attention to two things. First, the notion of interlocking oppressions refers to the macro-level connections linking systems of oppression such as race, class, and gender. This is the model describing the social structures that create social positions. Second, the notion of intersectionality describes micro-level processes—namely, how each individual and group occupies a social position within interlocking structures of oppression described by the metaphor of intersectionality. Together they shape oppression.

At this historical moment we have something very momentous happening—the linking of three historically distinct areas of inquiry with a renewed commitment to theorize connections on multiple levels of social structure. To accomplish this goal, all must support a working hypothesis of equivalency between oppressions that allows us to explore the interconnections among the systems and extract us from the internecine battles of whose oppression is more fundamental. The intent of race, class and gender studies is to push to understand oppression (or in the more polite language of academia, "inequality" or "stratification").

"Doing Difference" claims the language of inclusivity, but decontextualizes it from the history of race, class, and gender studies. It strips the very categories of race, class, and gender of meaning and then recasts the problems of institutional power in the apolitical framework of how we might "do difference."

The authors achieve this intellectual sleight of hand impressively. Consider the order in which they construct the individual discussions of gender, race, and class. Despite criticizing others who use "additive" approaches, in constructing their argument the authors use this same approach of treating gender as the most fundamental, theoretical category and then "adding" on race and class. They lay out their theoretical argument within a gender-only framework and then generalize this argument to race and class. Note that there are no "experience" examples within the gender category; apparently gender speaks for itself and needs no examples. In contrast, the discussion of race has more "experiences" included, thus providing the unintended but nonetheless unfortunate outcome of constructing people of color as less theoretical and more embodied. Amazingly, the discussion of social class opens with an "experience," foreshadowing an unusual approach to social class. Their treatment of social class remains distinctive because the literature of social class, much more so than that of gender and race, has long been grounded in questions of institutional power. After all, it is hard to discuss global capitalist markets as performances and representations.

By the end of the article, I found little evidence that the authors had really proposed a new way of thinking. Instead, they managed to transform the interlocking systems of oppression of race, class, and gender that produce positions characterized by intersectionality into, as British cultural critic Stuart Hall puts it, "a difference that didn't make any difference at all" (1992, 23).

To recast race, class, and gender politics as an issue of postmodernist difference is indicative of some problems of the politics of postmodernist discourse overall. The construct of difference emerges from social constructionist views of self/other where the self is constructed against the difference of the other, but this is not the use of difference we encounter in this article. Social institutions, especially analyses of the institutional bases of power shaping race, class, and gender, are dropped from the analysis, leaving a plethora of postmodernist representations in their wake. Recasting racism, patriarchy, and class exploitation solely in social constructionist terms reduces race, class, and gender to performances, interactions between people embedded in a never ending string of equivalent relations, all containing race, class, and gender in some form, but a chain of equivalences devoid of power relations.

This all leads to the puzzling question of why this is happening. It is one thing to say that manipulating "difference" comprises one effective tactic used by dominant groups to maintain control—this insight is closer to the actual meanings of Williams, Spelman, and myself. It's quite another to wring one's hands about the "problem of difference," laying the groundwork for handling difference as the real problem, instead of the power relations that construct difference.

Since not all social groups appear to find difference to be such a meaningful concept, I'm left wondering who is worried about it? Thinking through the meaning of difference hasn't much concerned people of color, poor people, and all the other people deemed "different" who disappear from this article. Attention by oppressed groups to the meaning of difference remains firmly rooted in the question of the use to which differences are put in defending unequal power arrangements.

Despite the well-intentioned goal of the authors, "Doing Difference" and similar efforts to infuse race, class, and gender studies with postmodernist notions of difference leave us on dangerously thin ice. What type of oppositional politics emerge from a focus on difference devoid of power? What types of directions emerge from theories stressing representations over institutional structures and social policies as central to race, class, and gender relations? Already, I see far too many students who see resistance to oppression as occurring only in the area of representation, as if thinking about resistance and analyzing representations can substitute for active resistance against institutional power. Quite simply, difference is less a problem for me than racism, class exploitation, and gender oppression. Conceptualizing these systems of oppression as difference obfuscates the power relations and material inequalities that constitute oppression. Doing away with thinking about difference will clarify the real problem.

* * *

LIONEL A. MALDONADO

West and Fenstermaker's (1995a) argument is engaging and provocative. They propose extending the use of an ethnomethodological formulation for understanding gender to also include race and class factors. They argue that their approach is a way to understand the social construction of gender, race, and class and contend that the common distinction between "micro" and "macro" levels of analysis is a false distinction. This point is made in their discussion of "accomplishing" race, but presumably is extended to gender and class. They imply that their formulation is sufficient to understand the processes regarding social inequality, generally, but their argument is not entirely convincing. There are two issues that I believe need to be addressed more fully regarding their social construction of race, class, and gender—the focus on both *social* and *construction*.

First, on the *social* part of this construction. I agree that people make their own history. They do so, however, within the confines of the circumstances and conditions they encounter. For example, Michael Mann (1993) has documented how military, political, and economic conditions of different periods configure the nation-state and influence the experiences of individuals and groups. Out of this context, socially constructed definitions, interpretations, and their rationales are produced. The formulation by West and Fenstermaker shifts our attention from these historical circumstances. The authors' position would be strengthened in more formally acknowledging the constraints imposed by these macro-level forces in the social environment.

My second point is that since reality is *constructed*, we need to be clear whose construction is being given attention. West and Fenstermaker's discussion leaves the impression that reality somehow is monolithic. They do this in spite of an early acknowledgment that the feminist movement did not address the needs and conditions of working-class women and women of color, nor did it recruit them; this rendered the movement less than inclusive. Clearly, groups and their members can, and often do, have very different (even diametrically opposed) beliefs about what is "real," "objectively true," "good," and "desirable." Much of this depends on the place each occupies in the social structure. How West and Fenstermaker's conception would accommodate this lack of consensus on social construction is not clear. Good examples on whose ideology wins out in this battle include Andrew Scull (1993) on the treatment of lunacy in Great Britain, George Sanchez (1993) on the development of the Chicano community in Los Angeles, and Paula Giddings (1984) on why Black women were not drawn to the feminist movement of white, middle-class women. West and Fenstermaker's argument would be enriched by consideration of such works.

* * *

DANA Y. TAKAGI

In *The Ethics of Authenticity*, a pithy book about identity, politics, and modernity, philosopher Charles Taylor (1992) defines three grand malaises of modernity: loss of meaning, loss of ends, and loss of freedoms. Taylor admits these are jumbo-sized themes, and he restricts his discussion to the first malaise—loss of meaning—hoping that others will be persuaded by his analysis and encouraged to take up analysis of the remaining two. Taylor's point is a simple one: namely, that contemporary debates about modernity fail to get to the heart of the problem—an analysis of the moral weightiness of the ideal of authenticity. Indeed, according to Taylor (1992), in spite of the tremendous amount of disagreement between, for example, universalists and relativists, the discussion in toto reveals an "extraordinary inarticulacy" about authenticity as "one of the constitutive ideals of modern culture" (18).

Like Taylor, West and Fenstermaker are interested in grand malaise. Although they never invoke his discussion, the parallel between their essay and Taylor's book is striking. As if on cue, they pick up Taylor's second grand malaise, "loss of ends," and illustrate how *some* feminist technologies of understanding race, class, and gender are animated by mathematical metaphors—intersections, additivity, and overlapping circles of Venn diagrams. By "loss of ends," Taylor is referring to the "primacy of instrumental reason" in economic, social, and political life. For West and Fenstermaker, arithmetic models, although providing neat diagrams of intersectionality, tend to ignore the socially produced nature of difference.

The problem of mathematics is more than the stammering of language, that is, of fumbling through the list of "inter-" descriptors—intersection, interwoven, interaction, intervening—to grasp the doings of race, class, and gender. The authors quite rightly point out that verbiage about simultaneity is an after-the-fact discussion that says next to nothing about the *mechanisms* that produce inequality.

Their essay, which documents structural and representational aspects of inequality, will be taken, I hope, as an argument for balance between what is currently seen as interactional consequences and interactional productions. The former should not be confused with the latter; consequences refers to outcomes and "effects," whereas the former constitutes the latter.

Their discussion should not be read, as I fear it might, simply as a plea for a new technology, ethnomethodological vision, for thinking about difference. Approaches to difference must be distinguished from visions of difference. Like technique, approach focuses on apprehending difference. Contrastingly, vision conjures up perspective, utopia, and even that category about which many of us feel ambivalent—science. West and Fenstermaker are offering us the latter, a vision of ethnomethodological gains as a means for understanding the mechanisms of doing difference. Their choice of terms, *mechanisms,* is both an appeal and rebuff of science metaphors about society. Mechanisms that are not mechanical refer to situated conduct, interactional accomplishments, and contextually specific interactions.

What is engaging about this essay for me as a sociologist is their move to divide scholarship about difference into metaphors and mechanisms.

West and Fenstermaker's notion of mechanisms is not completely at odds with some feminist thinking about difference. Their compelling argument to decenter math metaphors and privilege "situated conduct" is mostly complementary with Haraway's (1991) exposition of situated knowledges and partial perspective, but, whereas Haraway's project is to reclaim and rearticulate notions of science and objectivity for feminist perspectives, West and Fenstermaker appear less sanguine about such a possibility.

If *they* are not keen on math metaphors, then what should we do about the fact that the rest of the world steeps in the language of math, science, and biology? Or put another way, academics are not the only ones who embrace the metaphors of additivity and other mathematical relations. Discourses of science and math, and of instrumental reason, characterize popular understandings of inequality, too.

If interactional accomplishments are mechanisms of doing difference, then perhaps the language of mathematics is part of that accomplishment as well.

* * *

BARRIE THORNE

West and Fenstermaker's perceptive discussion of metaphors led me to reflect upon the authors' own imagery for conceptualizing relations among gender, race, and class. Instead of mathematics, West and Fenstermaker evoke the sphere of serious effort or work: *"doing* gender" (race, class); "difference as a *routine, methodical,* and ongoing *accomplishment"*; "the local *management* of conduct in relation to normative conceptions"; race, class, gender as *"mechanisms* for *producing* social inequality" (West and Fenstermaker 1995a, 9).

This imagery of daily interaction as a process of production focuses the argument that basic categories of difference and inequality are socially constructed. "Doing gender" is a compelling concept because it jolts the assumption of gender as an innate condition and replaces it with a sense of ongoing process and activity. The process, according to West and Fenstermaker, starts with "normative conceptions," such as "the moral conviction that there are only two sexes" and related assumptions about the "nature" of women and of men; actors sustain these conceptions through the practice of holding one another accountable as men or women (or Black men or working-class white women). West and Fenstermaker argue that the work of "doing difference"—the repeated act of holding one another accountable to cultural conceptions—is the basic mechanism that connects gender, race, and class.

The upholding of cultural conceptions keeps categories in place, and, turning to the dynamics of racial formation, West and Fenstermaker's framework can help account for the creation and inhabiting of racial categories, but it cannot explain the ways in which racial categories are "transformed and destroyed" (Omi and Winant 1994, 55). Nor does the ethnomethodological approach grapple with historical changes in the organization, meanings, and relationships among gender, race, and class. West and Fenstermaker, like Garfinkel and Goffman, analyze social phenomena with a functionalist tilt, emphasizing the maintenance and reproduction of normative conceptions but neglecting countervailing processes of resistance, challenge, conflict, and change.

Other contemporary theorists image the construction of gender not as work but as performance and even as parody. Pursuing an insight similar to the one that propels West and Fenstermaker's thinking, the philosopher Judith Butler (1990) writes, "Because there is neither an 'essence' that gender expresses or externalizes nor an objective ideal to which gender aspires, and because gender is not a fact, the various acts of gender create the idea of gender, and without those acts, there would be no gender at all" (140). Butler writes within the tradition of poststructuralism and seems to be unaware of sociological analyses of the construction of gender, which predated her work by more than a decade (S. Epstein 1994). Like West and Fenstermaker, but with a central emphasis on the heterosexual marking of gender, Butler (1990) discusses the routine acts that sustain binary gender categories. Unlike West and Fenstermaker, however, Butler emphasizes possibilities for transgression, looking for ways to "trouble the gender categories that support gender hierarchy and compulsory heterosexuality" (x).

The dramaturgical approach that feminist sociologists left behind when we discarded the conception of "sex roles" has reappeared in Butler's writings and in the humanities and queer theory more generally. Dramaturgical metaphors seem to fare better in their hands, perhaps because of a shift from reified noun ("role") to verb ("perform") and a cascade of evocative images—masquerade, parody, gender as a fabrication and a persistent impersonation that passes as the real—that provide an engaging counterpoint to the more earnest sociological approach.

But gender extends beyond daily cultural performance, and it will take much more than doing drag and mocking naturalized conceptions to transform it. Gender—and race, class, and compulsory heterosexuality—extend deep into the unconscious and the shaping of emotions (note the cognitive focus of the "doing difference" framework) and outward into social structure and material interests. R. W. Connell (1987b), who writes about a "field of gender relations," attends to this scope and insists on a theoretical approach that opens toward history. His reflections on structure and practice and on the organization of gender relations and meanings as a going but contested concern give dynamism to the core argument that gender is a social construction. He and his colleagues (Kessler et al. 1985) lay out a chain of suggestive metaphors when they write that class and gender "abrade, inflame, amplify, twist, negate, dampen, complicate each other" (42). To grasp complex relations among gender, race, class, and sexuality, we need a range of metaphors and theories honed in many sites of analysis. By itself, the construct "doing difference" won't stretch far enough.

* * *

LYNN WEBER

West and Fenstermaker build an analysis of race, class, and gender from the following foundation: a critique of the metaphors in the emerging scholarship on race, class, and gender; a critique of gender scholarship that ignores race and class; and an ethnomethodological approach, which is not grounded in gender, race, or class analysis. These three building blocks contain the strengths and the weaknesses of their perspective.

Grounded in ethnomethodology, West and Fenstermaker conceptualize race, class, and gender as emergent properties of social situations not reducible to a material or biological essence, and therefore not properties of individuals or some "vaguely defined set of role expectations" (25). They highlight the simultaneity of experience of race, class, and gender by focusing on how these emerge in face-to-face interactions. These are the greatest strengths of their approach: that race, class, and gender are socially constructed simultaneously in interaction and are not reducible to biological or material characteristics of individuals.

Metaphors aside, the fundamental contrast between race, class, and gender scholarship and "doing difference" is that West and Fenstermaker obscure rather than illuminate the mechanisms of power in the production and maintenance of racism, classism, and sexism. For race, class, and gender scholarship, social relations of dominance/control and subordination/ resistance are the cornerstones of theory. Because of its exclusive attention on face-to-face interaction, macro social structural processes such as institutional arrangements, community structures, and even family systems are rendered invisible in most observations based on an ethnomethodological analysis. This has several consequences. First, it obscures the freedom from constraints and the access to material resources that frame privileged group members' face-to-face interactions with each other and the control they exert in interactions with oppressed group members. In this way, it subtly reproduces the bias in perspectives that emanate solely from positions of privilege. Second, it conceals the collective involvement, connection, and consciousness of oppressed group members that arise in the struggle for survival within the context of systemic constraints.

A central element of privilege and power is freedom from constraints on material, political, and ideological resources, options, and opportunities. When options are not restricted, face-to-face encounters can take on greater significance in the lives of the participants. For example, in our study of Black and white professional-managerial women, Elizabeth Higginbotham and I asked women to describe any differential treatment or discrimination they experienced at work. Women in female-dominated occupations (teachers, nurses, librarians) talked in detail about structural discrimination against the entire occupation—low wages, lack of respect, and so on. Women in male-dominated occupations (lawyers, professors, business managers) instead talked about face-to-face interactions in the workplace, such as sexist and racist comments, being left out of key work informational networks, and having bosses who did not appreciate their talents. Wages, which were significantly different across these groups, were rarely mentioned by the women in male-dominated occupations. Instead they focused on individual, everyday, face-to-face relationships both to define their problems and to think about solutions (e.g., switch offices, change the way they interacted, and so on). Without attention to macro social structures that enable privilege in ideological and political as well as material/economic domains, we understand less about the processes that are unspoken or not problematic in face-to-face interactions.

From the perspective of subordinate groups, failing to analyze macro social structures and community ties has the effect of producing a static theory of conformity and not a dynamic theory capable of revealing resistance and social change. Race, class, and gender are pervasive social arrangements, and fundamental social structural changes in these arrangements cannot be fully captured in the attitudes and actions of a few unremarkable actors in everyday interactions. When West and Fenstermaker analyze interactions involving dominant and subordinate group members, they can consequently see only the actions of oppressed group actors—whether conforming or resistant—as reinforcing the existing race, class, and gender hierarchy.

Recall the example of the African American man who was stopped by the cop. West and Fenstermaker argue that if he acts passively and accepts the ticket without question, the race, class, and gender hierarchy is reinforced. If he chooses to resist, however, he brings on greater sanctions and reinforces the ideology about violent Black men that got him stopped in the first place. In that situation, there is no possibility for social change because the forces that could change expectations and behaviors are not always represented in isolated one-on-one interactions. What the Black driver encountered in that situation was more than a set of stereotypes or expectations in another individual's head. He encountered a cop with a gun that he is legitimately authorized to use by his position in a macro political system that preserves the privilege of those in power through the use of force. The approach, as currently conceived, ignores both the material realities in the situation (the gun) and the macro structures that lend force to the police action.

It also hides the connections of African Americans to a community of resistance, because in this situation we can see the driver as having no options only if we assume that he is isolated from others—the tendency when face-to-face interaction is the sole focus of attention. Imagine, instead, that the driver is the '90s version of Rosa Parks, and he is sent down that highway as bait by a consortium of African American civil rights organizations, some of whose representatives are strategically planted with video cams to document unfair police treatment of African American men on the highways. When stopped, the driver might protest and receive harsh treatment, which does not reinforce the status quo, but rather galvanizes the African American community to demand that the officer be fired, the police be monitored for selective enforcement of traffic laws and citizen abuse, the local sheriff be recalled, and so on. This scenario can happen only when we recognize the connection between an individual's collective consciousness, collective action, and macro social structural change.

Besides taking a different stance with respect to power and macro social structures, West and Fenstermaker argue that the mathematical metaphors commonly used in scholarship on race, class, and gender are inadequate and in some ways inaccurate. As West and Fenstermaker note, all of these metaphors imply that race, class, and gender can be isolated from one another in people's lives, a contention that is fairly uniformly rejected by the same authors who employ them (cf. Andersen and Collins 1994; Baca Zinn and Dill 1994; Collins 1990). They also point out that authors sometimes reduce gender, race, or class to a material or biological essence even while asserting that each is socially constructed, as when Collins (1990, 27) suggests that social constructions of gender are based on clearer biological criteria than constructions of race are. By articulating biology as a difference among the dimensions, Collins undercuts the argument that they are socially constructed.

While West and Fenstermaker correctly note the limits of the mathematical metaphors, I think they incorrectly assume that the insights of a race, class, and gender perspective have been seriously restricted by the use of less than perfect metaphors. For example, mathematical metaphors have the most direct relevance to positivist, quantitative research where race, class, and gender are treated as variables in an equation allowed to represent social reality. None of the authors cited here employ that approach and, in fact, are critical of it; furthermore, these authors use not only mathematical metaphors but also many others. Literary images are also quite common:

the wall at the end of Brewster Place (Baca Zinn and Dill 1994) or "holding back the ocean with a broom" (Gilkes 1980). The fact that these images do not fully depict the complexities of race, class, and gender in social structural arrangements and lived experience does not inhibit these authors from attempting to do so in the totality of their writing on the subject. In fact, West and Fenstermaker themselves offer no metaphor to illustrate their perspective; instead, they describe the accomplishment of race, class, and gender in social interaction—which is not a metaphor/representation of the thing, but the thing itself—as they see it. They would probably be very hard-pressed to find some other image that would accurately stand for the processes they attempt to describe.

West and Fenstermaker contend that we must analyze gender, race, and class in the *context* in which it is accomplished, and that *is* precisely what race, class, and gender scholarship does—presents systematic observations of the lives of people of color, women, and the working class. By developing a "doing difference" approach from a critique of race, class, and gender metaphors and ethnomethodology—instead of the systematic observations they call for—they obscure the central dynamics of power relations in the micro and macro structures of oppression.

* * *

HOWARD WINANT

Candace West and Sarah Fenstermaker (1995a) do some marvelous work in their article "Doing Difference." They give us a thoughtful account of the dynamics of gender-, race-, and class-based forms of "difference," which is to say of the dynamics of social inequality and injustice. They also employ ethnomethodology in a creative fashion, producing a wide range of political insights and helping us to reconceptualize some very thorny problems in contemporary U.S. politics.

Their principal achievement is their extension of the ethnomethodological account of difference, almost up to the frontier of a hegemony-oriented analysis. Their account of gender, race, and class as accomplishments, projects from which human agency is never absent, helps explain better than any other approach I know the contradictory character of these dimensions of identity.

By "contradictory character" I mean what Du Bois described nearly a century ago as the "veil" that divided and complicated blackness, the "peculiar sensation" of being "both an American and a Negro." Although he spoke of a racial distinction, his analysis resonates with oppressions of various kinds. "One ever feels his [*sic*] twoness," Du Bois wrote ([1903] 1989, 5). Awareness of the distinctive character of Black identity in a white society did not permit any transcendence of the veil, but it did facilitate a survival strategy: One had to divide oneself, to see oneself from both within and without, in order to anticipate and thus withstand the degradation that white supremacy constantly heaped upon its "others."

The contradiction is that to render this survival strategy effective, one has to emulate the oppressor, to think like him, to become him, at least up to a certain point. The Du Boisian analysis explains the "internalized oppression" much denounced by nationalists; more to the point here, it also explains the reproduction of racism as a price of surviving, and of resisting, racism. There are many implications one could draw from such an analysis: Freudian, Marxian, and Foucauldian approaches could all develop further the rich account Du Bois offers. So too can ethnomethodology, in the capable hands of West and Fenstermaker.

What I think is most useful about their work is its ability to stretch the ethnomethodological approach politically. Since Garfinkel, ethnomethodology has understood social relationships in terms of an "experiential technology," a set of tools available to actors to make sense of their interpersonal relations, their "lifeworld" in the Schutzian phrase. I do not think I am exaggerating when I suggest that West and Fenstermaker burst these bounds.

Take this statement,

> While individuals are the ones who do gender, the process of rendering something accountable is both interactional and institutional in character: It is a feature of social relationships, and its idiom derives from the institutional arena in which those relationships come to life. (21)

Or this, immediately following,

> Gender is obviously much more than a role or an individual characteristic: It is a mechanism whereby situated social action contributes to the reproduction of social structure. (21)

This is what I mean by reaching the frontiers of a hegemony-based analysis. As I understand them, West and Fenstermaker argue that there is something generalizable about the production of difference in regular, situated, human interaction. The linguistic regularities (what they call "idiom") through which difference is recognized and the patterned repetition (what they call "mechanism") through which individual characteristics become collectivized produce the divided and unequal social whole. This is a real extension of the traditional ethnomethodological perspective, whose focus was restricted to the generation and confirmation of shared perceptions of interaction. Only if this expanded view of the production of social structure is in place, I suggest, can we begin to talk of the politics of difference.

Yet, is it fully in place? I have spoken of the "frontiers" of a hegemony-based analysis because I think some significant problems persist in West and Fenstermaker's approach. Their account of the institutional dimensions of difference, of the social structures we label gender, race, and class, remains limited. For them, structure is only that which can be shown to be constantly reproduced from moment to moment. It has no ongoing, relatively independent existence.

An important dimension of hegemony is therefore neglected in the ethnomethodological view of difference as situated conduct. In my view, social structure must be understood as dynamic and reciprocal; it is not only a *product* of accreted and repeated subjective action but also *produces* subjects. As an example consider the commodity form of value. Without necessarily embracing the entire Marxist schema, we can readily see that capitalist classes and their members (as well as most of the other relationships and, consequently, the social roles we take for granted in the postmodern world) would be inconceivable without this structure; yet, it would be difficult to argue that the commodity form exists solely in the ways in which it is presently reproduced. On the contrary, it has a formidable inertia, a historical weight, which is crystallized in innumerable institutions, customs, and laws. It has been engraved in time and space, made into a truly "deep structure"—a result not only of contemporary repetitions but also as a legacy of past labor and past action (Sewell 1992, 25–6). It can produce subjects only because it has acquired its weight, its ubiquity, over epochal stretches of time.

To understand difference in terms of hegemony, then, we must conceive it both as situated conduct that repeats and thus supports systems of power and as a consequence of a pre-existing "structure in dominance" (Hall 1980). Indeed, hegemony is the synthesis of these two "moments" of power: Reproduced by the limited and situated agency of its subjects, it also concedes to them a limited but real autonomy. This is a situation that Gramsci (1971) described as one of "equilibria in which the interests of the dominant group prevail, but only up to a certain point" (1982).

This leads me to my final point concerning social change. To theorize difference as I have done so far—as situated conduct plus institutionally conceded autonomy—remains inadequate because neither of these accounts can explain the disruptive, oppositional character of difference. It is striking how both the ethnomethodological and hegemony-based approaches to gender, race, and class argue that these social distinctions are relatively static features of domination and inequality. Whether routinized through "experiential technology" or conceded in limited fashion by the powerful, the agency that "does" difference is conceived as limited and collusive in its own subordination.

Looking at racial difference, for instance: If race consists of "situated conduct" through which actual human subjects necessarily reproduce their subordination, how can large-scale sociopolitical change *ever* occur on racial lines? How was Dr. King able, to pick just one example from a virtually infinite list, to mobilize 6,000 black children(!) to march against the dogs, fire hoses, and truncheons of the Birmingham police one day in 1963? Weren't those children, and their parents, as "situated" as everyone else?

On the other hand, if "structures in dominance" are able to maintain hegemony by judicious concessions of autonomy to the subordinate, how is it that concepts of emancipation, liberation, and freedom have proved so hard to eradicate? The various dimensions of difference—gender-, racial-, and class-based, as well as others—retain an oppositional character that always exceeds the grasp of gestures made to contain it. Even the elimination of inequality (utopian as that might sound at this reactionary political juncture) would not justify the liquidation of difference. The project of self-emancipation, what Du Bois called "the conservation of races," would still await realization. (Once more, I am speaking in the context of racial difference, but I think the insight has wider application.) This work is already visible, prefigured in those aspects of "situated conduct" that do not preserve, but rather subvert, the established "experiential technology" of acquiescence to subordination (Kelley 1994), as well as in counterinstitutions and countercultures of various sorts.

In this respect, difference is not something that one "does" or many "do," but rather something that one "is" and many "are." The permanence of difference, situated and structured, but above all oppositional, still points toward freedom.

Reply—(Re)Doing Difference

We are honored to have "Doing Difference" as the subject of this symposium. It is extremely gratifying to have our article read so seriously by Professors Collins, Maldonado, Takagi, Thorne, Weber, and Winant and to have this opportunity to respond to their remarks. Together, they raise three important concerns to which our reply will be focused. In the space allotted to us, we try to rearticulate the fundamental distinction between process and outcome so crucial to understanding our perspective and then reassess the implications of this distinction for the questions of (a) face-to-face interaction versus structural discrimination; (b) history, institutions, and social structure; and (c) opposition, resistance, and change.

PROCESS VERSUS OUTCOME

Our overarching concern in "Doing Difference" is social inequality, in all its invidious manifestations. We take it as our starting point that the effects of patriarchy, racism, and class oppression have been amply and eloquently demonstrated by the scholars in whose footsteps we follow—and that no one would dispute these. We therefore begin with the assumption that these are well documented (by those who have commented on our article, among others). Our purpose is not to further document the effects of these *outcomes* but, rather, to understand the processes that produce them. In pursuit of this goal, we do not conceptualize difference per se as that which must be overcome: We agree that difference qua difference is not the problem. We believe, however, that a meaningful description of a system in which the bases of inequality *interact* with one another requires attention not only to the troublesome outcomes of the system (e.g., poverty, physical violence, punitive social policies, and so on) but also to the workings of the social relationships that produced those outcomes.

The criticisms raised by our commentators highlight the greatest challenge we faced in writing the article, namely, how to articulate the crucial distinction we advance between the processes and outcomes of social inequality. We tried to clarify this (see West and Fenstermaker 1995a) first on page 9: "while gender, race, and class . . . exhibit vastly different descriptive characteristics and outcomes, they are, nonetheless, comparable as mechanisms for producing social inequality." We tried again on page 19: "The goal of this article is not to analyze situated conduct per se but to understand the workings of inequality." And we tried again on page 25: "Despite many important differences in the histories, traditions, and varying impacts of racial and sexual [and class] oppression across particular situations, the mechanism underlying them is the same." Despite such efforts, the comments of our critics suggest that we have failed to spell out this important distinction adequately and that the implications of our formulation are likely to be misunderstood.

We conceive of gender, race, and class as ongoing interactional accomplishments (i.e., processes) that make patriarchy, racism, and class oppression possible. The accountability of persons to sex category, race category, and class category is, from our perspective, the heart of the matter. By "accountability" we do not mean the act of persons holding one another individually accountable, but the ubiquitous *possibility* of persons being held accountable—of having their actions, their circumstances, and even their descriptions characterized in serious and consequential ways (Heritage 1984, 136–7). Lest we be seen as merely substituting passive for active voice in making this distinction, we reiterate that (a) the notion of accountability pertains to activities that conform to prevailing cultural conceptions as well as to those activities that deviate; (b) the process of rendering some action accountable is an interactional—used in the broadest sense of the term—rather than an individual accomplishment; and (c) accountability is both interactional and institutional in character. . . . Thus, the agencies involved are institutions as well as individuals engaged in interaction with others.

FACE-TO-FACE INTERACTION VERSUS SOCIAL STRUCTURAL ANALYSIS

Given the above distinction between the processes of accomplishing gender, race, and class and the outcomes of those processes (i.e., patriarchy, racism, and class oppression), the question of face-to-face interaction "versus" structural discrimination becomes somewhat moot. We do not intend to use a postmodern concept of difference as a way to erase or minimize the concrete institutionalization of oppression that exists. This is so because we do not conceive of interaction as standing apart from the production of gender, race, and class divisions but, rather, as integral to the production of those divisions in the first instance (as both "the shadow *and* the substance," in Goffman's terms [1976, 69–77; italics in original]).

At any given moment, of course, theoretical attention may focus at different levels of concern. As with different lenses of a camera, foreground and background may shift in clarity and salience. So too with a set of theoretical lenses: The role of interaction may momentarily shift the focus from more macro, social structural forms; nevertheless, both are always at work and serve as manifestations of each other. This is why we take issue with Weber (1995), who argues that our perspective is limited by a focus on "a few unremarkable actors in everyday interactions" (501).

To be sure, our analytical perspective on gender, race, and class *is* different from any individual's experience of these dynamics (including our own). As we noted earlier (West and Fenstermaker 1995a, 33, n. 4), "a woman who is Latina and a shopkeeper may experience the simultaneous effects of gender, race, and class, yet identify her experience as only 'about' race, only 'about' gender, or only 'about' class." When asked to describe any differential treatment or discrimination she experiences at work, this woman might cite the lack of respect accorded to those in her occupation or the racist and/or sexist comments she encounters in her shop, depending on how she sees her experience. Regardless of how she views it, the fact that she can be categorized as a woman, a Latina, *and* a shopkeeper provides the possibility that she may be held accountable for her actions—in ordinary interaction and by the institutional workings of society—as a member of any (or all) of these categories (see Winant's [1995, this chapter] discussion of Du Bois). It is this possibility that provides our sense of patriarchy, racism, and class oppression as enduring and pervasive social arrangements.

Here we should note that since accountability is a feature of social relationships (not individuals), participants in any interaction are equally vulnerable to others characterizing their activities in ways that take notice of those activities and place them in a social framework (Heritage 1984, 136–7). For example, the police who stop Black men on the street or pull them over may also be held accountable for *their* actions as members of their sex category, race category, and class category. Indeed, public opinion about the police officers who apprehended and assaulted Rodney King in Los Angeles was shaped largely by public categorization of the officers as white men from suburban, working-class communities outside the city. The explosive reaction to the "not guilty" verdicts in the first trial of these officers leaves little doubt that their actions were seen to support the oppressive practices of the criminal justice system and the existing social order. In short, insofar as sex category, race category, and class category are omnirelevant to social life, no one is immune from being held accountable for their actions as an incumbent of particular categories.

HISTORY, INSTITUTIONS, AND SOCIAL STRUCTURE

With process and outcome distinguished from one another, it should be clear that the accomplishments of gender, race, and class rest on and are situated in history, institutional practices, and social structure, rather than disembodied from people's lives. Of course, the organization and meanings of gender, race, and class change over time, as do relationships among them. By viewing these as accomplishments, however, we can see how situated social action contributes to the reproduction of social structure at any particular sociohistorical moment. The challenge we face—theoretically and empirically—is to describe a system that manifests great interactional variation *but, at the same time,* rests on far more stable structural and historical legacies. Our focus on ever-changing, variously situated social relationships as the sites for the doing of difference does not denude those relationships of the powerful contexts in which they unfold. We argue only that the impact of the forces of social structure and history is realized *in the unfolding of those relationships.* . . .

OPPOSITION, RESISTANCE, AND CHANGE

Where is the possibility of people working at various levels of self-consciousness to resist oppression and promote change? Must we, as Thorne (1995) asserts, "[emphasize] the maintenance and reproduction of normative conceptions, but [neglect] countervailing processes of resistance, challenge, conflict, and change" (498)? After all, we have argued that to the extent that sex category, race category, and class category are fundamental criteria for differentiation, the accomplishments of gender, race, and class are unavoidable. This is so because of the social consequences of sex category, race category, and class category membership—the allocation of power in domestic, economic, and political arenas as well as the broad domain of social and institutional relationships; yet, even though gender, race, and class are ubiquitous, they are not identically salient in every set of social relationships in which inequality is done. Here, we believe, is where our formulation differs from the "monolithic" view Maldonado (1995) describes. Contrary to his description, our focus on the process of doing difference (to complement a focus on its outcomes) promotes a clearer perspective on the many moments of resistance that daily play themselves out in social relations. We argue that since difference is "done," there is both activity (including resistance) and agency at its foundation. Indeed, it is likely that resistance is as ubiquitous a feature of the shaping of inequality as is the doing of difference itself. We would agree with Winant (1995) that "the permanence of difference, situated and structured, but above all oppositional, still points toward freedom" (505).

What about lasting social change? For one, we contend that social action that confounds the possibility of differentiating persons according to sex category, race category, and/or class category membership undermines the legitimacy of existing institutional arrangements. Consider, for example, the growing public and scientific interest in the problems associated with race categorization today. As we write this, the *San Jose Mercury News* (among many other newspapers) has published a front-page story announcing that genes do not define race (Alvarado 1995, A1ff), and *Newsweek* has published a cover story on the changing meaning of *Black* as a category (Morganthau 1995, 63ff). Among the highlights of these stories are the public announcements of the facts that, from a genetic standpoint, "race" does not exist (Alvarado 1995, A1) and existing racial classifications do not capture changing demographic realities (Morganthau 1995, 65). Even the U.S. federal government has joined the debate, with the Office of Management and Budget sponsoring a series of public hearings on the topic of revising its statistical categories of race and ethnicity (Lewis 1994, A1). To be sure, none of these sources is proposing that race category be abolished. The consequences, they suggest, would be too dire (e.g., eliminating formulas used to distribute federal aid and to support the Voting Rights Act through districting regulations in congressional elections); however, by raising the untenability of existing "racial categories" as a matter of public debate, they are calling public attention to the question of why we seem so determined to divide humans into mutually exclusive groups to begin with (Begley 1995, 69). Such questioning can not only weaken the accountability of conduct to existing racial categories, but it can also offer the possibility of more widespread loosening of accountability in general (West and Zimmerman 1987, 146).

A second prospect for opposition, resistance, and change lies, of course, in social movements. When individuals are involved in "doing difference" appropriately, they simultaneously sustain, reproduce, and render legitimate the institutional arrangements that are predicated on sex category, race category, and class category (among others). If they fail to "do difference" appropriately, they as individuals—not the institutional arrangements— may be held to account (for their motives, character, and predispositions); however, social movements (e.g., those that oppose patriarchy, racism, and class oppression) can furnish the ideology and impetus to question existing arrangements and the social support for individual exploration of alternatives to them (West and Zimmerman 1987, 146). Valerie Jenness observes, "many social movements, and certainly. . . 'new social movements' have relied upon the accomplishment of race, class, and gender in exactly the same terms that the perspective implies" (personal communication March 4, 1995; see also Taylor and Whittier's [1992] discussion of "collective identities" as a critical resource for mobilizing contemporary social movements). As a result, social movements may call institutions themselves to account for *their* motives, character, and predispositions.

CONCLUSION

"Doing Difference" is a relatively modest attempt to map the dynamics of gender, race, and class as they unfold in social relations. We intended it to provide, as Takagi (1995) puts it, "an argument for balance between what is currently seen as interactional consequences [on the one hand] and interactional productions [on the other]" (496). We engaged with the general and ongoing project of many scholars to meaningfully link the workings of a system of oppression in order to understand the nature of social domination and possibilities for change. We rejected the notion of a hierarchy of oppressions, and we sought to understand simultaneity as more than a periodic collision of socially determined categories with unpredictable outcomes. Toward this end, we asked how inequalities are produced *together*.

There is a good deal to criticize in this first theoretical statement and much more work is needed to improve on it. We outlined a number of suggestions for further work in the article itself; here, we offer a few more. First, we have not fully articulated how the accomplishment of gender, race, and class actually link the realms of institutional and face-to-face interaction. Second, the dynamics of class inequality, although perhaps not qualitatively different from one another, are different enough in their interaction with other categories to warrant much more investigation. As Bettina Aptheker has noted in response to our article, "'Class' is the most problematic—not because it is not true, but because it is either (apparently) overshadowed by race (most often) or more complicated since it is not necessarily (inherently) immediately identifiable" (personal communication, November 8, 1994). We believe that the question of "inherence" deserves much closer attention, with respect to class as well as other categorical identities, as they operate in confluence with one another. Third, and most important, the ideas we advance in this article must be translated into empirical research. With empirical attention to the mechanisms that produce social inequality, no single theoretical statement will be asked to bear all the weight (and the freight) of the complexity of these social relationships and the politics of studying them; moreover, only in empirical work will Thorne's (1995) call for "a range of metaphors and theories honed in many sites of analysis" (499) make sense.

We agree wholeheartedly with Collins (1995) that there is a great deal at stake: Efforts such as this one have grave consequences for how scholars undertake a collaborative dialogue and for how those who also work directly to end oppression conceive of and realize coalition. Of all the criticisms and praise leveled at our article thus far (prior to publication as well as afterward), however, we would most take issue with the idea that a focus on the socially constructed character of oppression reduces it to "performance" or text, minus the weight of history, torment, struggle, and resistance. A focus on the situated, dynamic, and quintessentially social character of inequality does not deny, dilute, or erase the very real consequences of domination. To the contrary, it can further clarify how much really *is* at stake.

NOTE

1. This symposium and the reply to it were originally published in 1995 in *Gender & Society* 9 (4): 491–513.

Section II   **EMPIRICAL**

APPLICATIONS

CHAPTER SIX

Work and Gender (from The Gender Factory)

SARAH FENSTERMAKER

I began with the well-worn story of "who does what" in the market and the household.[1] Judging from the literature, and the descriptive statistics in chapter 3, it looked as if there wasn't much variance, or even much of a story to tell: Husbands are the primary breadwinners, so-called, and wives the household workers. When wives take outside jobs, they add those hours to their work in the home. Such generalizations are, of course, accurate if imprecise. And that is where the analysis began. Another story was unearthed by positing a set of work relations that operate within the household and are determined by the unexamined terrain of *household* productive capacity. That is, how much was done at home, at work, and who did it were conceived to be different, albeit related, phenomena. Moreover, how work was allocated was presumed to operate in the context of, and conditional on, the establishment of the total amount of household and market work.

The more accurate picture that emerged was still one of little variance, but the sources of that variation were revealed. First, a great deal of the variance in individual contributions to the home and to the labor market is captured by the context of the work itself. That is, the household "pie" places its own demands on household members and helps to determine household labor and market time allocations. Second, however, and just as crucial to an understanding of household work relations, is the vast (and largely uncharted) normative backdrop that influences the mechanisms by which work is apportioned to household members and that renders household work relations as gender relations. Thus, as only one example, the total amount of work established for the household had a large and significant bearing only on the wives' tasks and time. These findings cannot be dismissed simply by invoking some version of a "natural order"—of either an economic or a biological variety.

It is the premise of this final chapter that the division of household labor represents a process whereby both gender and work shape and are shaped by each other. Moreover, the results of this analysis demand a reconceptualization of household production that takes account of the imperatives of work and gender and of the sense that the members make of them.

* * *

THE STRUCTURES OF HOUSEHOLD LABOR

The analysis has made clear that how families come to allocate their household labors depends on a great deal more than the prior, simplistically conceived models suggest. Hardly a question simply of who has more time, or whose time is worth more, who has more skill, or who has more power, it is clear that a complicated relation between the structure of work imperatives and the structure of normative expectations attached to the work as *gendered* determines the ultimate allocation of household members' time to work and home. That complex relation has been only roughly approximated here, but its presence in the findings is undeniable. Separately, these household labor "structures" determined the particulars of the results, and taken together, they articulate the complexity of these work relations.[2]

THE STRUCTURE OF WORK IMPERATIVES

This analysis rested on a presumption that the determinants of the tasks and the time of the household may be different from the determinants of their allocation. Analytic models were constructed to address the expectation that the market and household pie would impose its own influence on how work was apportioned among household members.

In chapter 4, it was clear that a variety of factors independent of household member preferences affects the nature and amount of work to be undertaken. For example, children exert the greatest impact on the tasks and time of the household. Whether through the demands that come with their dependency or through the contributions that they make to the household as productive members, children leave their mark on this work site in profound ways. Any other influence exerted by characteristics of the home, characteristics of the members, or their preferences pales in comparison with the influence of children on the household and (indirectly) the market pie.

Such a conclusion would be of no interest if the household labor pie had little effect on the members' contributions to household labor. But, in fact, and to reiterate a bit . . . by far the most important determinant of the wives' contributions to household tasks or time was the *total* tasks or time presented to the household unit. In addition, recall that these forces had no impact on the husbands' contributions.

Regardless of the asymmetry of the effects, the fact remains that what is to be done and the time it takes to do it constitute the context in which the allocation of household labor to all members occurs; this context imposes crucial constraints on the process by which household labor is divided. Indeed, there lies the variance to be explained. No matter what the work to be done, who does it or even how it must be allocated is in part a question not of what the members may wish, but of what the demands of people and tasks require. And it is in this context that any normative structure operates.

For example, even the *contemplation* of what is fair or unfair can be eclipsed by the sheer number of the tasks that constitute infant care.[3] Yet, patterns of work allocation established to respond to the demands of tasks during a *particular* period in the life cycle of a household may remain long after the relevant circumstances have changed. With the arrival of a new baby, a wife may leave the workplace for a time and take primary responsibility for both infant care and the work of the household. After all, it is she who spends her days in this work environment, and in practice, it may be impossible to differentiate her work as strictly child care or strictly household labor.[4] Once she is back in employment, however, the logic of the arrangement that was so apparent earlier is gone; nevertheless, what "worked" before becomes the way-we've-always-done-it, and thus the way-we-do-it. Note, too, that when wives return to employment, it is only *their* circumstances that have changed. Thus, any change in the division of household labor in response to new circumstances would logically imply more household labor from the *husbands*. Old habits and routines die hard, precisely because change requires so much effort.

THE NORMATIVE STRUCTURE OF HOUSEHOLD LABOR

We have no direct evidence of how members' perceptions of who *should* do what affects who *does* do what. . . . The actual mechanisms by which the normative structure of gender imposes itself on this work site can be discerned only indirectly, and not without some speculation. Yet, the circumstantial evidence surrounding the "gendered" nature of this work and its allocation is overwhelming. . . .

On a more general level, however, and over and above the obvious worker concerns of marginal productivity, the clear presumption existed that the wives were responsible for the work of the household. It is this overarching normative orientation that found its way into the few measures that tapped it and that, more important, drove these patterns to their consistent asymmetry. This sort of normative structure—resting as it does on gender relations—lends a kind of solidity to the arrangement of work that, in principle, could be organized in many different ways or might be subject to substantial influence from pressures external to the household but is not.

The normative structure that motivates these work patterns may provide some ballast for an otherwise problematic set of activities for household members. Yet, it is hardly the intention of this analysis to suggest that household labor could be accomplished *only* within this sort of normative structure. Indeed, one doesn't need a degree in the New Home Economics to build a strong case against workers arranging production so that, regardless of the time commitments of the members, *one* member will invariably do the lion's share of the work. Simple logic argues otherwise. Therefore, one must wonder what it is that motivates a continued dependence on this way of organizing household labor. Any answers (or at least an approach to them) carry implications for the role of individual choice and possible change in our work lives. At the risk of overdrawing their positions (and exaggerating some obvious shortcomings) but as a useful starting point nonetheless, I will briefly return to traditional sociological and neoclassical economic perspectives.

MECHANISIMS OF CHOICE AND CONSTRAINT

What might be a sociological account of the findings concerning the allocation of market and household labor? To begin, institutional and normative forces combine to limit severely the choices of all members of the household. To return to a prior example, the overwhelming demands of an infant child, the rigid organization of employment, and the clear cultural message that only a mother can truly satisfy a child's physiological and emotional needs provide little incentive to parents to elect full-time employment and to share the rearing of their children. The sociological world is "lumpy"; when movement occurs, it comes in discrete states: One is employed, or not; one is married, or not; one has children, or not. This (often binary) world is portrayed as imposing a set of impersonal forces on the individual who must negotiate her or his choices accordingly.

This perspective becomes most problematic when it tries to account for individual variation over time. Any form of social science explanation that presupposes a social world where individual human action is often incidental to it faces trouble when confronted with variation and change. Moreover, constraint is surely not the only dimension worth considering in the study of household work.

Another vantage point, which is no less a reality in the data, is that aspect of household labor best appreciated from the neoclassical economic standpoint. Here, the actors become the whole story, and social (or normative) structures are a relatively trivial feature of their functioning. Rather than being weak and ineffectual, individual experience and choices are crucial and continuous, constantly balancing all sorts of complicated opportunity costs within a single full-income constraint. For example, wives do not decide whether or not to get a job; they decide to work more or fewer hours per week. This more hydraulic model counters the "actorless" world of the sociologist, as individual choice operates to produce the everyday practices surrounding household labor. Yet, unlike explanations of the sociological variety, the economic models ignore the material and cultural context of choice and thus face trouble when they face data. In the case of the present analysis, one finds very little variation that might be introduced by individual choice, regardless of circumstance or biography. This story is one of constancy, not variation.

Quite obviously, neither traditional sociological nor economic explanations of the division of household and market labor make it easy to give formal attention to the two realities of choice *and* constraint. In their failure to handle the direct experience of work creatively, these perspectives reduce the mechanisms of the organization of household labor either to a social system that is fully constraining or to one that knows only the individual (and therefore somewhat questionable) choices of institutionally unconstrained members.

How does one combine the two perspectives and thus improve on their ability to account for the workings of these social relations? Both sociology and the New Home Economics must be reintroduced to the complexities of the social systems that they wish to explain. The nature of the household production process itself must be reconceptualized, so that households become considerably more complicated than Gary Becker's "small factory" metaphor would suggest. This reconceptualization would attend to both the work and the normative structures of household labor.

RETHINKING HOUSEHOLD PRODUCTION

Let us return to a much-criticized assumption from the New Home Economics: Households are "at the margin" in their organization of production, and thus, given a set of resources and an efficient "production function," resources are optimally allocated within the household. With this assumption, and the data, one is forced to contemplate how the members could rationally establish the arrangements that they do solely for the production of household goods and services. Moreover, even if such arrangements were optimal, why would the workers consider them fair? If only on the grounds of efficiency, might one not instead expect a greater effort by wives and husbands to equalize the division of household labor? One answer is that one might expect such effort if the division of labor were brought to bear only on efficient production, or if household goods and services were *all that were being produced*. In short, if we retain the assumption that the lopsided arrangements surrounding the allocation of household work are optimal for *some* production process, we must again ask the simple question, What is being produced?

At least metaphorically, the division of household labor facilitates *two* production processes: the production of goods and services and what we might call the production of gender. Simultaneously, household members "do" gender, as they "do" housework and child care, and what I have been calling the division of household labor provides for the joint production of household labor and gender; it is the mechanism by which both the material and the symbolic products of the household are realized.

THE PRODUCTION OF GENDER

If we are to speak of the "production" of gender, the traditional and static notion of sex or gender "role," with its rather vague behavioral referents, must be abandoned. (For a discussion, see Hochschild 1973; Lopata and Thorne 1978; Thorne 1976; Tresemer 1975.) Increasingly, the concept of gender "role" as a set of learned and enacted sex-linked expectations has been slowly supplanted by a conception of gender as an active, behaviorally based, and demonstrable accomplishment, a "situationally accountable feature of sexually categorized human beings" (West and Zimmerman 1984).[5] To appreciate gender as an ongoing accomplishment, Goffman's concept of gender display (1977, 1979), as well as a recent (West and Zimmerman 1984) critique and extension of it, is instructive.[6]

Goffman (1977) conceived of gender as constituted by a family of behavioral displays, or "sex-class-specific ways of appearing, acting, feeling" (303) that serve to establish or reaffirm members' categorical identity and essential nature, and to "align" members to each other in social situations. As Goffman (1979) noted,

> If gender be defined as the culturally established correlates of sex (whether in consequence of biology or learning), then gender display refers to conventionalized portrayals of these correlates. (1)

West and Zimmerman (1984) have elaborated on Goffman's notion of gender displays as "indicative" behaviors, in order to consider the mechanisms by which gender is accomplished normatively. They argued quite convincingly that the "doing" of gender does not simply mean that, through a set of behavioral displays (e.g., a husband "helps" his wife carry heavy grocery bags, and a wife "nags" her husband about cleaning the rain gutters), we affirm our *categorical* status as male or female. . . . For West and Zimmerman, and as demanded by this analysis, the normative structures embedded in human activity (including household labor) become crucial because, as they noted,

The task of "measuring up" to one's gender is faced again and again in different situations with respect to different particulars of conduct. The problem involved is to produce configurations of behavior *which can be seen* by others as normative gender behavior. (19–20; emphasis in original)

Thus, it can be argued that the allocation of household labor—implying as it does a fairly complicated process of coordinating work efforts—involves interactions that, in West and Zimmerman's terms (1984), "pose gender relevant issues" (30). The production process itself is defined through the production of household commodities *and* through the production of gender. The combination of the two results in a new production function as well as a set of household commodities bred from the fusion of household work and gender.[7] This may prove a way to reconceptualize the joint production of household goods and services and gender relations, but we must still question the *nature* of the gender relations produced through the allocation of household labor. West and Zimmerman (1984) directed us to an answer:

Thus when talking about the relationship of categorical identity [male or female] to gender (accountable maleness or femaleness), it may be that the primary category-bound activities are, for men and women respectively, dominance and submission. The practical problem, then, for members who seek to render their activities accountable in such terms is to devise out of the stuff of mundane interplay situationally responsive means of doing dominance and submission. (28)

Instances of "doing" dominance and submission are surely frequent in work settings other than the household and are obviously not necessarily tied to heterosexual gender relations. Likewise, not all household labor involves displays of dominance indicative of the doing of gender. For example, we know that both men and women sometimes speak of "how different" or "how easy" it was when, prior to marriage, they lived in same-sex roommate arrangements. One might argue that not only are the demands of work likely to be lighter in that sort of arrangement, but more important, the process by which the labor is divided is subject only to considerations of *the work itself,* as that is all that is being produced. The production of gender relations through the exercise of dominance and submission is largely irrelevant in such arrangements; as a result, the work of a "single" life seems so different and so uncomplicated. Yet, it may be that, in households where the appropriation of *another's* labor is possible, in practice the expression of work and the expression of gender (dominance and submission) are inseparable.

When the production of household goods and services and the production of gender relations are combined in a single setting, the mechanisms by which their joint production is arranged may be problematic for the household members. After all, through the daily practice of household activities, the wife and husband face the constraints imposed by the demands of household labor and the situational exigencies posed by gender practices. From this dual production process emerges the variety of individual members' adaptations to household arrangements and the members' perceptions of choices made and contemplated. Gender ideals shape the way in which the production of gender will manifest itself in daily practice. Similarly, the particulars of the household production function affect how household work will unfold. Thus, child care (or laundry, or household repair, and so on) can become the occasion for producing commodities such as clean children (or clean laundry, or new light switches, etc.) and a reaffirmation of one's *gendered* relation to the work and to the world. In short, the "shoulds" of gender ideals are fused with the "musts" of efficient household production. The result may be something resembling a "gendered" household-production function. Here, it will be helpful to identify at least some rough reflections of a system where the division of household labor poses both work- and gender-relevant issues for the members. They are found in the daily concerns of household life.

WORK AND GENDER: SOME ILLUSTRATIONS

Thirty open-ended interviews conducted with the wives in an earlier phase of our project at least hint at how the division of household labor may involve the production of both work relations and gender relations.[8] These brief illustrations—by no means meant to be systematic or intended to represent all the qualitative data from which they are drawn—are the responses of six women to the question "What household work does your husband do?"

First, the division of household labor became "gender relevant," usually implicitly, but sometimes more obviously. Below are the responses of three women to the question.

> He puts dishes away, does the laundry, and in dire emergencies, he picks up toys, vacuums, mows the lawn. He usually only does those things if we're having company and I can't get to them. I'm also generally responsible for outside-the-house jobs. He just shovels snow on the outside.

> He helps out regularly. Twice a week he plays games with the kids. He helps [daughter] with her [multiplication] tables three times a week. He sleds with the kids and ice skates with them, too. My sister

and I go to visit my mother in a nursing home every Sunday, and he watches the kids. Sometimes he takes them bowling.

Never. He never helps me. I suppose I should say "rarely." That's a better word to describe it. He hangs up his clothes once in a while. He puts his dirty socks down the laundry chute. In extreme circumstances, he makes the bed. He does nothing. He doesn't have to. It's not his job. People should do what they like.

Goffman (1977) described gender ideals as the essential source for maintaining gender differences because they "provide . . . a source of accounts that can be drawn on in a million ways to excuse, justify, explain, or disapprove the behavior of an individual or the arrangement under which he lives" (303). Thus, a more interesting and subtle process for household members is one where gender intervenes to influence directly the division of household labor. It may be argued that because gender relations—the doing of dominance and submission—are an everyday proposition, then gender may serve as a warrant for household members' claiming particular relationships to, or stances toward, household labor. When the time comes to allocate the household members' labor, there are available a host of "good reasons" that husbands, *regardless* of other considerations, should be market specialists, and wives either household specialists or modern-day generalists, devoting time to both work sites. Obvious examples emerge in the quotes to follow, where the wives' acceptance of their husbands' claims to incompetence in (or obliviousness to) household labor is striking:

He doesn't do much. I get irritated at him at times. He's unaware that there are things for him to do. . . . He'd leave the paper on the couch, but now he picks it up. He does this for a month, forgets, and then I have to remind him.

He tries to be helpful. He tries. He's a brilliant and successful lawyer. It's incredible how he smiles after he sponges off the table and there are still crumbs all over.

The imperatives posed by the production of gender relations mean that the division of household labor not only is concerned with the rational sorting and optimal matching of tasks and time to household members, but is also centered on the symbolic affirmation of the members or their "alignment" with each other as husband and wife, man and woman, brother and sister. Nevertheless, how much is gender and how much is work is hardly the question. Instead, it is clear that, as gender and work are "done," already existing patterns of both are ratified by household members. The way household labor is divided is brought into line with an image of how it *should* be divided.

> If my son is dirty and needs his diaper changed, my husband says, "'Honey, you do it." It's like he has dibs on not doing it.

Having "dibs" depends, of course, on an active acceptance of a particular gendered relationship to the world of work. And although it perplexed the young mother above, she nevertheless perceived her husband's claim as legitimate. Ultimately, then, and from day to day, work and gender combine, and the division of household labor becomes the activity around which the two can determine and capacitate each other.

Thus, if we return to the problem of household decision making, we can see more clearly that questions of how to allocate the time and tasks of the household members (between home and market and among the members) must attend to the demands of this hybrid production process. In practice, this means that the rationales taken as legitimate and the considerations defined as pertinent to decision making involve issues of both gender and work.

The mechanism by which such decisions are made in this work environment may constitute a real—and more complicated—process barely hinted at by the New Home Economics. In addition to seeking the combined optimal allocation of resources, under the dual constraints of time and income, household members' time and task contributions are apportioned as well to "align" what is happening in the situation with normative notions of what *should* be happening in the situation. In short, how household and market work *should* be allocated (according to the dictates of gender and work ideals) is brought to bear on how the work *can* be allocated (subject to the constraints of income and time). The joint production of work and gender represents a maximization process with a *new* mix of incentives, tasks, and perceptions of opportunity costs. It is this maximization process, with its complicated agendas involving work and gender—the material and the symbolic—that effectively guarantees the asymmetric patterns found so often in studies of the division of household labor. And ultimately, it is within these two interwoven structures that household members make their choices and get the business of living done.

It is no surprise that all this goes on without much notice being taken. As one respondent noted in her household-work diary,

> Some things are done so many times a day and for so many years that it is difficult to assess my true reaction to having to do them. They are taken for granted and done without thinking about them.

The taken-for-granted quality of these work arrangements clearly extends to a lack of voiced concern about their equity. Notions underlying equity theory would have it that the perceived "fairness" of the division of labor results from an evaluation of the fit between the contributions made and the benefits received. (For a more extensive discussion, see Walster, Walster, and Traupman 1978.) Earlier, it was somewhat perplexing to learn that, despite some real lopsidedness in household contribution, most wives and almost all husbands thought the division of labor in their households fair. This finding proves to be consistent with what little empirical research there is on couples' assessments of the equity of various aspects of their marriages. For example, Schafer and Keith (1981) found that wives were more likely than husbands to report inequity in the performance of household roles, but that, in the main (and increasing over the course of the relationship), couples reported high levels of marital equity. These simple findings notwithstanding, the prior discussion would suggest that there is more to marital equity than the "pop bottle" calculus of whether one gets a return on one's deposits.

Quite obviously, whether one perceives a work arrangement to be fair depends fundamentally on what alternatives are conceivable and are judged viable. After all, if no alternative arrangement is thought possible, then an acknowledgment of inequity may be psychologically untenable. Nevertheless, any perceptions of equity in the division of household labor are obviously structured by and prove conditional on the experience of both the production of gender and the production of household goods and services. In this case, the fusion of the two militates against alternative ways of allocating the work. If the doing of gender provides a framework by which husbands and wives reaffirm their relation to each other and to work, as competent members, then departures from these normatively circumscribed ideals are ruled out. After all, doing gender serves to guide and thus limit the members, not to expand on already complicated human affairs. A gendered household production function may be efficient, free of the risk of even implicit social sanction, safe, and certainly familiar. It can serve as a refuge for almost all of us—the cowardly or the simply tired. Yet, with this comes the reiteration of the status quo and thus a more limited vision of alternatives. Once alternative ways of arranging household labor are ruled out, the probability that inequity will be perceived and acknowledged is lowered. Goffman's (1979) remarks are instructive once more. Of gender display, he wrote,

> The expression of subordination and domination through this swarm of situational means is more than a mere tracing of symbol or ritualistic affirmation of the social hierarchy. These expressions considerably constitute the hierarchy; they are the shadow *and* the substance. (6; emphasis in original)

Thus, perhaps it is only researchers who are preoccupied with the question of "how fair" household work arrangements are. Such questions are rarely contemplated by household members, and when they are, the constraints posed by the way in which the work and gender are accomplished day to day determine the perceived viability of the alternatives.

A FINAL NOTE ON CHANGE

Although exhibiting near-uniform patterns, the prior chapters imply that how members allocate their efforts to home and market is nevertheless subject to change. Yet, even the rough sketch of the work-gender production process offered here suggests that impetus for change is unlikely to come from within. Again, the nature of production itself imposes critical constraints on the ability of household members to effect fundamental change. The production of household goods and services—and with it, the production of gender—may serve to thwart the efforts of any member to transform her or his household work life. It is especially difficult when, as is often the case, a lone voice calls for change. As one mother wrote in her household diary,

> I wish there were some accurate way to record and describe how much work it is to get others to do their work—children dressing for school, or putting away toys, for example.

Rather, a reorganization of household production is more likely to find its origins in forces outside the household. That is, demands emanating from extra household commitments will, in "collision" with household production demands, promote change in the organization of that production.[9] Indeed, in earlier chapters, it was suggested that market demands can directly affect total household labor time, and that the introduction of children into the household can significantly increase household labor tasks and time. Nevertheless, although these exogenous forces clearly affect the size of the household and market pie, they do little to transform who does what and how much.

Our cross-sectional sample of 335 couples was certainly not of sufficient size to allow us to address the question of change adequately, but some unsystematic observations may prove provocative. A search for those husbands who were household labor "outliers" unearthed some interesting characteristics. The criterion employed for the definition and selection of the "outlier" husbands . . . was a level equivalent to the *mean* household-task or household-time contribution of the sample wives. When that criterion was applied, roughly 10 percent of the sample of husbands was selected.

These husbands and their households did indeed differ in important respects from the larger sample. First, they had greater numbers of children—especially small children—so that they were slightly younger (and poorer) than the larger sample of husbands. Second, and more important perhaps, more than half the outlier husbands had wives who were employed full time. Thus, a majority of these men had preschool children *and* full-time-employed wives. These husbands lived in what might be called labor-intensive households; they did more, there was more to be done, and along with their wives, they had little choice in the matter.[10]

What this may indicate is that, subject to new constraints imposed from *outside* the household or external to the members' preferences (e.g., increased employment, more children, and illness), the particular production function of the gendered household may change. Whether the everyday enactment of gender dominance and submission will continue is not at issue. Just as household work will go on, so, too, will the production of gender. Under some circumstances, however, exogenous pressures could force a change in the gender "production function," where, for some harassed couples, "doing" gender in traditional ways becomes a luxury. Or for others, a greater number of household goods and services may be purchased outside the household, partially severing the close connection between the production of household commodities and the doing of gender. Thus, depending on class position, household members may face either an insurmountable budget constraint or the resources to opt out of household production. In either case (perhaps for the very poor or the very rich), a change would result in the number of "gender-relevant" occasions posed by household labor. Where this leaves the *middle-class* household, where production is neither as economically constrained nor as easily marketized, is less clear. But it may be that in the future, husbands and wives will have no choice but to shift the locus for the doing of gender away from the allocation of household members' labors, or to de-emphasize one production process in the interests of the other. Still, such speculations on the "degendering" of household work raise serious and unresolved questions about the intractability of the dominance and submission orchestrated around gender and about the precise interplay between work and gender relations among family members. Moreover, although analytically separable, such convenient distinctions between the accomplishment of gender, dominance and submission, and the organization of society's work obscure actual experience. A more rigorous articulation of these issues remains a crucial research agenda.

Even were change likely, it would be a dangerous distortion of reality to suggest that men and women experience household and market production in the same way. Halfhearted protestations to the contrary, men benefit directly from the labors of women and from the system of male dominance within which those labors occur. Thus, whatever change does result will come from the new bargains struck between those who stand to gain and those who face no better deal (Goode 1982). Only then will the production of household well-being become more complicated, more uncertain, and more equitable.

NOTES

1. The original version of this chapter is the conclusion in Fenstermaker's 1985 *The Gender Factory: The Apportionment of Work in American Households*, Plenum Press: 185–211.

2. For this concluding discussion, I focus primarily on the determinants of the division of household labor, and, of necessity, I neglect the determinants of market-time allocation. The relation between household members' allocation of time to home and market, however, remains crucial to an understanding of the work imperatives imposed on household members.

3. As one young father of an infant said, "For the first six months, the question of fairness became a real problem—we were *both* doing more than was fair."

4. Nevertheless, women sometimes express strong feelings about the difference between the two. Note these two examples: "I'm a mother and wife first. I'm a housewife last. There's a difference when I do things with the children"; "You have to understand—children are why we do housework. They are why we are in therapy; they are why we're not working; they are why we're here at *all*."

5. I do not suggest that socialization to gender-appropriate behavior is trivial or developmentally inconsequential. On the contrary, learning how to "do" gender is crucial to achieving the identity and the status of a component member of a social group. (For review and discussion see Cahill 1982.)

6. A complete exegesis on the importance and the implications of this reconceptualization of gender cannot be presented here. The reader is directed to a number of instructive first statements (e.g., Cahill 1982; Henley 1977; Lopata and Thorne 1978; West 1982).

7. Of course, Gary Becker (1981) might reply that here gender would simply represent one more household commodity produced through a single household production function. Yet, this sort of response is vacuous and sidesteps the fact that it is the *joint* production of household work commodities and gender that is at issue. In the speculative model proposed here, joint production is not (as Becker might have it) an occasional theoretical inconvenience. Quite the opposite, the joint production of household work commodities and gender is fundamental and endemic to the production process; this model rests on joint production.

8. A more systematic treatment of these data may be found in Berheide et al. (1976) and in Berk and Berheide (1977).

9. For a similarly underdeveloped argument concerning these catalysts of change, see Eisenstein (1981, 201–14).

10. It is perhaps unnecessary to point out that the *relative* position of the wives and the husbands in labor intensive households remained similar to that of the larger sample; both the wives and the husbands did more, with husbands contributing a significant but nevertheless small fraction of the total work done.

CHAPTER SEVEN

Accounting for Cosmetic Surgery: The Accomplishment of Gender

DIANA DULL AND CANDACE WEST

Within the United States, physicians claim a professional mandate to define the nature and treatment of disease (Hughes 1958; Thorne 1973).[1] For most surgeons, this mandate includes the right to evaluate patients' complaints, to determine what should be done about them, and to assess post-operative results.[2] For plastic surgeons, however, the mandate is not so clear. The field of plastic surgery encompasses two categories of operations: (1) reconstructive procedures, which restore or improve physical function and minimize disfigurement from accidents, diseases, or birth defects; and (2) cosmetic procedures, which offer elective aesthetic improvement through surgical alterations of facial and bodily features (American Society of Plastic and Reconstructive Surgeons 1988). In the case of reconstructive surgery, the professional mandate rests on the surgeon's ability to improve physical function and minimize disfigurement. But in the case of cosmetic surgery, the evaluation of patients' complaints, the determination of what should be done about them, and the assessment of post-operative results must be negotiated in relation to *what* "aesthetic improvement" might consist of, and to *whom*. This, then, is the central dilemma of cosmetic surgery.

The disproportionate number of women who undergo cosmetic operations suggests the importance of gender to understanding how this dilemma is resolved. For example, in 1988 more than half a million people in the United States had cosmetic surgery, with the available evidence indicating that the vast majority were women.[3] Although official statistics do not distinguish between cosmetic and reconstructive operations, they do indicate a decided bias. In 1985, 61 percent of all rhinoplasty (nose surgery), 86 percent of all eyelid reconstruction, and 91 percent of all face-lifts were performed on women (U.S. National Center for Health Statistics 1987). The American Society of Plastic and Reconstructive Surgeons estimates that 90,000 men opted for cosmetic surgery in 1988, but that number represents only 16 percent of the total cosmetic operations identified.

Our purpose in this paper is to examine how those involved in cosmetic operations resolve the central dilemma of cosmetic surgery. Our analysis of surgical screening and decision making focuses on how the medical profession comes to enter a terrain that would seem so clearly beyond its mandate—that is, constructing appearances and performing surgery that, by its own definition, is unnecessary. We show how surgeons who perform cosmetic procedures justify their entry into this terrain and how people who elect such procedures make sense of their decisions to do so. Finally, in conjunction with these activities, we show how women are constituted as the primary frontier for this territorial expansion through the accomplishment of gender—in this context, the assessment of "good candidates" for surgery in relation to normative conceptions of men's and women's "essential natures" (Fenstermaker, West, and Zimmerman 1990; West and Fenstermaker forthcoming [published 1993]; West and Zimmerman 1987).

METHODS

Our primary data consist of interviews with surgeons who perform cosmetic surgery and with individuals who have undergone such operations. By law, any licensed medical doctor may perform cosmetic surgery, but we limited our study to surgeons certified to do so through boards recognized by the American Board of Medical Specialties. Eight of the 10 surgeons in this sample are certified by the American Board of Plastic Surgery, and two by the American Board of Otolaryngology. We obtained these interviews through a snowball sample, yielding one woman and nine men surgeons, all white. With the exception of one surgeon outside California (whom we interviewed by phone), we conducted all our physician interviews in person at surgeons' offices. Each interview was recorded on audiotape and lasted approximately one hour.

Given the sensitive nature of the topic, we gave people who had undergone cosmetic surgery two interview options. The first option, chosen by 7 of the total 23, was to be interviewed on audiotape face to face. The second option, chosen by 16 of the 23, was to complete an open-ended questionnaire with a follow-up discussion over the phone if clarification was needed. In the analysis that follows, we found no differences among people's perspectives on cosmetic surgery according to which of the options they selected. These interviews were also obtained through a snowball sample.

Nineteen of the 23 persons interviewed were women whose surgical experiences included face-lifts, upper and lower eyelid reduction, rhinoplasty, chin implantation, breast augmentation, breast reduction, and liposuction of the hips, thighs, and knees. Two of the interviews were with men who had undergone eyelid reduction or face-lifts. Our secondary data consist of two further interviews with men who ultimately decided against cosmetic surgery. Given that both had seriously contemplated aesthetic rhinoplasty and were among only four men we were able to locate who had ever consulted plastic surgeons, we decided to include their views with those of our other interviewees—setting them off in our analysis as anomalous cases.[4] Four of the women and one of the men had undergone more than one surgery, and in at least two cases later operations were performed in order to correct the results of an earlier procedure.

At the time we interviewed them, individuals in this sample ranged in age from 24 to 67. Nine had had surgery before turning 35; seven more, between 35 and 50; and seven more, when they were 51 years old or older. While face-lifts were confined to those who were 50 and older, the other procedures were reported by people across different age groups. Six people were single, two were divorced, and ten were married (with five failing to indicate marital status). Nine of them, including one who was single, had children. All of them were white; two identified their ethnicity as Jewish, and one as Italian. They held a variety of jobs, including those of dentist, bookkeeper, and administrative assistant. One, a retired medical assistant, had formerly been employed in the offices of two different cosmetic surgeons; another, also retired, had worked as a medical editor in a large health care facility.

Our analysis of these data is qualitative and inductive. In the tradition of grounded theory (Glaser and Strauss 1967), we did not set out to test specific hypotheses but rather to generate them from the entire corpus of material.

SURGERY AS A "NORMAL, NATURAL" PURSUIT

In routine descriptions of their circumstances and activities, people provide names, formulations, characterizations, excuses, explanations, and justifications for the circumstances and activities, thereby situating them in a social framework (Heritage 1984). Among those who had undergone cosmetic surgery, many described their desires for such surgery as "normal" and "natural," explicitly comparing their inclination to buying makeup and having their hair done. They extolled the benefits of cosmetic surgery by characterizing their actions as what anyone would do. Hence, patients' descriptions of their activities were formulated as justifications for those activities. For example, a woman who underwent breast augmentation observed,

In this age, with all the technology possible, changing something less than perfect about one's looks seems so easy, so normal. It's unfair that cost keeps such a wonderful thing from so many people. . . . I would recommend this procedure to anyone.

A woman who underwent a face-lift stated,

I mean, if it is your body and you want to have it done, why not? And if it helps your vanity, what's wrong with it? . . . Women buy makeup and have their hair done—what's the difference?

We might expect such descriptions from people who have undergone cosmetic surgery, insofar as they are accounting for having done so in the course of being interviewed. However, such descriptions were not unique to former patients. Many surgeons also categorized cosmetic surgery as a "normal," "natural" pursuit. For example,

There is a certain natural order to things. A person who is 25 years old does not need a face-lift, but they need a breast augmentation. Well, "need" is relative, obviously, but for purposes of discussion . . . there's a certain order of what you go through psychologically and what you might need. . . . If it makes them happy and gives them a boost, then it's no different than going on a two-week vacation as far as I'm concerned. (Italics added.)

Or, as another surgeon remarked, "It's not any vainer than wearing makeup or changing your hairstyle. If you think those things are vain, then plastic surgery is vain too."

To be sure, those descriptions contained numerous contradictions. First, some patients who characterized their surgery as what anyone would do nonetheless reported that they agonized over their decisions to have surgery. Second, surgeons and former patients who compared cosmetic surgery with other mundane activities often advanced claims with defensive overtones (for instance, assessing surgery as "no vainer than" other attentions to one's appearance). Third, even while surgeons and former patients referred to the desire for surgery as "normal" and "natural," they implied that the desire was "normal" and "natural" only for women. They did not, for example, draw parallels between cosmetic procedures and shaving one's face or trimming one's beard. Thus, the claim that cosmetic surgery was a "normal," "natural" pursuit was a deceptively simple one.

"OBJECTIVE" INDICATORS

A more complex picture began to emerge as interviewees described "criteria" for particular surgical procedures as if these were objective indicators for surgery. As Zimmerman (1978, 11) observes, we can examine "properties of social life which seem objective, factual, and transsituational" as "managed accomplishments or achievements of local processes." Such examination provides a preliminary understanding of how surgeons and former patients could reach the conclusion that cosmetic surgery was "normal" and "natural," namely, by formulating facial or bodily features as "objectively" problematic.

For example, like the surgeon who suggested that a 25-year-old person does not "need" a face-lift, many patients alluded to "self-evident indicators" for surgery in accounts of their decisions. One woman "explained" her upper eyelid reduction by noting,

> At about 45 [your eyelids] start to come down. And that's when you start to notice that you're losing elasticity and you get the fold in your upper eye . . . by the time you get to be my age, it was certainly time to do it.

The same woman described her subsequent decision to undergo liposuction under her chin by adding,

> In your late fifties and sixties you start to get a lot of "crepeyness" in your neck. Just all of a sudden it's just there. And it's just, you know, not attractive. And your jowls, of course. Mine weren't that bad, but they were coming down.

In these excerpts, we find a concrete empirical description of the "natural order to things" described earlier. While this woman's description is perhaps more chronologically detailed than most, other patients were just as explicit in their references to "heavy eyelids," "droopy necks," and "baggy chins" as "objective" grounds for their decisions to have surgery.

Interestingly, surgeons were the ones who suggested that "objective" signs of aging—and their relationship to cosmetic surgery—might not be so objective. For example, when asked about the relationship between age and cosmetic surgery, many intimated that "age" was in the eye of the beholder. While a 20-year-old woman might look terrific to the person on the street, she may well look "too old" if she is competing in front of the camera.

The youngest lady I've done was a younger lady in her twenties who was a model and was losing it to the teenagers. So I did her face and eyes. . . . To you and me, she looked great. But to the camera and to the people who wanted to shoot the teenage look, she looked too old. . . . It was a modest facelift, but it was enough to put her right back there on the front page of the magazine. . . . She was perfectly realistic. She showed me her shots and shots of the kids and said, "This is where the industry is going, and I want to stay in it." You see, the perceived deformity relates to that person's particular situation in life. Their jobs or their perceived role.

Although many surgeons acknowledged that procedures such as face-lifts were more easily and effectively performed on someone who is young, one surgeon remarked,

You're never too old for it. The best answer to the question of when you need it or when you should do it, is when you need it. . . . I've done a face-lift on a 93-year-old.

Thus, the surgeons took patients' individual perceptions and livelihoods into account in their perspectives on "objective" signs of aging. Surgeons were not always so sociologically reflective when it came to other dimensions of identity such as race and ethnicity. For example, more than a few of them averred that patients' racial or ethnic features constituted "objective" problems. Through references to what people, particularly women, of color "have" and "need," these surgeons invoked race and ethnicity as factual, transsituational grounds for surgical interventions in appearance (cf. Zimmerman 1978).

I've had one Black patient . . . it was a lip reduction. . . . I guess there are more Black people that have big lips than white people. . . . I had a lot of Black patients back in [the South] . . . breast reduction was a tremendously common procedure . . . because . . . a lot of Black women have huge breasts. . . . The usual cosmetic procedures were, with the exception of rhinoplasty, very uncommon. You know, Black women don't usually have the aging changes that white women have—they don't get the fine wrinkles. . . . Orientals don't either.

Or, as another surgeon remarked,

The Black people that I have operated on have had . . . mostly their noses [done]. The Black people have big flared nostrils and would like that smaller. The Orientals don't seem to have much of a bridge, so they, you know, [have] kind of a dish face.

On the other hand, some surgeons implied that "problems" with racial and ethnic features were—at least in part—subjectively determined. They acknowledged, for example, that patients' conceptions of their racial features were often derived from their groups.

> There are not that many Black flat women compared to Caucasians. . . . But another flip side—how many flat Asians do you see? Females? Lots! They're all over the place. For them, that's accepted. I do very few Asians. Very few Blacks. And my theory is that most of the Blacks don't need it. And my theory is for Asians, flat is still in.

One surgeon contended that whatever a patient's racial or ethnic features, the surgeon's task was to improve the appearance of the individual patient, rather than to force fit it according to some universal criteria.

> I saw a Black lady today who I had done her eyelids and a face-lift. And she came back, and she wanted a forehead lift. And uh, you know . . . that was fine. . . . But this was just to make this lady look better. . . . Basically, it is just trying to make them look better, rather than to have them fit a mold.

In this regard, the most complicated claims we heard were those that acknowledged "objective" differences between the racial or ethnic "characteristics" of different groups, but attributed desires for changes in such characteristics to the patients' individual perceptions—not to the characteristics themselves. Changes in such characteristics might result in a "different" appearance but not necessarily a "better" appearance.

> I mean, if you've got a great big old honker, and it looks like somebody hit it with three passes of the sword and it comes down your face like a "Z" or a "W," you want to look better. . . . Now, contrariwise, if you just happen to have a big nose because you come from an Armenian background or some very recognizable ethnic appearance and you want to change it, that's cosmetic surgery. . . . Michael Jackson is leading the way on changing Negroid characteristics to Caucasian characteristics.

Patients' descriptions of their surgeries in relation to their ethnic backgrounds were more complex still. They expressed their desires for surgery through references to subtle alterations to—rather than total transformations of—their "ethnic features." For example, one woman of Italian descent said that prior to her rhinoplasty,

> I didn't like my nose in photographs. (Now) I have a cute profile and my nose is not tiny but in proportion to my face. . . . I think I look softer (now) and not as exotic as before.

A Jewish woman said of her pre-operative consultation with a surgeon for rhinoplasty, "He wasn't going to give me a cute little WASPy nose, but one in proportion to my face. I was very satisfied." Through such carefully worded descriptions, patients implied that they were essentially satisfied with their "ethnic appearances," despite their desires to have particular features surgically changed. Notwithstanding these nuanced claims, we observed that surgeons and former patients only specified "problems" with racial and ethnic features in the marked case: in the case of individuals who were not white, Anglo Saxon, and Protestant. Some former patients referred to their "big Jewish" noses, but none ever referred to their "puny gentile" ones. Some surgeons alluded to "Caucasian" eyelids or lips, but only when contrasting them with "Oriental" or "Negroid" ones. Thus, even in these carefully worded descriptions, race and ethnicity were invoked as "objective," transsituational grounds for surgery.

Of course, patients' class backgrounds might also be seen as "objective" indicators for cosmetic surgery insofar as these determine who is—and who is not—able to afford it. Since insurance companies, health maintenance organizations, and state-funded health care programs exclude virtually all elective aesthetic procedures from their provisions for patients' care, prospective patients must be prepared to pay for their surgeries themselves.[5] A woman to whom $2,000 is "nothing" is in a far better position to finance her upper eyelid reduction than a person to whom $2,000 is a substantial—or inconceivable—outlay. For example, one patient reported,

> In South America, they say that everyone in the upper class has had this surgery. I mean, it's automatic, like you go to the dentist. And to me, it was like, you buy a car. You pay eight thousand to twelve thousand dollars for a car, and four years later, it's worth nothing. . . . So what's two thousand dollars? Nothing. And it's going to last a lot longer than a car.

Or, as another patient put it,

> It's sort of like wearing braces—it's sort of a status thing. Everybody's doing it. If one of (your) friends does it and looks good, well, how are

(you) going to let her get away with that? [You're] going to have it done too. It is a status thing: "I had so and so do mine" —"Oh, did you? How did you like him? I had SO and so do mine."

But our data indicate that while limited economic resources may *hinder* the pursuit of cosmetic surgery, they do not necessarily *prevent* that pursuit. For instance, one woman who underwent breast augmentation took out a personal loan for $3,000 to finance her operation, a loan she worked very hard to pay off for a year following her surgery. Another woman received her breast augmentation "as a present" from her husband for her thirty-second birthday after ten years of wanting it. Other people we interviewed scrimped and saved for their operations on their modest salaries as bank tellers or secretaries. Thus, although class differences influenced people's perceptions of their operations as "luxuries" or "investments," they did not explain people's desires to pursue surgery in the first instance.

ASSESSING "GOOD CANDIDATES"

As surgeons described their screening procedures they revealed a complex sequence of assessments with a course they did not determine by themselves. For example, most described their first task as finding out what patients "really want," as opposed, presumably, to what patients think they want or say they want. Some surgeons employ computerized questionnaires to help them elicit such information, but even then, they cannot rely on what patients tell them as prima facie evidence for surgery. Like surgeons who function without computers, they then assess whether patients' expectations are "realistic," that is, consistent with what surgeons expect they can do for patients. Though photographs may be employed as visual aids, it becomes clear that "having realistic expectations" results from extensive negotiations *between* surgeons and their prospective patients.

> The first thing I've got to find out is what the patient really wants. Then I have to find out whether the expectations are realistic or not. That sort of goes into what they want and what I can do for them. Once we've established that, then I tell them the way I do it . . . and I give them real informed consent. . . , [discussing] potential complications, the kind of procedures and what they're going to be going through. Then they have to make up their mind whether they're going to go ahead with it.

As another surgeon put it, gauging whether a patient has realistic expectations is not a one-shot determination he makes by himself, but a "two-way interview" with the patient. If surgeons *can* establish that prospective patients "have realistic expectations," they can then solicit patients' informed consent and accept them as candidates for surgery. Even then, as many surgeons note, would-be patients have to make up their minds to go through with it.

As we noted earlier, where cosmetic procedures are concerned, the surgeons' mandate rests solely on their ability to provide elective "aesthetic improvement." Thus, surgeons involved in cosmetic procedures must negotiate the evaluation of patients' complaints, the determination of what should be done about them, and the assessment of post-operative results in relation to *what* "aesthetic improvement" might consist of, and *to whom*. Even individuals who are not deemed as "in need" of aesthetic improvement by the first surgeon they consult may be subsequently accepted as patients by another. Approximately one-third of the patients we interviewed said that they had consulted more than one surgeon prior to their operations, with several indicating that they had been refused surgery by the first surgeon they consulted. Our data suggest that the determination of *what* "aesthetic improvement" might consist of revolves in large part around patients' displays of "appropriate" levels of concern.

APPROPRIATE LEVELS OF CONCERN

All of the surgeons advanced the view that there were "appropriate" and "inappropriate" levels of concern for particular patient problems. They advanced this view with explicit references to when patients should exhibit concern—and how much concern patients should exhibit—for the specific problems that bring them to the surgeon's office. They saw it as inappropriate, for example, for patients to wait until they were middle-aged before seeking surgical alteration of features that had bothered them all their lives.

> Say they're fifty years old—why have they waited until now? There may be some good reason—maybe they couldn't afford it or they couldn't get the time off. But the reason may also be that this woman's husband is leaving her, and she thinks it may be her nose and puts undue attention on this one thing without paying attention to the other things—it can be very dangerous to operate on someone like that.

Moreover, they saw it as very inappropriate for patients to display concern for problems that were insignificant in relation to the whole.

> Say some absolutely gorgeous woman has some eeny-teeny little wrinkle right here, and she's just invested her whole life to getting that wrinkle away. Well, I know almost one hundred and ninety-nine

percent that no matter what happens to that little wrinkle, she's going to fix on something else afterwards to, uh, grope after. And those are real tough patients to help out.

Of course, one of the dangers involved in doing surgery on patients who show "inappropriate" levels of concern is the possibility of subsequent suits for malpractice. Plastic surgeons are among the four types of surgical specialists (the others are neurosurgeons, obstetrician/gynecologists, and orthopedic surgeons) most likely to lose malpractice insurance due to lawsuits or negligence (Schwartz and Mendelson 1989). Among surgeons we interviewed, there was general consensus that "problem" patients (cf. Lorber 1975a) who display "inappropriate" levels of concern are, most often, men. For example, when asked why so few men sought cosmetic surgery, surgeons responded,

> I think that male patients are more difficult. They're harder to deal with. Ten years ago when I was beginning to train, the dictum was "you don't do male cosmetic surgery" because they're all problems. They all have enough emotional instability to one, either sue you, or two, be a surgical disaster.

And

> I've turned a couple of males down. They were just totally unrealistic—totally secretive, which is fairly typical for males. Didn't have a good sense for what they wanted at all. Just totally edgy, jumpy sorts of people.

Such descriptions suggest that surgeons rely on a proportionate analysis of patients' concerns in relation to patients' sex categories and surgeons' own perceptions of patients' problems. The claim that there are "appropriate" levels of concern for specific problems sustains the belief in objective, factual, transsituational grounds for aesthetic improvement—even as these are constructed from the particulars of the case at hand.

DOING IT FOR THEMSELVES

More complex still was the determination of *to whom* a particular surgical intervention might constitute an "aesthetic improvement." Surgeons implied that they determined this on the basis of evidence that prospective patients were seeking cosmetic surgery "for themselves." They described "good candidates" for surgery as those who think surgery will increase their self-esteem and improve their self-image, not those who think it will help them attract a younger lover or maintain their spouse's attention. Through these means, surgeons located the impetus for aesthetic improvement within patients themselves. As one surgeon explained,

> Married female patients, especially with breast enlargement, have a lot of antagonism from their husbands. . . . [A husband may say,] "You look fine to me, I don't know why you want to do this." The comment the ladies make is, "I don't feel good about myself, that's why I want to do it. I've had two or three babies, and I used to have a nice figure and now I don't, and I just don't feel good about myself and I'm having my breasts increased."

However, surgeons' expressed preferences for patients who "do it for themselves" were not without contradiction. For instance, most surgeons agreed that it is perfectly reasonable for people to seek surgery in order to meet the requirements of their jobs.

> You know, I do a lot of theatrical people. . . . [Those] who earn a living by their appearance are pretty legitimate. I've had many of them tell me . . . that they wouldn't do this unless it were important for them to make a living.

Moreover, many former patients indicated that they were influenced in their decisions to seek surgery by significant others. One woman who had undergone rhinoplasty at 14 years of age said,

> My father was physically and psychologically abusive to me, and part of his abuse was about how ugly I was, how I didn't deserve to be alive, how he wished I was dead. But a lot of it was on my looks, and I looked identical to him. I probably even had the same size nose as he did—that's where I got my nose—and he used to say that I looked so much like his mother. . . . He hated his mother.

The woman who had worked for two different plastic surgeons told the following story:

> The first doctor I worked for . . . one day he came into my office— this was after I had been there about three or four years—and he sat there and he looked at me and said, "One thing I have found out," And I looked at him and said, "And that is?" And he said, *"Every* surgeon in town has done his girls." And I was the only girl! So he said, "When are we going to do you?" . . . Well, he never let me alone!

Finally, I let him [perform a face-lift]. I just figured, "Well, if it'll make him happy and it will help his practice, I'll do it . . ." because he needed an example to show patients. He was thrilled to have done me. . . , and I just loved him and his family, but I tell you, I would *not* have had it done.

Finally, surgeons' own accounts indicated that under some conditions, they might advise their would-be patients to consider particular surgical procedures that they did not come in for. For example, one surgeon confided,

I personally feel that the patient should tell me what procedures they want—what they feel a need for, that's what they should tell me. Now, if they ask me if there's anything else that I feel could use improvement, I'll give them an opinion.

Thus, our data show that patients "with realistic expectations" do not always generate those expectations from within. Surgeons' stated preferences for patients who are "doing it for themselves" obscure a range of outside influences (including friends, family members, and employers) on people's decision to seek "aesthetic improvement." Moreover, once in the surgeon's office, those considering surgery may be influenced by further recommendations as to what they might "need." Through these means, "patients with realistic expectations" are *created* as well as "found" (cf. Conrad 1976; Conrad and Schneider 1980).

REDUCING THE BODY INTO PARTS

For the surgeons and former patients we interviewed, a primary means of creating patients with realistic expectations was the reduction of would-be patients' faces and bodies to a series of component parts. To be sure, reductionism is a key to scientific, and therefore medical, reasoning, and surgeons are encouraged to develop the capacity for it in the course of their professional training. Given that surgical practice is predicated on the subdivision of patient "parts," it would be odd if the surgeons we interviewed did *not* display an orientation toward reductionism in their descriptions of their activities (cf. Guillemin and Holmstrom 1986; Scully 1980). But our data indicate that surgeons also look for evidence of this orientation in prospective patients. One surgeon explained his approach as follows:

There's two groups of people. Ones that will come in and say, "Make me beautiful" —those are very poor candidates. And somebody [who comes in] and says, "I don't like my nose." And you say, "What don't you like?" And he says, "Well, I don't like the lump and it's too long" —if they can describe what bothers them, and you know that it can be surgically corrected, then those are excellent candidates for surgery.

Most former patients provided ample evidence of their orientation toward seeing their bodies in parts. For example, one woman described her "pre-rhinoplasty" appearance as follows:

> I had a very Roman nose, straight, kind of broad. I mean, it was perfect, but kind of big. When the first guy operated, I had scars in here (pointing to nostrils in the drawing she has made of her nose). There was more of a stereotype of Jewish women [and] big noses. . . . So I thought, what better thing to do than have my nose made smaller?

Another woman specified the benefits of her face-lift in this way:

> I got what I wanted. A clear forehead, no heavy eyelids and bags under my eyes (my eyes weren't too bad to begin with [but] my forehead was heavily lined). No furrows around my mouth. No wrinkles. Neck is great.

Still another itemized the pluses and minuses of her breast augmentation by saying,

> I am very pleased with the results. Sometimes I fluctuate on wondering if I should have chosen an even larger size in breasts, but I inevitably return to the same conclusion: that this is perfect proportionately. I see no scar whatsoever on the left nipple; there is a slight trace of scar along the edge of the right nipple, but I don't think anyone else would ever notice, it is so slight.

Here, patients demonstrate such well-honed abilities to reduce their bodies to parts that they can offer pre- and post-operative drawings of the parts in question, itemize the benefits of their procedures part by part, and even identify subtle traces of scars that no one else would notice. Clearly, reductionism plays an important part in these patients' own views of their experiences.[6]

We might ask why this orientation becomes so central to accounts of people who undergo cosmetic surgery and those who perfom it. Our data suggest that reductionism is essential to problematizing the part (or parts) in question and establishing their "objective" need for repair. For example, throughout these interviews, surgeons and patients alike alluded to technically normal features as "flaws," "defects," "deformities," and "correctable problems" of appearance. Surgeons referred to patients as "needing" face-lifts and breast augmentations, while patients referred to the specific parts (or parts of parts) that they had "fixed." Through such terminology, they constitute *cosmetic* surgery as a *reconstructive* project. Ultimately, they may even dissolve the distinction between the two categories of plastic surgery—suggesting, for example, that to someone with "an ugly nose or prominent ears," cosmetic surgery may be "just as important as reconstructing somebody after cancer removal." Thus, reductionism provides a means of resolving the central dilemma of cosmetic surgery—defining the nature and treatment of "disease." By jointly reducing patients' bodies to a series of parts and focusing on the parts that require "correction," surgeons and patients forge a *mutual* basis for evaluating patients' complaints, determining what should be done about them, and assessing post-operative results.

Of course, there were minor variations on this theme. For example, one surgeon argued that *patients*, not he, perceived their features as deformed:

> I'm perceiving it as a shape, a structure, as whatever you want to call it . . . this *person* perceives it as a deformity. I just perceive it as the way they look. And they're asking me, "Can you change the way I look to something I don't perceive as a deformity?" So I'm basically treating their attitude towards their own appearance.

Two other surgeons characterized their work as "improving the patient's self-esteem" and "giving them more confidence." However, whether surgeons conceptualized the deformity as on the patient or in the patient's head, they took surgical means to repair it.[7]

There are several apparent inconsistencies in the evidence we have presented so far. For example, if the pursuit of cosmetic surgery is—as surgeons and patients claim—"normal" and "natural," why are objective indicators needed to justify it? And if the objective grounds for surgery are sociologically variable, what sense does it make to describe them as "objective" in the first place? Finally, if surgeons prefer patients who are doing it for themselves, why do they accept patients whose decisions to have surgery are clearly influenced by others' (including surgeons') opinions on their problems? Below, we address what we see as the "missing link" in our analysis so far: namely, the accomplishment of gender.

THE ACCOMPLISHMENT OF GENDER

* * *

In the data presented in this paper, we find that accounts of cosmetic surgery rest ultimately on the accomplishment of gender. For example, throughout our interviews with surgeons and former patients, we found implicit claims that what was "normal" and "natural" for a woman was *not* normal or natural for a man. Surgeons were united in the view that women's concerns for their appearance are *essential* to their nature as women. They observed that women are, after all, taught to look good and disguise their real or imagined "defects." Hence, they said, it is taken for granted that a woman "wants to primp and look as pretty as she can." Her desire may not be biologically ordained—as they noted, she *is* a product of our society and how she was brought up. But, they pointed out, by the time a woman has been "brought up," her consciousness of her appearance as a matter of self-image is "intrinsic" to her nature *as a woman* (cf. Cahill 1982, 1986a, 1986b).

By contrast, surgeons characterized men's concerns for their appearance as extrinsic to their nature as men. They observed that men are taught "to deal with little defects here and there," and that therefore, "they don't have the psychological investment in it that women do." They further observed that men must rely on their wives to buy their clothes or tell them what looks good and that men attend to their appearance only in instrumental fashion, for example, to attain a more prestigious job.

> Women are more concerned about their appearance than men are as a basic rule. Now that is not something you can apply to every person. Obviously you'll see that the success level is related to their appearance level. People who don't take some care in how they appear don't seem to be in supervisory or professional positions. And I guess people, as they're educated, I guess, as they attempt to reach some goal in life, find that their appearance relates to achieving those goals. Women, conversely, are intrinsically . . . concerned about their appearance, not just in a goal-oriented fashion, but as a matter of self-image.

Here, a surgeon notes that educated "people" (meaning men) may discover that their appearance has an impact on their "attempt to reach some goal in life," but he does not attribute that discovery to any natural order of things. In fact, a concern for appearance is so unnatural for men that, as another surgeon notes, some men may deliberately misrepresent it in surgeons' offices, for example, complaining that they "can't breathe" to cover up their wishes for "a better-looking nose."

Our interviews with former patients also suggested that what was "normal" and "natural" for a woman was not normal or natural for a man. As noted above, women referred to cosmetic surgery as what "anyone" would do, extolled its benefits for "everyone," and compared it to "wearing makeup" or "having your hair done." By contrast, the only grounds on which men characterized the pursuit of cosmetic surgery as "normal" were job-related concerns. One man, a cosmetologist who underwent upper eyelid reduction, said he felt that his upper lids were a distraction in his work. Another, who had undergone a face-lift, explained that as a dentist, he thought patients liked "younger persons working on them." Still another man we spoke with who underwent reconstructive rhinoplasty for a deviated septum—but decided against cosmetic alteration—stated that he would only consider cosmetic surgery if he "were disfigured or something." And a man who consulted a surgeon about cosmetic rhinoplasty—but then decided against it—told us,

> I like my nose. It's a little on the large side, and I was teased about it when I was younger, but it's the nose I grew up with. . . . Besides, would I lie to the kids I have some day? They're going to grow up with these noses and say, "Where did this come from?" My philosophy is that you work with what you've got.

Of course, the men in the last two excerpts were accounting for something they did not do, while those in the first two excerpts were accounting for something they did. We can, therefore, understand why the last two excerpts would emphasize good reasons for not having surgery, and the first two, good reasons for having it. But what is noteworthy in all four descriptions is the assumption that a desire for aesthetic improvement must be *justified* (either on the basis of job-related concerns or in the case of "disfigurement"). Clearly, it was not seen as "natural."

Our interviewees further distinguished women from men in their descriptions of "objective" indicators for surgery. Many surgeons acknowledged that our culture and its double standard of aging are responsible for women's and men's differential experiences as they get older. Thus, they explained the fact that a man with wrinkles looks "acceptable" while a woman with wrinkles does not on the basis of cultural conceptions, rather than any objective standard. Surgeons, however, relied *on those same cultural conceptions* to select candidates for surgery.

> Our society has got a very strange double standard and it can be summarized that when a man gets old, he gets sophisticated, debonair, wise; but when a woman gets old, she gets old. A man with a wrinkly face doesn't necessarily look bad in our society. A woman with a wrinkly face looks old. So when a man comes in and he wants a face-lift, I have to be able to get considerably more skin than I would on a woman. . . . And usually there is something else going on. . . . Usually, they're getting rid of their wife.

In requiring "considerably more [excess] skin" for men than women the surgeon constructs an "objective indicator" for doing surgery—as well as "objective differences" between women and men.

Another surgeon contended that there *are* objective differences that make women more likely to "need" surgery:

> Men don't seem to have the lipodystrophy [i.e., deposition of fat in tissue] that women do. They don't have subcutaneous fat layers and, uh . . . I guess I've only done one man with love handles. . . . I think it is more of a gender-related difference than, uh, psychological. . . . Men dermabrade their face with a razor every morning. You have thick hair follicles that support the skin so it doesn't get wrinkled . . . like your upper lip, for instance. Men hardly ever have any problem with that and women, sometimes by age 50, need their lip peeled or something.

Our concern here is *not* the physiological differences this surgeon attests to (although we note that he ignores potbellies in this description). Rather, we are interested in how these differences are invoked to legitimize one course of activity and discredit another. If women's bodies are seen as *essentially* "in need of repair," then surgery on women can be seen as a moral imperative instead of an aesthetic option. But if men "hardly ever have any problem with that," then surgery on men will require elaborate justification.

Such justification was apparent in our interviews with men who had undergone cosmetic surgery. For example, in contrast to the woman patient who said that "when your eyelids start to come down" and "you start to get that 'crepeyness' in your neck" it is simply "time to do it," one man said that *his wife's appearance* motivated him to have a face-lift, as he did not want his wife "to look much younger." Here, he eschewed a description of "objective" signs of aging for an explanation of how he might appear in relation to his spouse. Another man stated that following his upper eyelid reduction, he "once again looked like [his] old self." As a result, he indicated he "felt better" and did not "get as tired," attributing the difference to psychological effect.

The notion of gender as an interactional accomplishment also advances our analysis of how race and ethnicity were constituted as "objective" grounds for surgery. References to Michael Jackson notwithstanding, the descriptions of most surgeons focused on what *women* in various racial and ethnic groups "have" and "need," not on men. Even while former patients relied on white, Anglo-Saxon, Protestant features as the unmarked case, they described their post-operative benefits as looking not only "less exotic," but also "prettier" and "more attractive to men."

In short, we contend that our interviewees' accounts would not have been possible without the accomplishment of gender. This is the mechanism that allows them to see the pursuit of elective aesthetic improvement as "normal" and "natural" for a woman, but not for a man. The accountability of persons to particular sex categories provides for their seeing women as "objectively" needing repair and men as "hardly ever" requiring it. The fact that gender is an *interactional* accomplishment explains why surgeons prefer patients who are "doing it for themselves" but actively participate in the construction of patients' preferences.

The evidence indicates that the selection of "good candidates" for cosmetic surgery relies not merely on the creation of patients with "appropriate" levels of concern and the reduction of patients' faces and bodies to a series of component parts. It also relies on the simultaneous accomplishment of gender. Following Fenstermaker Berk (1985), we contend that there are actually *two* processes here: (1) the selection of "good candidates" for surgery and (2) the accomplishment of gender. The "normal," "natural" character of each process is made sensible in relation to the other, and since they operate simultaneously, the relationship between the two processes and their outcomes "is virtually impossible to question" (West and Fenstermaker forthcoming [published 1993]). Thus, the assessment of "appropriate levels of concern" ensures patients who will agree with a surgeon's perceptions of their problems, and, at the same time, it furnishes the opportunity to affirm the pursuit of cosmetic surgery as an essentially "gendered" activity.

> A lot of guys come in and the classic one is that they want their nose fixed. And you look at the guy and he's got this big, God-awful nose. So does Anthony Quinn! Uh, a man can get away with that kind of nose. So what is normal for a man would not be . . . well, let's say what is *acceptable* for a man would not necessarily be acceptable for a woman.

The point, then, is not merely that pursuing cosmetic surgery is seen as something women do, but that for a woman to seek it while a man does not displays the "essential" nature of each.

CONCLUSION

* * *

In this chapter, we have examined how surgeons who do cosmetic tions account for their activities and how people who elect such o make sense of their decisions to do so. Our data indicate that su patients "explain" their involvement in these activities by extend inition of reconstructive surgery to include cosmetic procedu

DOING

ing patients' faces and bodies to a series of component parts, surgeons and patients together establish the problematic status of the part in question and its "objective" need of "repair." This process affords them a mutual basis for negotiating the evaluation of patients' complaints, the determination of what should be done about them, and the assessment of post-operative results. But this process operates in tandem with the accomplishment of gender, allowing surgeons and patients to see the pursuit of cosmetic surgery as "normal" and "natural" for a woman and *not* for a man. Without the accountability of persons to sex categories, women could not be established as "objectively" in need of repair, nor men, as "objectively" acceptable.

We advance our findings as hypotheses rather than generalizations. Indeed, we present them in a spirit of invitation—with the hope of stimulating among sociologists a broader range of interest in the topic we sought to address. We do not know, for example, how prevalent these processes are among surgeons and patients at large. Nor do we know how these processes might operate in other clinical domains, such as orthodontia (for some suggestive leads, see P. Davis 1980) or cosmetic dentistry.

We do know that our findings contribute to the existing literature on medicalization by identifying a new frontier for expansion of the medical mandate. Beyond work on the appropriation of "bad" behavior and on the usurpation of natural processes, our findings point to the expropriation of the aesthetic realm as a third arena of medicalization. We also know that our findings yield a new direction for research on the social construction of the body: illustrating that bodies are not merely adorned and altered, but physically *reconstructed* in accord with prevailing cultural conceptions. Finally, we know that at least among the surgeons and patients we interviewed, accounting for cosmetic surgery depends on the accomplishment of gender (West and Zimmerman 1987). In offering accounts of their pursuit of surgery, patients enact their "essential natures" as women or men. In offering accounts of their surgical decision making, surgeons uphold normative attitudes and activities for particular sex categories and, hence, become co-participants in the accomplishment of gender. In addition, surgeons act as technological facilitators of gender's accomplishment and as cultural gatekeepers in the fine-tuning of gender's presentation. Thus, cosmetic surgery emerges as an institutional support for "doing gender."

NOTES

1. The original version of this chapter was drawn in part from a paper presented at the annual meeting of the American Sociological Association, Chicago, 1987. The original article appeared in February 1991 in *Social Problems* 38 (1): 54–70.

2. The surgeon's mandate to assess post-operative results works in at least two ways. First, it affords surgeons the authority to appraise likely outcomes of operations in advance of their occurrence (and thereby, to determine whether operations should be performed). Second, it affords sur-

geons the authority to judge results of particular procedures after the fact (and thus to pronounce procedures as "successful"). The latter mandate is especially important in cases of malpractice suits where the expert testimony of other surgeons weighs heavily in litigation.

3. This figure should be treated as a conservative estimate insofar as it includes only operations performed by the 2,550 active physician members of the American Society of Plastic and Reconstructive Surgeons. However, statistics on the actual incidence of cosmetic surgery are virtually impossible to maintain. For example, the U.S. National Center for Health Statistics reports figures independently of physicians and surgeons, board affiliations and society memberships, but it does not include operations performed outside hospitals. Since 95 percent of cosmetic procedures are said to be performed in private offices or clinics (American Society of Plastic and Reconstructive Surgeons 1988), the National Center for Health Statistics offers an even less reliable estimate of their actual incidence.

4. Ideally, we also would have obtained interviews with women who consulted plastic surgeons but decided against cosmetic surgery. We were unable to locate such women through our snowball sample. However, insofar as the accomplishment of gender involves the *accountability* of persons to particular sex categories (not deviance or conformity per se), this "gap" in our data does not constitute a problem for our analysis.

5. Until July of 1990, military personnel and their families were an exception to this rule. Prior to that time, military physicians and surgeons performed aesthetic procedures on members of the U.S. armed forces under the general provisions for health care of those personnel "to sharpen their skills as surgeons in preparation for wartime duty" (*Parade Magazine* 1990, 14). The Pentagon has introduced new regulations to prevent the use of appropriated funds except for "the correction of birth defects, the repairing of injuries, or the commission of breast-reconstruction procedures following mastectomies."

6. Of course, the capacity for reductionism has received considerable attention in feminist analyses of the politics of appearance. Freedman (1986), for example, suggests that women develop an overall image of their bodies from the detailed scrutiny of particular parts. In cases where women suffer from "poor body image," they "generalize from one bad feature to their whole appearance, while ignoring the ways they are attractive" (25).

7. Here, we do not mean to be glib. But these surgeons' claims to be engaged in "surgery of the self-image" are belied by their own participation in the formulation of patients' preferences and by their limited expertise in techniques of psychological assessment. For example, most surgeons said that "specific" psychiatric and/or psychological training had not been a part of their medical education and that patient selection was ultimately a "judgment call" based on their "gut feelings."

CHAPTER EIGHT

Accountability and Affirmative Action: The Acccomplishment of Gender, Race, and Class in a University of California Board of Regents Meeting

CANDACE WEST AND SARAH FENSTERMAKER

On July 20, 1995, the University of California Board of Regents held a heavily attended and widely broadcast meeting in San Francisco.[1] There, Regents decided (by a vote of 15 to 10) to end UC's affirmative action policies for hiring and contracting, and (by a vote of 14 to 10, with one abstention) to end its affirmative action policy for admissions. This decision was described as historic and likely to have major implications for hiring and admissions practices across the United States.[2] And, in the weeks following the decision, a great deal of public attention centered on the identities of those responsible for it. News magazines concentrated on the two best-known politicians who attended the meeting: (then) California Governor Pete Wilson, "suburban avatar of the angry white male," and the Rev. Jesse Jackson, "who arrived in the open-necked shirt he favors when he's in his Third World Leader mode" (Fineman 1995). Newspapers concentrated on individual Regents, such as "Ward Connerly, the black Sacramento housing consultant, who, as a regent appointed by Wilson, spearheaded the move to repeal affirmative-action programs" (Kurtzman and Thurm 1995, A26) and "UC Regent David Lee, the Chinese immigrant who runs a telecommunications equipment firm in Milpitas" (Kurtzman 1995, A22).

Clearly, journalists' reports of the UC Regents' meeting sorted out decision makers by sex ("male"), race ("black"), and class (the "Sacramento housing consultant," the "immigrant who runs a telecommunications equipment firm") in making sense of their actions. Journalists thereby took notice of those actions (e.g., naming, blaming, describing, excusing, or merely acknowledging them) and situated them in a social framework with other actions, like and unlike. This is hardly surprising, given that one of the jobs of journalists is to make sense of the events they report to their readers and given that categorizing persons by sex, race, and class is deemed essential to making sense of the world in which we live. But the fact that people's actions *can* be described in such ways leads to the possibility of engaging in action with an eye to how it might be described, for example, as appropriate or inappropriate for a particular "kind" of person. Thus, expectations can matter to people's behaviors.

What then, of participants in the Regents' meeting that ended affirmative action policies at the University of California? Here, we examine audiotapes and videotapes of the meeting proceedings to see how participants characterize themselves and one another in relation to their conduct. We find that, by characterizing themselves, one another, and their actions in relation to gender, race, and class, participants invite others to make sense of their remarks as appropriate—or inappropriate—for "people like them." Insofar as our accountability to sex category, race category, and class category is what renders the institutional arrangements based on these "normal" and "natural" (West and Fenstermaker 1995a; West and Zimmerman 1987), these data provide a richly detailed picture of how the most fundamental divisions of society are legitimated and maintained.

Below, we briefly reiterate our understanding of "difference" as an ongoing interactional accomplishment (West and Fenstermaker 1995a). We then describe our methods of analysis, including our choice of the UC Regents' meeting as the source of our data. Next, we present our findings on how participants characterized themselves and one another on the particular occasion of this meeting. In discussing our results, we focus on the forms of conduct by which participants at this meeting *do* gender, race, and class— and thereby show their orientation to difference as a significant feature of the interactional context in which they find themselves (Schegloff 1997, 182).

DOING DIFFERENCE: A BRIEF REITERATION

In everyday life, those of us living in Western societies take for granted that there are two—and only two—sexes. We also take for granted that people are "only naturally" (and irrevocably) one sex or the other (Garfinkel 1967, 122). When we interact with others, we assume that each of us has a manly or womanly nature—a nature that derives from our sex and one that can be detected from the "natural signs" we give off (Goffman 1976, 75). These assumptions constitute our normative conceptions about the properties of normally sexed persons.

As members of Western societies, we also take for granted that race is an enduring and essential property of a person. We share preconceptions about what those in particular races "look like," as indicated by comments such as "Odd, you don't look Asian." Moreover, we share deeply rooted beliefs about what those in particular races *are* like, and we are apt to be confused when those we interact with "do not act 'Black,' 'Latino,' or 'white.'" These comprise our normative conceptions with respect to the "seemingly obvious, 'natural' and 'commonsense' qualities of the existing racial order" (Omi and Winant 1986, 62).

Our dominant ideology in Western societies tells us that class is very different from sex and race. In the United States, for instance, we believe that our society is classless, that class is something one achieves, and that anyone can, in theory, make it to the top. At the same time, though, we

> believe in luck and on closer examination, it certainly is quite a coin-
> cidence that the "unlucky" come from certain race, gender and class
> backgrounds. In order to perpetuate racist, sexist and classist out-
> comes, we also have to believe that the current economic distribution
> is unchangeable, has always existed, and probably exists in this form
> throughout the known universe, i.e., it's "natural." (Langston 1991,
> 146)

For example, if someone is quite rich, or merely well-to-do, we presume that it is the result of their own effort, talent, and initiative. But if someone is quite poor, we presume that it is because of something they did or failed to do: They did not work hard enough, they lacked ambition, and so on. Certainly, these beliefs *look* less deeply rooted than our views of womanly and manly natures or our convictions about characteristics of particular racial group members; even so, they presume that a person's economic lot in life is determined by the *qualities of that person*. We therefore see initiative as inherent to those who have and lack of initiative as inherent to those who have not. While we do not espouse the view that "classed" qualities (such as industriousness, ambition, charm, and willingness to sacrifice) have "natural signs" (Goffman 1976, 75) as race and sex do, our view of these as personal traits shapes the way we interact as members of particular classes.

Scientific grounds for our beliefs about gender, race, and class simply do not exist. For example, scientists have determined that there is no basis for linking class to the biological characteristics of persons (despite numerous early attempts to link pauperism with heredity—see, for example, Rafter 1992). There is considerably less agreement about race (compare, for exam-ple, Aguirre 1979, Montagu 1975, and Stephans 1982 with Herrnstein 1994). But, while the United States is only one of several Western societies to generate theories of racial character, its theories (like those of other Western societies) are not grounded in any scientific criteria for reliably dif-ferentiating members of different "racial" groups. Michael Omi and

Howard Winant (1986, 57) offer ample evidence of the confusion this has generated, such as California's decision in 1854 to categorize Chinese persons as "Indian." Biological criteria *are* used in the initial process of sex assignment (classification of persons as either females or males at birth). Yet the criteria for sex assignment can vary (e.g., chromosome type before birth or genitalia after birth), they sometimes don't agree with one another (e.g., hermaphrodites), and they display considerable cultural variation (Kessler and McKenna 1978). As Harold Garfinkel points out (1967, 116–8), it is our *moral conviction* that there are two and only two sexes that explains the relative ease with which sex assignments are produced. It is this conviction that gives females and males the status of "natural" and unequivocal beings, whose distinctive social and psychological tendencies follow from their reproductive functions (West and Zimmerman 1987, 127–8).[3] In short, sex, race, and class are social constructions—not straightforward reflections of biological "facts."[4]

Nevertheless, in everyday life, people can and do classify themselves and others in relation to sex category, race category, and class category. *Sex categorization* does not involve any well-defined set of criteria that must be satisfied in order to classify someone as a woman or a man; instead, it involves treating appearances (deportment, dress, and bearing) as if they were the expression of some underlying biological reality (anatomy, hormones, and chromosomes). Nor does *race categorization* involve any well-defined set of criteria. In the United States, for example, the relatively recent emergence of the category "Asian American" misrepresents the very different histories, geographic origins, and cultures of Cambodian, Chinese, Filipino, Japanese, Korean, Laotian, Thai, and Vietnamese Americans. Despite important differences among these groups, "the majority of Americans cannot tell the difference between their members" (Omi and Winant 1986, 24). Thus, "Asian American" operates as a device for categorizing persons by race in everyday life.

To be sure, there *are* reliable criteria for distinguishing people's positions within the system of distribution that structures our access to resources. It is possible to sort people out using these criteria and it is the job of many public agencies (within the United States, for example, the Legal Aid Society, the Human Services Agency, and even the Internal Revenue Service) to do so. In everyday life, though, we rely on commonsense understandings of how class "will tell" in the most mundane of social doings (see, for example, DeMott 1990, 1–27). *Class categorization*, like sex categorization and race categorization, involves treating appearances (very broadly defined) as if they were indicative of some natural state of affairs. . . .

Thus, we contend that doing difference means *creating* differences among members of different sex categories, different race categories, and different class categories—differences that are hardly "natural." These differences are then invoked to maintain the "essential" distinctiveness of categorical identities as well as the institutional arrangements they support. The accomplishment of difference makes the social arrangements based on sex category, race category, and class category understandable as normal and natural, that is, as legitimate ways of organizing social life. Distinctions among persons that are created by this process can then be portrayed as fundamental and enduring dispositions. From this point of view, patriarchy, racism, and class oppression can be seen as responses to the differences— the social order being merely a way of accommodating "natural differences" among human beings.

Below, we explain how we analyzed the accomplishment of gender, race, and class by participants at the UC Regents' meeting.

METHODS

Our data consist of audiotapes and videotapes of the meeting proceedings: thirteen hours of deliberations over proposals to end affirmative action policies for hiring, contracting, and admissions at the University of California. The proceedings were held in a large auditorium, in which members of the Board of Regents sat around long conference tables in the front of the room; speakers addressed the Regents while standing at a nearby podium; and members of a large audience sat in tiers of raised theater seats, which extended to the rear of the auditorium. The proceedings were aired on television and radio; hence, there were broadcast journalists operating cameras and sound equipment throughout the auditorium, with large groups of them around the Regents down in front.

After a roll call of the Regents in attendance, the meeting started with an address by (then) California Governor Pete Wilson, who was also the president of UC's Board of Regents. Then, 31 elected officials and public figures addressed the Regents, followed by members of the public, who were selected by lottery from more than 140 people who wanted to speak. Regent Clair Burgener, the chair of the board during the morning session of the meeting, conducted the lottery at the meeting's onset, stipulating that all speakers (after Wilson) would be limited to three minutes for their remarks. A beeper sounded when speakers reached their three-minute limit; however, many continued for considerably longer (e.g., then Speaker of the California Assembly [and now mayor of San Francisco] Willie Brown spoke for more than 12 minutes).

Videotapes of these deliberations were produced by Bay Television (and subsequently, made available to us by the UC Regents' Office). Periodically, the focus of these tapes shifted from the meeting participants to various TV news reporters, interviewing people whose opinions about the proceedings might be of interest to viewers. When this happened, we depended on the audiotapes alone as a record of the proceedings. Sooner or later, the audiotapes needed to be turned over or replaced; when this happened, we relied on the videotapes.

Our transcripts of the audio and videotapes employ a set of transcribing conventions (see Appendix), the aim of which is to capture as close to a verbatim description of interaction as possible.[5] For purposes of this analysis, we focus on the first two hours of the UC Regents' meeting, containing addresses by the elected officials and public figures represented in 120 pages of transcript.

We had little idea of what we might find when we began the analysis of these data. Our theoretical conceptualization of difference as an accomplishment did not easily translate into clear-cut operational definitions of the phenomena in which we were interested. Moreover, neither of us could attend, watch, or listen to the full 13 hours of the UC Regents' meeting on the day it took place. For these reasons, we proceeded quasi-inductively, scanning the tapes and transcripts for possible practices of naming, describing, blaming, excusing, and merely acknowledging actions, and placing them in a social framework with other activities, like and unlike (Heritage 1984, 136–7).

As many people have observed, of course, this meeting "was less a marathon decision-making occasion than a rhetorical circus" (Don Zimmerman, personal communication). A full day before the proceedings, word reached many of us that Wilson "had the votes" and would preside at the meeting. Given this, it might appear that the meeting itself was a largely scripted affair: After all, most participants addressed the Regents with carefully prepared speeches (many of which were circulated in advance); a chair moderated who would speak next, about what and (in theory) for how long; and the outcome of the meeting was predetermined. How, then, is this meeting a logical place to explore the *doing* of gender, race, and class in social interaction?

We have three answers to this question. First, and most obvious, because UC's affirmative action policies (prior to this meeting) relied on classifying people by sex category, race category, and class category,[6] we would expect these to be relevant issues for participants and that participants would orient their conduct to them. Second, even speeches (no matter how carefully they were scripted in advance) comprise occasions of social interaction when they are delivered. Rules for who will speak next and for how long must therefore be invoked *on the occasion* of a speech being spoken, audience responses (such as applause or booing) must therefore be negotiated *on the occasion* of a speech being delivered (cf. Atkinson 1985; Clayman 1991), and "a range of phenomena that are integral to naturally-occurring speech . . . intonation, pitch, pacing, volume, filled and unfilled pauses, nonlexical vocalizations, false starts, repetitions, interruptions and overlaps between speakers" (Mishler 1984, 21) appear *on the occasion* of that speech's delivery, not in the text of the speech the speaker prepared in advance. Third, and most important, if sex category, race category, and class category are, as we have argued (West and Fenstermaker 1995a) potentially *omnirelevant* to social life, then persons involved in virtually any activity (scripted or not) may be held accountable for their performance of that activity in relation to their category membership. Our focus was not the relative salience of gender, race, and class to the proceedings, but rather, how participants might orient their conduct to these as the proceedings unfolded. Below, we present our findings on how sex category, race category, and class category were made to matter for the conduct of participants at the meeting.

SELF-CATEGORIZATION

The first pattern we observed on the tapes (a pattern so striking that we could hear it without looking at a transcript) was that many speakers explicitly prefaced their remarks by characterizing themselves in relation to race category, or race category and sex category. For instance, speakers used explicit self-categorization *to introduce themselves* at this meeting.[7]

California Assembly Member Barbara Lee (76: 2019–28)

Lee:	((audio only)) <u>Than</u>k you. uh Mister Chairman?
	u [h: Mister]= <u>Governor?</u> Mister President (1.0).
	<u>Than</u>k you for the oppor<u>tun</u>ity to <u>speak</u>
	with you today. (1.4) I <u>stand</u> before you as a
	member of the California <u>Legis</u>lature? representing
	<u>Oak</u>land? (.4) Ale<u>me:</u>da? (.2) and <u>Pied</u>mont?
	(1.2) As the im<u>me</u>diate <u>past</u> <u>chair</u> and
——->	representative of the California Legislative Black
——->	<u>Cau:</u>cus? (1.8) A <u>wo:</u>man?
	(1.0) ((video comes on again, with a close-up shot of Lee, an apparently Black woman, at the podium))

California Assembly Member Nao Takasugi (94: 2497–2503)

Takasugi:	[°Good morning, Mister <u>Governor,</u>] Mister Chairman,
	(1.2) ((camera shifts to Takasugi, an apparently Asian man, looking up)) members of the Regents ((looks down)) (2.8)
	My name is <u>Nao</u> Takasugi,=I'm (.4) an assemblyman
	from the thirty-seventh <u>dis</u>trict. ((looks down)) (.8) The

-------> ((looks up)) only A:sian face in the uh hundred twenty
seven member: (1.0) state legislature toda:y. ((looks
down)) (2.0)

Former Speaker of the Assembly, Willie Brown (17: 431–40)

Brown: ((audio only)) Mister Chairman (3.0) Governor Wilson,
            President Peltason, (1.8) Mister Leach hh (5.2)
            distinguished members: (.8) of the Board of Regents
            of the University of California. (2.0) I have the great
            honor, (.8) and plea:sure (1.8) of serving with you, (.8) at
            least- one or two of you,=Frank Clark, (1.2) Regent
            Campbell, (.2) one or two others (1.0) for a period of
            almost fifteen ye:ars. (.4) On this distinguished body.
-------> (1.0) Having been the first, (.4) as I understand it, (1.0)
-------> African American (1.0) appointed directly to this body in
            September. (.8) Of nineteen eighty. (1.2)

We noted that none of the speakers in these examples (or indeed, at any
point in the first two hours of the meeting) was a prospective student or
employee of the University of California, that is, someone whose chances of
being admitted to or hired by the university might be affected by changes in
its affirmative action policies. Thus, we could not explain speakers' explicit
self-categorizations by race, or by race and sex, as a function of how the university would classify *them* for purposes of admission, contracting, or hiring.

Another thing we noted was that those speakers who explicitly used
race category, or race and sex category, to introduce themselves came from
both sides of the debate about changing UC's affirmative action policy. For
example, Lee, who introduced herself as "immediate past chair and representative of the California Black Legislative Caucus" and "a woman,"
argued against ending affirmative action.

California Assembly member Barbara Lee (82: 2178–82)

Lee: I ur:ge each and every one: of you (.8) to defeat (.4)
            each ((gesturing with her right index finger)) and every
            one: of Mister Connerly's proposals before you today.
            ((casting her eyes over in Connerly's direction again, then
            looking down))

Takasugi, who introduced himself as "the only Asian face in the hundred
and seventy member state legislature today," argued in favor of ending affirmative action.

DOING GENDER, DOING DIFFERENCE

California Assembly Member Nao Takasugi (96: 2535–8)

> Takasugi: Let us be clear toda:y, what we are discu:ssing. (2.0)
> With UC's (.) ((looks up, then down)) special
> preferential admissions policy (.4) ((looks up, then
> down)) nothing more or less than state-mandated
> ((looks up)) discrimi<u>nation</u>. (.6) ((looks down)) Based on
> <u>ra</u>ce. (.2)

And Brown (UC Regents' Meeting, 26: 677–85), who introduced himself as "the first African American appointed directly to this body," later contended,

> Brown: To <u>vote</u> to change affirmative action. (.) Ahead of
> the <u>peo:ple</u>? Ahead of a court order? Ahead of a
> constitutional amendment? A<u>head</u> of any statutes?
> (.6) Would BE: to mo:ve the <u>Regents</u> I:Nto the <u>are</u>na of
> politics. (.6) And once there, (.8) extrication (.2) becomes
> an impossibility.

Thus, we could not explain speakers' explicit self-classification by race category, and by race category and sex category, as a function of their position on UC's existing affirmative action policy (pro or con).

What *did* explain speakers' explicit self-classifications in introducing themselves were their apparent race category and apparent sex category memberships. Among the elected officials and public figures who addressed the Regents during the first two hours of this meeting, those who introduced themselves with explicit references to their sex category and race category memberships (e.g., Lee) were, apparently, women of color; those who introduced themselves with explicit reference to their race category membership alone (e.g., Takasugi and Brown) were, apparently, men of color.

To be sure, women of color did not *always* introduce themselves using race and sex categorization. For example, California Assembly Member Marguerite Archie-Hudson and California Senator Diane Watson (both Black women) introduced themselves as follows:

California Assembly member Marguerite Archie-Hudson (67: 1782–89)

> Archie-Hudson: Thank=you=Mister=Chair=and=the=members,=let=
> me=first =say=for=the=<u>record</u>=that=As<u>sem</u>bly=Member=
> Juanita=MacDonald=who=will=<u>not</u>=address=you=today
> has <u>asked</u> <u>me</u>: to let you know that she joins in these

remarks. (.4) Mister <u>Chair</u> and <u>MEM</u>bers of the
Board
———-> of <u>Re</u>gents of the University of Cali<u>for</u>nia (.6) I <u>COME</u>
———-> before you to<u>day</u> as <u>chair</u>=of=the=Assembly=Committee=
———-> on=Higher=Edu<u>ca</u>tion, to <u>UR:GE</u> you to de<u>FEAT</u> the
resolutions proposed=by=Mister=Connerly=before=you=
to<u>day</u>. (.2) The <u>RES</u>olutions are <u>at</u> <u>BE:ST</u>, premature.

California Senator Diane Watson (27: 704–6)

Watson: ((camera locked on her)) My name is <u>Sen:</u>ator Diane
———-> Watson, <u>na</u>tive of this state. (.8) I <u>speak</u> to you this
———-> morning as a <u>prou::d</u> alumna (1.2) of the University (.6) of
———-> California (.4) at Los Angeles. (2.0) Why <u>now,</u> (4.)
Mister Connerly. (1.0) Why <u>now</u>, Regents. (.8) Why <u>now</u>.

Above, Archie-Hudson invokes her position as "chair of the Assembly
Committee on Higher Education" to introduce herself, and Watson invokes
her status as "a proud alumna of the University of California at Los
Angeles" (in addition to referring to herself as "senator" and "a native of this
state").

But, while women of color did not always introduce themselves with
explicit references to their sex category and race category membership,
those speakers who *did* introduce themselves this way were all (apparently)
women of color. The one exception to this rule was California Assembly
member John Vasconcellos, who introduced himself as follows:

California Assembly member John Vasconcellos (53: 1396–1404)

Vasconcellos: (1.2) I come as a native Cali<u>for</u>nian? (elected here)
twenty nine <u>years</u>? (1.2) chaired both stage(s) of the
<u>Mas</u>ter Plan? ((looks down briefly at notes, then up ———
———-> again)) and as a <u>white</u> ma:n, ((looking straight at the
camera)) (1.2) ((microphone noise)) <u>RAIS</u>ed to believe
that we: are <u>one</u> people?

Here, Vasconcellos, whose appearance we could not readily categorize as
either white or Latino (he is of Portuguese descent), explicitly introduces
himself as "a white man."

One reason Vasconcellos's introduction attracted our attention is that
none of the speakers whom we *could* readily classify as "white men" used race
category or sex category membership to introduce themselves. For example,
California Senator Bill Leonard (35: 922–30)

Leonard: I=appreciate=your=making=the=time=available for
             me to (speak)
             (.)

Some man: Hear, hear!=

Leonard: =in support of Regent Connerly's: resolutions. (.2) To
             eliminate race based admissions and hiring practices (.2)
             at the University of California. (.2) I come before you as
             state senator representing the people of Riverside and=San
             Bernadino=Cou:nties, a:nd personally, as an alumnus
             of UC Ir:vine.

California Senator Tom Hayden (40:1046–9)

Hayden: ((looking down at his notes)) I have distributed a (.2)
             written version of these comments, uh- Mister
             Chairman (.2) uh Governor (.2) members=of=
             the=Regents: (.2) Good morning. (1.0) I uh (.8) am here
             to uh (.4) ask you to defer action on this measure, and
             urge that you try to reframe the debate, on affirmative
             action.

California Senator Tom Campbell [now Representative Tom Campbell of
the U.S. House of Representatives] (47: 1254–7)

Campbell: ((with camera locked in on him, looks up at camera and
             not at notes)) My name is To:m Ca:mpbell. I am a state
             senator. (.6) I also had the very high ho:nor of clerking
             for Justice (.2) Byron White (.4) the year Bakke was
             decided.

California Assembly member Phillip Isenberg (UC Regents' Meeting 60:
1601–4)

Isenberg: (.2) I appear to you today as chair of the Judiciary
             Committee in the Assembly.=In January we will begin
             hearing on propo:sed constitutional amendments, (.2)
             to prohibit or modify affirmative action in the state of
             Califor:nia?

California Assembly member Bernie Richter (85: 2243–50)

Richter: Governor Wilson, (1.2) Regents, (1.4) it's a pleasure to be: here and I want to congratulate first of a:ll (.2) the Governor (.8) and Ward Connerly for having the cou:rage (.8) to carry this issue to the people and to bring it to this board. ((licks his lips)) (1.2) ((looking down now, as if starting to read)) Af [firmative action has-become] a code word for preferential policie:s, so:das, quo- ((still looking down, as if reading)) quotas and set asides.

And, of course,
(former) California Governor Pete Wilson (3: 78–83)

Wilson: Thank you Mister Chairman. This institution has a long and a proud tradition. Of generating and- tolerating diverse opinions and perspectives. We will ((voice quavers)) carry on ((quaver subsides)) that tradition today. But as Regents of the university of California, we cannot tolerate University policies or practices that violate fundamental fairness. Trampling individual rights to create and give preference to group rights.

In the excerpts above, Leonard introduces himself as "state senator" and as "an alumnus of UC Irvine," Campbell introduces himself as "a state senator" and as someone who was "clerking for Justice Byron White the year [the] Bakke [case] was decided," and Isenberg introduces himself as "chair of the Judiciary Committee in the Assembly." Moreover, Hayden, Richter, and Wilson launch their remarks without *any* introduction of themselves in categorical terms: Hayden presents himself simply as someone asking the Regents to "defer action on this measure," Richter does not introduce himself at all, and Wilson invokes the *institution* of the University of California in speaking about the tradition "we" will carry on. In fact, the only (apparently) white man who verged on introducing himself in relation to race category (but not sex category) was Assembly member Charles Poochigian, who presented himself as follows:

California Assembly member Charles Poochigian (106: 2804–10)

Poochigian: ((looking up at Regents)) President Peltaso:n (.8) Mister Chairman and members of the ((looks down)) (.8) Board of Regents, (1.8) as an American ((looking up)) of Armenian descen(t) (.8) [I'm] very- ((looking up at Regents))awar:e and proud (.6) ((he blinks during this interval)) of my heritage.

Above, Poochigian bypasses both race category and sex category, and instead introduces himself as a member of a particular ethnic group ("an American of Armenian descent").

As a first step toward explaining these patterns in our data, we propose that explicit self-classification by race category or by race and sex category in the context of speakers' introductions is a means of proposing *that the speakers see themselves as accountable* for the remarks to follow in relation to their race category or race and sex category memberships. Thus, Lee, who urges "each and every one" of the Regents to defeat "each and every one of Mister Connerly's proposals," does so not merely as "Assemblywoman Barbara Lee" (as Chair Burgener introduced her) but, rather, as "immediate past chair and representative of the California Black Legislative Caucus" and as "a woman." Takasugi, who describes UC's existing affirmative action policy as "nothing more or less than state-mandated discrimination based on race" does so not simply as "Assemblyman Nao Takasugi" (as the chair introduced him) but as "the only Asian face in the hundred and twenty seven member state legislature today." And Brown, who cautions the Regents that "to vote to change affirmative action ahead of the people, ahead of a constitutional amendment and ahead of any statutes would be to move into the arena of politics" does so not only as "former Speaker Willie Brown" (as the Chair said) but also as "the first African American appointed to this body." Through these means, speakers characterize their remarks as appropriate, and further, invite others to hear them, as "only natural" for a member of their race category or race category and sex category.[8]

We find further evidence for this interpretation in cases where self-categorization occurred not in speakers' introductions of themselves (in what conversation analysts might describe as a "pre-topical" position [Maynard and Zimmerman 1984]) but in terms that were used to take special notice of some activity and place it in a social framework. For example, consider San Francisco Supervisor Mabel Teng's explicit references in the following excerpt:

San Francisco Supervisor Mabel Teng (UC Regents' Meeting, 113: 2980–5)

```
Teng:       It is inSULTing ((looks down, closes her eyes for
            an instant)) for me: ((looking up toward Regents)) as an
——->        A:sian ((shifting her eyes toward the auditorium
——->        audience)) American, (.6) ((looks down, then up at
——->        audience)) as a ((looks down)) wo::man (1.0) ((looking
            up at auditorium audience)) to hear some of the previous
            ((shifting her eyes over toward the Regents)) speakers'
            ((looking down)) remarks.
```

By explicitly invoking her race category ("Asian American") and sex category ("woman") memberships in the context of a turn characterizing "some of the previous speakers' remarks" as "insulting to hear," Teng conveyed the unequivocal message that it is "only natural" *for an Asian American* and "only natural" *for a woman* to be offended by them.

If this analysis is correct, how do we explain the fact that the apparent white men in these data did not mention race category or sex category in introducing themselves (or indeed, anywhere in their remarks)? Simply as follows: that they did not see themselves as accountable *as white men* for what they had to say. Their lack of self-categorization in introducing their views (in the context of a meeting in which race categorization and sex categorization were explicit topics of discussion) implied that it was "only natural" for *anyone* (no matter what their sex category membership or race category membership) to see things the way that they did. They might be accountable as "a state senator," as "chair of the Assembly Judiciary Committee," as someone who was "clerking for Justice Byron White the year [the] Bakke [case] was decided,"[9] or as someone who speaks on behalf of "this institution" itself—but *not* as white men.

Three further bits of evidence support the analysis we have so far. First, the only (apparently) white woman to speak during the first two hours of the UC Regents' meeting introduced herself with no mention whatsoever of her race category membership and only indirect reference to her sex category membership.

California Assembly member Marilyn Brewer (100: 2644–55)

Brewer: ((smiles—possibly laughs inaudibly—and looks down)) Governor Wilson ((looks up toward Regents, then down)) (.6) <u>ho:n</u>ored Regents ((looks up toward Regents)) and distinguished ((looking down)) visitors ((looks up toward auditorium audience, then down)) (1.2) As a <u>Califor:n</u>ian concer:ned about ((looking down)) public education, (.) ((looks up toward auditorium audience)) As a <u>law:</u>maker concerned ((looking down)) about ((looking up toward auditorium audience)) our <u>state</u> ((looks down)) (.2)

——->   ((looks up and shifts her face toward the Regents)) and as
——->   a <u>bu:</u>inesswoman concerned abou:t our <u>future</u> ((looking down)) (.4) ((looks up at auditorium audience)) I am here today to ((looking down)) speak in sup<u>port </u>((looking up toward camera)) of Regent Ward Connerly's ((looking down)) propo:sal.

Introducing herself as "a businesswoman concerned about our future" (as well as "a Californian concerned about public education" and "a lawmaker concerned about our state"), Brewer identifies herself as a woman only indirectly—in the context of "business."[10] Second, with the exception of Vasconcellos, no apparent man of color introduced himself with explicit reference to his sex category membership. Takasugi, like Brewer, employed an indirect reference in his introduction ("an assemblyman from the thirty seventh district"), and neither Brown nor (Steve) Phillips (an apparently Black man, a law student at Hastings, and member of the San Francisco Board of Education) mentioned sex category in their introductions at all. If the lack of self-categorization in a speaker's introduction implies a *lack* of accountability in relation to particular category membership (e.g., Brewer's whiteness), then indirect self-categorization in a speaker's introduction surely implies a muting of it (e.g., Takasugi's maleness). And third, Vasconcellos only characterized himself as "a white man" in the context of a turn at talk in which he selected Ward Connerly (out of all those listening to Vasconcellos's remarks) as the intended recipient of his utterance.

California Assembly member John Vasconcellos (53: 1396–1404)

> Vasconcellos: (1.2) I come as a native Cali<u>for</u>nian? (elected here)
> twenty nine <u>years</u>? (1.2) chaired both stage(s) of the
> <u>Mas</u>ter Plan? ((looks down briefly at notes, then up
> ——> again)) and as a <u>white</u> ma:n, ((looking straight at the
> camera)) (1.2) ((microphone noise)) <u>RAIS</u>ed to believe
> that we: are <u>one</u> people? (1.0) who <u>need</u> to ex<u>TEN:D</u>
> ourselves to each other, ((looks over to (viewer's) far left
> ——> at Regent's table)) <u>War:</u>d, ((presumably, Ward Connerly))
> (.8) ((with camera locked on him)) to be sure we are
> in<u>clud</u>ed.

Although Vasconcellos's introduction serves as a means of presenting himself to all parties present, his explicit self-categorization as "a white man" occurs where he addresses "Ward" (a Black man) in particular. We see this as one of the few instances of the wholly intentional use of rhetorical strategy in our data: Vasconcellos's description of himself as "a white man" is notable (coming next in a series after Wilson's, Leonard's, Hayden's, and Campbell's failures to describe themselves as white men). His subsequent use of Connerly's first name in public ("Ward") further marks his opposition to the adversaries of affirmative action.

Although some speakers did not see themselves as accountable for their actions in relation to their race category or race category and sex category memberships, this did not prevent them from being held accountable by others. Below, we turn to cases of other-categorization in our data.

OTHER-CATEGORIZATION

In the first two hours of the UC Regents' meeting, no participant ever called another participant to account for his or her conduct by explicitly invoking that participant's race category or sex category membership. Although some made charges that could best be described as denunciations of other participants,[11] none ever did so with explicit reference to the race category or sex category of the persons they denounced. This is certainly understandable; after all, if one participant were to charge another with doing what they're doing (or saying what they're saying) *because* of their category membership (e.g., as "a white man," as "a Latino" or as "a woman"), the participant so charged could deny it and/or accuse the person making that charge of prejudice.

By contrast, consider the subtlety and effectiveness of the implicit other-categorization just below:

California Senator Diane Watson (33–34: 882–3)

Watson:	((looking at camera)) Because if this university (1.0) reverts (.8) to an a:ll white male and Asian male university, (1.2) closing the doo:rs on the people who are: California, (.8) why should we: (.2) ((looking at Regents)) as taxpayers (.2) want to support (1.2) why:: should we want to support a university
——->	((looking at camera)) that has a person who wants to
——->	sta:nd (1.4) in the doo:r (.) reminiscent of George Wallace (.6)
(A man):	°Whoa!=
Watson:	=An' say to Di [ane Watson,]
Audience:	[((applause and "whooping"))] (.4) ((Watson looks at Regents))
——-> Watson:	[You no longer can enter.]
Audience:	[((applause and "whooping"))]

Here, Watson never explicitly states who the "person" *is* "who wants to stand in the door and say to Diane Watson (a Black woman), 'You no longer can enter.'" She simply likens him to George Wallace—a white man, who, while governor of Alabama in 1963, stood in the door of an Alabama schoolhouse to prevent Black students from registering. But the significance of her indirect reference is hardly lost on the unidentified man who exclaims softly ("Whoa!"), or on members of the audience, whose applause following this remark lasts for 22.8 seconds.[12]

George Wallace was not the only white man whose name was employed in indirect categorical references. Thomas Jefferson's name came up repeatedly during these proceedings.[13] For example,

California Assembly member Marguerite Archie-Hudson (68: 1805–18)

> Archie-Hudson: ONLY TWo: days ago, . . . the pre:sident (.) of this
>   Board of Regents (.) the <u>GOVERNOR</u>(.2) of this state
>   of Cali<u>for</u>nia, made CLE:AR in a <u>press</u> release, that the
>   <u>vote</u> to<u>day</u> is a <u>ce:n</u>tral <u>el</u>ement (.6) of his presi<u>den</u>tial
>   ca [mpaign.]
> A man: [(((unintelligible))]
> Archie-Hudson: HE has de<u>cla:red</u> affirmative action to be <u>quote</u>
>   THE <u>DEAD</u>ly <u>VI</u>rus of <u>TRIBAL</u>ism, close quotes= He
>   has-<u>ASK</u>(ed) that
> ———> the PRIN [CIPLES of] <u>Thom</u>as <u>Jeff</u>erson, [(((gavel
>   pounding?))]
> Archie-Hudson: a <u>slave</u>holder, (.2) who believed that BLACKs <——
>   -were in<u>HER</u>ently in<u>FER</u>ior, be the ba<u>ro:me</u>ter   <——
>   by which this <u>iss</u>ue is measured.

Above, Archie-Hudson is the epitome of indirection, using Wilson's titles ("the President of this Board of Regents," "the governor of this state of California") rather than his name, and using the third-person singular ("his," "He") to refer to him.[14] Even so, by calling him to task for asking that "the principles of Thomas Jefferson, a slaveholder, who believed the Blacks were inherently inferior, be the barometer by which this issue is measured," she clearly implies that he is accountable for his conduct as a white man— like Thomas Jefferson.

The most dramatic example of indirect other-categorization in these data is one that raises Thomas Jefferson's name once again. Because it so vividly demonstrates the *interactional* nature of the process of rendering someone accountable for a course of action, we present it in its entirety.

California Assembly member Barbara Lee (79–80: 2103–31)

> 1———> Lee: Eh- <u>Mis</u>ter Gov:ernor, (.2) <u>I</u> am con<u>vin</u>ced that <u>you</u>
>   (.2) understand this
>   ((camera shifts back to close-up of Lee))
> Lee: <u>clea:r</u>ly. In <u>your</u> <u>public</u> statement on <u>July</u> eighteenth
>   nineteen ninety <u>fi:</u>ve, as As<u>sem</u>blywoman
> 2———> Marguerite=Archie=Hudson=said, you quote Thomas
>   Jefferson's

3————->	((camera shifts to close-up shot of Pete Wilson, looking at Lee))
Lee:	statement (.2) <u>equal</u> <u>ri:ghts</u> for <u>all</u>, spe:cial <u>priv</u>ileges for <u>none</u>= without re<u>mi::::nding</u>= <—-4 ((Wilson looks down, then up)) <—-5
Lee:	=the <u>citizens</u> of this <u>state</u> (.2) that when <u>Thom</u>as Jefferson <u>ma:</u>de this state- <u>statement</u> ((Wilson looks down, leans forward slightly in his chair and reaches toward the microphone with his right index finger as if to tap it))
Lee:	he was the <u>prou::::d</u> (.8) <u>ow:ner</u> (.6) of <u>slaves</u>.= <—-6
Wilson:	=((loud thumping noise from microphone)) <—-7 (1.0) ((laughter from audience in this interval))
Lee:	And he <u>also</u> considered African Americans <u>property</u>. (1.6) ((Wilson looks up at Lee again, crosses his arms on the table, "half" smiles, looks down, then up)) <—-8
Lee:	In <u>fact</u>, ((camera shifts back to close-up of Lee))
Lee:	Thomas <u>Jeff</u>erson in his seventeen eighty six <u>notes</u> <u>wrote</u> (.2) that in imag<u>ination</u> they are du:::ll, <u>taste</u>less and an<u>omo</u>lous. (.2) And are <u>inferior</u> to the <u>whi:tes</u> in the endowment of both <u>body</u> and <u>mind.</u> (1.4) So it's <u>not</u> surpri::sing that given your <u>all</u> out as<u>sault</u> on affirmative <u>action</u> you would <u>cite</u> Thomas <u>Jeff</u>erson as an ex<u>ample</u> of ideal <u>fairness</u>. ((shaking her head from side to side))

Although citing Archie-Hudson, Lee proceeds very differently from Archie-Hudson: she addresses Wilson directly ("Mister Governor") and uses second person singular in characterizing his conduct ("you quote Thomas Jefferson's statement equal rights for all, special privileges for none"). But then, after comparing Thomas Jefferson's conduct ("the proud owner of slaves," "considered African Americans property," and so on) with Wilson's conduct ("your all-out assault on affirmative action") she asserts that "it's not surprising" that Wilson "would cite Thomas Jefferson as an example of ideal fairness." Her implication is clear, we believe: "It's not surprising *for someone like you*."[15]

Now, what is the evidence for our contention that by "someone like you," Lee means *a white man*? First, there is the fact that Thomas Jefferson was, as a matter of historical record, a white man. Second, there is the fact that the overwhelming majority of those who owned slaves in the United States in Jefferson's time were white men. Third, the vast majority of those who regarded African Americans as property in the United States at that time were white men (in 1786, white women could not own property in their own names if they were married). Fourth, those who wrote (in 1786) that African Americans were "dull, tasteless and anomalous" and "inferior to whites in the endowment of both body and mind" were white men (U.S. women were barred from such public forms of address throughout the eighteenth and well into the nineteenth century). Fifth, and most important, *Wilson himself* demonstrates his accountability as a white man. Apart from his looking at Lee at arrow 3, thumping the microphone at arrow 7, and sitting back in his chair with a "half-smile" at arrow 8 (in the excerpt above), consider his actions the moment that Lee finished her speech.

California Governor Pete Wilson (83: 78–83)

Wilson:	[Mister] Chai:rman,=
	((Burgener looks toward the (viewer's) left; camera slides in that direction to a close-up shot of Wilson))
Wilson:	((his right hand holding the microphone, looking up toward Burgener)) Mister <u>Chair</u>man uh: (.6) <u>slight</u> poin(t) of personal pri:vilege, I would just point ou::t (2.0) ((looks down, then up)) that I am in very good <u>com</u>pany in quo:ting Thomas <u>Jef</u>ferson. (1.6)
Wilson:	.h ((turning toward the camera)) Doctor Martin Luther Ki [:ng] ((turning back toward Burgener))
A man:	[<u>No:!</u>]
Wilson:	found his remarks [so inspiring-]
Audience:	[((unintelligible shouts))]=
Burgener:	[((gavel pounding))]
Audience:	=((more unintelligible shouts, possibly including ["shut up!"))]
Wilson:	[Doc- Doc-]=
	=((clears throat)) Doctor <u>Ki:ng</u> found his remarks so inspiring (.8) that <u>he</u> quoted them. (1.0) He e<u>voke</u>d them in his ((casts eyes up toward camera, then down)) (.4) description of his <u>drea:m</u> ((casts eyes up toward auditorium audience, then down)) for this nation. ((looks down, then up at camera)) (1.0) ((camera shifts to a wide-angle shot of the audience in the rear of the auditorium))
Wilson:	He quoted [from thE] wor:ds (.2) of [Thomas]=
Someone:	[((cough))] [((cough))]
Wilson:	Jefferson in <u>writing</u> (.2) the Declaration of Inde<u>pen</u>dence. (.6) ((looking up, he presses his lips

together)) I think that's pretty good company.
((looking up and around with a half-smile, he leans back
in his chair and removes his hand from the microphone))

Having had his conduct put in a social framework with conduct such as owning slaves, regarding African Americans as property, and believing in the inherent superiority of whites, Wilson defends his quotation of Jefferson by aligning himself with Rev. Martin Luther King Jr., one of the most celebrated Black men to have lived in the last 50 years. If King, the moral leader of the Civil Rights Movement *and a Black man,* could quote Jefferson,[16] Wilson figures that he must be "in pretty good company." His defense strategy is clear to members of the audience, one of whom intervenes to protest ("No:!") just as King's name becomes recognizable (cf. G. Jefferson 1973).

CLASS CATEGORIZATION

There is an apparent absence of class-categorical references in the data we have presented. By now, readers may have correctly deduced that no participant in the first two hours of the UC Regents' meeting introduced himself or herself by explicitly invoking class category membership. No one claimed to "stand before" the Regents or "come before" the Regents "as a middle-class," "as an upper-middle-class" or even "as a very affluent and privileged" person. And no one likened his or her opposition in this debate to the actions of John Paul Getty, Nelson Rockefeller, or Horatio Alger. Even those who introduced themselves with reference to their means of earning a living—for example, Brewer, the "businesswoman," who later described herself as "a founder and co-owner of a manufacturing company . . . that gives jobs to over two hundred Californians" (103: 2723–4)—did not explicitly refer to their class category membership. The closest speakers came to explicit class categorization was describing themselves in relation to their educational background (e.g., Watson: "a proud alumna of [UCLA]," Takasugi: "my MBA at the Graduate School of Whorton School of Business Finance," and Brown: "entered this university, and graduated from law school") or, as in the case of Brewer's reference, by their relationship to their employees.

But, while no one explicitly referred to their class category membership, participants *did* speak at length of hardships overcome and challenges faced in the course of arriving at their current class-privileged positions.[17] For example, Brown described "the limited previous high school education" that prevented his acceptance to Stanford University in 1951; Takasugi told the story of how his "studies were interrupted by the outbreak of World War II" and how he was subsequently interned in a camp with other Americans of Japanese ancestry; and Poochigian spoke of "his people" being denied teaching jobs, admission to local clubs and associations, and the opportunity to own homes in certain neighborhoods "because of their [Armenian] heritage."

Each tale of hardship and disadvantage, however, ended with an aphoristic conclusion that portrayed the protagonist as triumphing over the odds by demonstrating the core qualities of middle-class persons: character, industriousness, and determination. For example,

California Assembly member Nao Takasugi (98: 2606–19)

> Takasugi: I've lived a:: <u>story</u> of hardships and challenges.
> (1.8) It's also one: of <u>goa:l</u>s achieved (.2) through hard work and merit.
> (1.8) ((camera shifts to close-up shot of Takasugi, looking down))
>
> Takasugi: .hhh This story also includes ((looking up)) my acceptance (.2) ((looks down)) to UCLA. (.8) An acceptance <u>not</u> <u>based</u> on (.2) the color of my ((looks up, then down)) ski::n? (.4) ((looking up)) but based on my ((looks up, then down)) ow:n personal ((looks down)) achievement. (.8) And((looking up)) I=wouldn't=wa:nt it (.2) any other way.

And,

California Assembly member Charles Poochigian (106: 2804–10)

> Poochigian: We must live in the <u>prom</u>ise of the future ((looking up at the audience)) (1.2) rather than ((turning toward the camera)) the sin:s of the past. ((looking down)) (2.0) What we must do is <u>work</u> together to make (.4) <u>rea:l</u> the promise ((looks up at camera)) (.8) of our wo:nderful country. ((looks down)) (.8) That <u>promise</u> is that a:ll men and women ((looks up toward Regents)) are created equal ((looking down)) (1.8) <u>guar</u>anteed an ((looking up)) opportunity ((looks down)) to preserv- to pur<u>sue</u> ((looks up)) <u>life</u> (.8) liberty ((looks down)) and happiness (.6) that <u>each</u> American (.6) ((looks up at Regents)) will be treated <u>fair</u>ly (.6)
> and <u>equal</u>ly. ((looks down)) The PROMise is that HARD WORK DETERMINATION and aCHIEVEmen(t) will receive their <u>just</u> reward.

Even Brown, who contends that "had there not been somebody years ago who offered affirmative action to Willie Brown," he would never have become a college graduate, demonstrates his "essential" middle-class character in his story of successfully overcoming the challenges confronting him.

Former Speaker of the Assembly, Willie Brown (17: 433–40)

Brown: He exTENDed on a conditional basis, admission to San Francisco: State University. (2.0) Within six weeks (1.2) I was performing (.8) equal to any other student in that body. (.8) And of course I graduated (.4) entered this university, (.2) and graduated from law school, (.2) and qualified as a- (.) practicing lawyer. (1.6) Affirmative action (.4) extended to me: the opportunity to do: that. (.8) Within six weeks ((gestures become more animated here)) (.2) from the time that I was there (.6) Duncan Gilles reLEASe(d) ((spreads his hand open, as if releasing something)) my hand. (.4) ((camera locked on him, gesturing and swaying in tempo with his words)) Just as we should do. (.6)In a::ll affirmative action programs. (.2) ((camera shifts from Brown to an apparently Asian male Regent, listing with his head up, lips pursed))

Brown: They should ON:ly stay (.6) as lo:ng as they are necessary (.2) to get me to the LI:ne of qualifications. (.2)Once I'm there, (1.4) ((somebody says something unintelligible in the background))

Brown: I the:n become (1.0) the competitive force based upon my ow:::n skills. ((camera shifts back to close-up of Brown))

Brown: ((camera locked on him)) My ow::n energy. My ow:n desire. An' my own intellect. (.8) That's what affirmative action has been, in this university. That's what it should be.

Just above, Brown describes nothing short of a miracle. Despite his "limited" previous education, "within six weeks" of his conditional acceptance at San Francisco State, he was "performing equal to any other student in that body." And *of course* he graduated from that university, *naturally* he entered this university (and graduated from law school); in light of this, it's hardly surprising that he then qualified as a practicing lawyer (indeed, we would have been surprised if he had not). Brown explicitly contends that, although affirmative action got him to "the starting line," he triumphed over all by virtue of *his own* skills, *his own* energy, *his own* desire, and *his own* intellect (that's the way it *should be*).

Here, as in our earlier work (West and Fenstermaker 1995a), we draw on Benjamin DeMott's (1990) observation that Americans conduct themselves on the basis of a most unusual assumption: that we live in a classless society. Admittedly, our everyday discourse is replete with categorizations of persons by class. Yet we believe that we in the United States are unique "in escaping the hierarchies that burden the rest of the developed world" (DeMott 1990, 29). Try as we might, we cannot see the stable system of distribution that structures our unequal access to resources. In everyday life, *the accomplishment of class* rests on our presumption that everyone is endowed with equal opportunity and, if not, once it is granted, real differences in the outcomes we observe must result from individual differences in properties such as intelligence and character. We locate accounts of our accomplishments (or lack thereof) squarely within the paradigm of individual achievement.

DISCUSSION AND CONCLUSION

In the past five years, a number of authors (Baxter forthcoming; Billig 1999a, 1999b; Schegloff 1997, 1999a, 1999b; Wetherell 1998) have debated how to address what Emanuel Schegloff (1991, 49) has called "the problem of relevance," that is, how to determine what is relevant among people's multiple ways of "characteriz[ing], identify[ing], describ[ing], refer[ing] to, indeed 'conceiv[ing] of' persons, in talking to others." As he points out (Schegloff 1997, 165, citing Sacks 1972 and Schegloff 1991), people who can be categorized one way—for example, as women or men—can also be categorized many other ways—for example, as young adults or old ones, as religious persons or atheists, and so on. As a result, the analyst cannot justify focusing on one set of category terms—such as women or men—by arguing that the persons so referred to are, after all, women and men.

Schegloff further notes that, just as people can be described in many different ways, so too can their conduct, and the contexts in which their conduct occurs (Schegloff 1997, 165–6). For example, one could describe Schegloff (1997) as building "an important defence of conversation analysis" (Billig 1999b, 543) or as launching "an attack on critical discourse analysis" (Billig 1999b, 543). One could describe the context in which his ideas are put forth as a paper presented at "the American Association of Applied Linguistics Annual Conference, 23–26 March, 1996, Chicago, Illinois" (Schegloff 1997, 185) or as a lead article in a journal (*Discourse & Society*). Given that each of these characterizations is accurate, the question is, which one is the right one, for analytical purposes?

Schegloff (1997) contends that, because the course of human events depends on the sense that participants make of those events, *that* is the sense (i.e., "the orientations, meanings, interpretations, understandings, etc. of the *participants* in some sociocultural event") which should concern the analyst. Consequently, he suggests:

> One line of analysis which could enrich both "formal" and critical discourse analysis would be the elaboration of the forms of conduct by which persons "do" gender, class or ethnicities of various sorts, and by which they may be shown to display and invoke participants' orientations to those features of the interactional context. (182)

In this chapter, we have attempted to do what Schegloff suggests.[18] When we examined the addresses of elected officials and public figures at the Regents' meeting, we found that participants frequently described themselves using explicit race and (or) sex categorization. Through these means, they marked the relevance of such categorization to the content of the proceedings (debate over UC's affirmative action policies) and, far more important, to the normative context in which their remarks should be heard (as appropriate or inappropriate for "someone like them"). Participants' race and sex categorizations of one another were less direct, but no less relevant to the course of these deliberations. Through implicit references to where others "stood" with respect to race and (or) sex category membership, speakers invoked (and were seen as having invoked) the normative conceptions to which those others were accountable. And, while none of the participants described themselves or one another in relation to class category, their tales of triumph over hardships and challenges provided abundant evidence of their "essential" middle-class characters.

Ultimately, participants' self-categorizations invoke those normative conceptions to which "someone like me" should be held accountable, and their other-categorizations invoked those to which "someone like you" should be held accountable. In both instances, normative conceptions impose structure on the proceedings as much as any set of rules regarding who may speak, about what, and for how long. Such structure ratifies notions of difference, dominance, and entitlement.

In closing, we note that a great many things were accomplished at the July 1995 meeting of the University of California Regents: presidential politics, regental business, demonstrations by outraged students, and even a novel redefinition of university governance. In addition to those accomplishments was the interactional process of rendering persons accountable—accountable to the differences that *make* a difference. Our findings suggest that explicit self- and other-categorizations render persons answerable to normative conceptions that legitimate social inequalities.

Accountability presents to each of us the ever-relevant possibility of evaluation with respect to our "essential nature." We therefore orient ourselves, our beliefs, and our behavior to the possibility of that evaluation. The result is all too familiar: Through our institutions, we establish, create, and reaffirm difference and the inequalities that result from it.

APPENDIX: TRANSCRIBING CONVENTIONS

The transcript techniques and symbols were devised by Gail Jefferson in the course of research undertaken with Harvey Sacks. Techniques are revised, and symbols added or dropped as they seem useful to work. There is no guarantee or suggestion that the symbols or transcripts alone would permit the doing of any unspecified research tasks: They are properly used as an adjunct to the tape-recorded materials.

1. I don' [know]
   [you] don't
   Brackets indicate that the portions of utterances so encased are simultaneous. The left-hand bracket marks the outset of simultaneity, the right hand bracket indicates its resolution.

2. We:::ll now
   Colons indicate that the immediately prior syllable is prolonged. The number of colons is an attempt to represent the length of the prolongation.

3. But-
   A **hyphen** represents a cutting off short of the immediately prior syllable.

4. CAPS
   Capital letters represent increased loudness of the utterances (or parts of utterances) so marked.

5. *italics* and <u>underscoring</u>
   Italics and **underscoring** are used to represent heavier emphasis (in speaker's stress) on utterances or parts of utterances so marked.

6. 'Swhat I said=
   =But you didn't
   Equal signs are used to indicate that no time elapsed between the objects "latched" by the marks. Often used as a transcription convenience, these can also mean that a next speaker starts at precisely the end of a current speaker's utterance.

7. (.)

The **period encased in parentheses** denotes a pause of one tenth of a second.

8. (1.3)

Numbers encased in parentheses indicate the seconds and tenths of seconds ensuing between speaker turns. They may also be used to indicate the duration of pauses internal to a speaker's turn.

9. ((very slowly))

Double parentheses enclose descriptions, not transcribed utterances.

10. (word)

Single parentheses with words in them indicate that something was heard, but the transcriber is not sure what it was. These can serve as a warning that the transcript may be unreliable.

11. . ? ,

Punctuation marks are used for intonation, not grammar. A period represents "falling" intonation, a question mark represents "rising" intonation, and a comma represents a "falling-rising" intonational contour.

12. °So you did.° I see.

Degree symbols represent softness, or decreased amplitude of the utterances they are attached to.

NOTES

1. A revised version of this chapter appears in *Discourse & Society*, forthcoming, 2002.

2. One year later (in the fall of 1996), California voters elected to change their state constitution by endorsing Proposition 209, which prohibits consideration of sex, race, religion, color, ethnicity, and natural origin in hiring. In the fall of 1998, Washington voters endorsed a similar measure. In the spring of 2001, UC Regents voted to *reverse* their actions of 1995. Although this vote was significant for its symbolic value, the passage of Proposition 209 made it effectively irrelevant.

3. Laqueur's (1990) book on the historical construction of sex raises the complex and intriguing question of whether two "naturally" defined sexes are necessary—or only sufficient—for the accomplishment of gender. For the purposes at hand, we temporarily sidestep this question.

4. This is not to say that biological "evidence" and scientific "evidence" amount to the same thing; there is an obvious moral component to the establishment of scientific facticity and scientific consensus. Moral convictions are, of course, part of the practice of science (Keller 1985), and people use biologically informed ideas quite independently of scientific consensus.

5. For readers' ease, excerpts of transcripts presented in this paper appear in simplified form.

6. Public attention from various print and broadcast media tended to focus primarily on race category and secondarily on sex category in depictions of the University of California's affirmative action policies (prior to July 20, 1995) in hiring and contracting and in admissions. A lesser-known fact is that UC Educational Opportunity policies relied on class category in administering pro-

grams for "economically disadvantaged" students. Many of the students who benefited from such programs were white men and white women.

7. Again, the conventions used to transcribe these data appear in the Appendix to this paper. As the following excerpts indicate, notations of speakers' *apparent* sex category and race category are included in double parentheses (designating them as descriptions, rather than transcriptions). Admittedly, this notation practice draws on the transcriber's ability to sort participants according to sex category and race category. But it also draws on participants' abilities to display themselves clearly and unequivocally as incumbents of particular categories (e.g., as a Black woman or as an Asian man). A symmetry of members' knowledge is involved here: the competent production of categorical displays, on the one hand, and the competent recognition of those displays, on the other.

8. A critic attuned to the oratory nature of these proceedings might argue that such self-categorizations are intentionally crafted rhetorical strategies, designed to establish the speakers as appropriately "credentialed" and thus legitimate. Perhaps so, but this does not preclude the use of self-categorizations as claims on "natural" entitlements to speak or as invocations of the normative conceptions in relation to which speakers may be held accountable. The notion of multiple "uses" for self-categorizations raises the question of how volitional such practices may be. We would argue that while self-categorizations are rhetorical resources (e.g., for introduction, framing of remarks, and achieving standing) their form and use depend fundamentally on the normative expectations surrounding categorical accountability.

9. By "Bakke," Campbell means the case of the *Regents of the University of California v. Bakke*, in which the U.S. Supreme Court ruled (in 1978) that quotas based on race are not permtted in public higher education. For an excellent analysis of the use of such context-bound and situation-specific "person-descriptions," see Andrew Roth's (1995) study of how broadcast news interviewers characterize their interviewees ("in terms of institutional roles that the interviewees embody, experience that they possess, actions that they have committed, or opinions that they hold") in the course of asking them particular questions. For a broader discussion of the universalizing function of such language, see Iris Young's (1990) work on citizenship and Ruth Frankenberg's (1993) analysis of "white" as outside race categorization practices.

10. Some readers may object to this interpretation on the grounds that, in the case of "businesswoman," the sex categorization is implicit in the word itself (after all, someone named "Marilyn" Brewer couldn't very well describe herself as a "businessman" in this day and age). In response, we would note that *Roget's International Thesaurus* (1979, 829.12–831.6) lists two columns of gender-neutral synonyms for "businessman" and "businesswoman" (including "entrepreneur," "merchant," and "business executive").

11. For example, Bernie Richter proclaimed that "UC officials lie::. I mean boldface lie::. About what they do to implement what are in fa:ct racial and ethnic quotas." (UC Regents' Meeting, 89–90: 2370–4).

12. Audience appreciation of Watson's indirect reference may have been heightened by Eva Patterson (executive director of the Lawyers' Committee for Civil Rights), who used the George Wallace metaphor in explicit reference to Pete Wilson some weeks earlier: "To me as a black woman, he is standing in the metaphorical door to progress" (quoted in the *San Jose Mercury News* [Kurtzman and Thurm 1995]).

13. At the time, reports of the DNA study that established Thomas Jefferson as the biological father of at least one of Sally Hemings's children had not yet appeared in the popular press (cf. Murray and Duffy 1998).

14. Perhaps as a harbinger of these practices, Archie-Hudson's opening statement did not include Wilson among those whose presence she acknowledged: "Mister Chair and MEMbers of the Board of Regents of the University of California (.6) I COME before you today . . ." (67: 1785–7).

15. "Not surprising" is, of course, a downgraded form of "appropriate," "normal," or "only natural."

16. In point of fact, King never cited Jefferson in particular in his "I Have a Dream" speech but, rather, "the architects of our republic [who] wrote the magnificent words of the Constitution and the Declaration of Independence" (King 1994). Moreover, he characterized their writing as "signing a promissory note to which every American was to fall heir . . . the promise that all men, yes,

black men as well as white men, would be guaranteed the unalienable rights of life, liberty, and the pursuit of happiness." From there, he went on to itemize the ways that "America has defaulted on this promissory note in so far as her citizens of color are concerned."

17. Certainly, anyone looking at the videotapes would be struck by the elegant dress and adornment of those who addressed the Regents during the first two hours of this meeting. From Former Speaker Willie Brown, in his designer suit, to Assembly member Marguerite Archie-Hudson, with her elaborate salon hairdo of "cornrow" plaits, each and every one of these elected officials and public figures was "dressed to kill." Moreover, while California senators and Assembly members do not earn six-figure salaries in their capacities as public servants, their incomes (quite apart from the benefits and "perks" of their jobs) do ensure that they live quite comfortably. By the "objective" indicators used to classify people's positions within the system of distribution that differentially structures our access to resources, most (if not all) would be described as members of the upper-middle class.

18. This includes comparison of the categorization practices we identify with a "naturally occurring" sample we found in local newspapers. There, we found routine self-categorizations by writers of letters to editors. Like those who addressed the Regents, these writers used the opportunity to identify themselves as a place to propose the accountability of the opinions they put forth to "people like them."

> As a Chicano freshman at UC Berkeley, I can tell you that simply being raised in a Spanish-speaking or partially Spanish-speaking home environment is not a guarantee of "breezing through" the SAT II Spanish exam. (Rocha 2001)

> As an American of Indian ethnicity and an advocate for equality, I have to ask how eight years in prison equates with the irreparable damage to the lives and self-esteem of a number of young girls and women and the death of one young girl due to carbon monoxide poisoning. (Dandavati 2001)

> As a single mother, a practicing family law attorney and a fathers' rights advocate, I have to applaud George Will for asserting an unpopular and politically incorrect truth: Our nation's children are in crisis, and in large part it is due to the changes and shifts which have occurred as a result of the feminist agenda foisted onto an unsuspecting maternal population. (Mitchell 2001)

And, just as former Governor Wilson spoke on behalf of the University of California, some letter writers spoke on behalf of institutions:

> As an association of families and friends of people with developmental disabilities who live in developmental centers, we have for more than 35 years advocated for the kind of facilities in which they live. (Chase, Member, Green Line Parent Group, Inc., 2001).

We even found self-categorizations reported in news stories (some distance from the opinion pages and letters to editors). Below, for example, a journalist quotes Junichiro Koizumi, the prime minister of Japan, justifying his controversial plan to visit the Yasukuni Shrine on August 15, 2001 (the official end of World War II):

> I think such a visit is only natural, as a Japanese citizen and the prime minister of Japan. (French 2001)

CHAPTER NINE

"Doing Gender" Differently: Institutional Change in Second-Parent Adoptions

SUSAN DALTON AND SARAH FENSTERMAKER

In 1987, Candace West and Don Zimmerman argued that using an ethnomethodologically based approach to understanding the social construction of gender allows one to view gender as a social production, something that takes on its social import, meaning, and consequences through social interaction. Thus, in their original formulation, "interaction" was put at the center of the social machinery through the everyday accomplishment of gender.

In 1995, West and Fenstermaker asserted that social scientists can expand this approach to explain the workings of race and class. In some contrast to critical responses when the formulation was confined to gender, their more extensive claim was met with resistance. For example, Collins (1995), Thorne (1995), and Weber (1995) objected that the "doing difference" approach obscures the ways systems of power—patriarchy, racism, capitalism—operate at the "macro" or institutional level to structure oppression.

In response to these criticisms West and Fenstermaker (1995b) reiterated that an ethnomethodological view does not confine social interaction to face-to-face exchanges. They asserted that institutional structures influence the nature, content, and meaning of whatever face-to-face interactions occur within them. The challenge, they insist, is to "theoretically and empirically . . . describe a system that manifests great interactional variation *but, at the same time*, rests on far more stable structural and historical legacies" (West and Fenstermaker 1995b, 509, emphasis in original). In other words, the task is to explore the meaning of face-to-face interactions in the specific context of the overarching social structures in which they occur; one cannot fully comprehend the former without situating it within the latter.

It should be noted that this is not a new assertion for West and Fenstermaker. In 1991, they and Don Zimmerman argued that the process of gender stratification "becomes at once both an individual and institutional practice, providing an interactional 'bridge' between different spheres of human activity" (290). They advocated the theoretical development of understandings of gender that "would allow for variation by setting, the actions of individuals, and prevailing institutional and cultural expectations," suggesting that the ethnomethodological framework can encompass so-called macro- and micro-level forces (Fenstermaker, West, and Zimmerman 1991, 291).

An additional critique forwarded by Winant (1995) holds that their formulation freezes the social order, thereby clouding our vision of the elements necessary to change how class, race, and gender hierarchies are accomplished. In this chapter we hope to demonstrate that it is in the situated accomplishment of categorical inequalities that opportunities for change present themselves and can be acted upon. We explore the role of "mere" interaction in fostering consequential shifts in the doing of gender by state-mandated institutional actors. We draw on Dalton's empirical work to explore the relationship between the interpersonal and the institutional.[1] We examine institutional changes that have recently transpired and were a result of a series of encounters between lesbians seeking to adopt children and social workers working in California's Department of Social Services (CDSS). This chapter examines how changes in what routinely occurs within the interpersonal interactions between an agency's personnel and their clients may effectively challenge normative practices traditionally invoked by agency personnel. In turn, over a period of time, these help determine shifts in the institutional practices of the agency as gender, race, and class are accomplished in tandem with the agency's daily business. We argue that individuals who elicit particular reactions from institutional actors may successfully challenge those responses and, by doing so, eventually alter the practices viewed as inviolable and inalterable.

Our analysis begins with a brief review of neo-institutionalism, specifically as it applies to institutional stability and change. We follow our review with a description of the legal adoption structure used by California's Department of Social Services and the institutional norms regarding gender and sexuality that are embedded within that institutional structure. We then discuss the anti-gay and anti-lesbian policies and procedures employed by the CDSS prior to 1986, focusing specifically on one lesbian couple's attempts to adopt two children. Examining subsequent interactions that occurred between lesbian parents and CDSS social workers between 1986 and 1999, we find literally thousands of interactions in which the mothers persistently challenged the normative standards imposed on them by the

CDSS via its social workers. Through these interactions, lesbian mothers were successful in persuading the social workers to assist them in subverting the CDSS's normative standards, eventually replacing them with standards more to their liking. Despite administrative and legal resistance, the mothers and social workers joined together to create a grass-roots model of institutional change, one that is fundamentally grounded in interpersonal interaction and one that has far-reaching effects.

NEO-INSTITUTIONALISM

Institutional theorists face the difficult task of simultaneously accounting for institutional stability and institutional change. On the one hand they argue that institutions act as socializing forces, ensuring the persistence of culture (see, for example, DiMaggio and Powell 1991; Jepperson 1991; Zucker 1983, 1986, 1981). For example, according to Zucker (1991) "social knowledge, once institutionalized, exists as fact, as part of objective reality, and can be transmitted directly on that basis" (83). Social practices become routine and pervasive as institutional actors develop a taken-for-granted approach to their implementation (Jepperson 1991). At that point, simple inertia plays an important role in institutional persistence and makes it extremely difficult to alter institutional norms and practices. Such practices can prevail even as changes in the surrounding social milieu make continued implementation of the status quo an impediment to the performance of institutional actors (Mathews 1986).

On the other hand, institutional theorists argue, institutional structures change over time, and such change is fostered by institutional actors (see Bourdieu 1977; Emirbayer and Mische 1997; Foucault 1965, 1978; Friedland and Alford 1991; Giddens 1984; Powell 1991; Powell and DiMaggio 1991; Sewell 1992). In an attempt to explain the social forces behind institutional change, Friedland and Alford (1991) focus on the multiple and often contradictory logics that emerge when institutions develop different normative systems and repertoires of behavior. They contend that contradictory logics may become tools for change when wielded by actors who are unhappy with existing normative structures of the institutional system in which they are operating. While institutional systems are, among other things, "systems of signs and symbols," the "patterns of individual and organizational behavior vary institutionally" and may be carried—via institutional actors—from one institutional system to another (243). With Friedland and Alford's model, human beings are situated actors who have the agency to facilitate institutional change because, as Emirbayer and Mische (1998) suggest, human beings possess the "capacity to imagine alternative possibilities" (963).

If we follow this reasoning to its obvious conclusion we can argue two points, in only apparent contradiction. First, accumulated institutional practices might socialize actors through interaction, leading them to accept and reproduce particular systems of normative logic (like patriarchy, racism, and capitalism) and to affirm existing social arrangements in interaction with one another. At the same time, however, institutional actors may exercise agency to challenge and even change institutional practices. Thus, the seeds of institutional change are found within the ubiquitous and seemingly fixed mechanisms by which the status quo is re-created and reaffirmed.

To anticipate the forthcoming analysis, we find that the process of creating institutional change occurs primarily within the context of interpersonal interactions. It begins when an actor—often a newcomer to (or client of) the institutional system—violates an institutional understanding so embedded within the institution structure that its presence is taken for granted as a "natural" result of human affairs. The "norm violator" may retreat in the face of the "natural order," or be dismissed or treated as "unsocialized" or otherwise neutralized. But in some instances the violator may challenge the normative institutional order. What happens next, institutionally speaking, accounts for why institutions change so slowly and with great difficulty. It falls to those within the *institution* to respond to the challenge: to first problematize the existing institutional order and then embrace a new way of doing things—"naturally." In short, they must help redefine and reframe the "natural" order to accommodate new institutional logics.

If the norm violator succeeds in convincing institutional representatives to reorder their perspective, institutional change can begin. Those representatives who incorporate new institutional logics into their repertoires and begin altering their responses to behavior previously identified as deviant are taking action that may, under the right conditions, eventually lead to change in the institutional structure. In the following example we highlight instances where the departure from normative (i.e., gendered) conceptions of parentage resulted in a change to institutional policies and practices.

THE INSTITUTIONAL STRUCTURE OF ADOPTION

In California (as in all states) adoption is an institution created by the state legislature for the purpose of providing legal parents to otherwise parentless children (Bartholet 1993, Hollinger 1996). The statutes are situated under the umbrella of Family Law which is predicated on "a paradigmatic family structure consisting of married heterosexual adults and their biological children" (for discussion, see Dalton 2001, 206; also see Bartholet 1993; Bartlett 1984; Butler 1990; Dolgin 1993, 1997).

Like many other states, California has a three-tier adoption system.[2] The top tier of the adoption hierarchy is the "summary adoption." Summary adoptions occur automatically upon the birth of a child when a married woman, living with a legal spouse, gives birth to a child who is not the spouse's offspring.[3] These adoptions require no state or judicial action.

The "stepparent adoption" occupies the second tier of the adoption hierarchy. Stepparent adoptions occur sometime after the birth of a child and must be initiated by the child's parent(s). The adoption occurs between the child and his or her legal/custodial mother's or father's spouse (the child's stepparent). Unlike summary adoptions, stepparent adoptions require state involvement—in the form of a minimal investigation of the adopting adult—and judicial approval.[4]

"Independent adoptions" occupy the third tier of the adoption hierarchy. These adoptions occur when a single adult or a married couple adopts a child from outside their immediate family.[5] Like stepparent adoptions, independent adoptions may be initiated only by the adopting adult(s) after the child's birth. These adoptions also require state involvement—a significantly more lengthy investigation of the adopting adult(s)—and judicial approval.[6]

Both the summary and stepparent adoption statutes require the child's legal parent (usually the biological parent but in the case of stepparent adoptions occasionally an adoptive parent) and the adoption petitioner be married. Both statutes prevent same-sex couples, who cannot legally marry anywhere in the United States, from legally protecting their parent-child relationships. By contrast, the independent adoption statutes do not require that an adopting adult be married, but they do require all existing legal parents (usually the child's biological parents) to relinquish their legal attachment to the child before the adoption is finalized. This requirement, at least on its surface, appears to block unmarried couples from using independent adoptions to secure both of their parent-child relationships simultaneously. In other words, an independent adoption would transfer custody of a child from the original parent to that person's partner, divesting the original parent of parental rights and responsibilities while investing those rights and responsibilities in the adopting parent.

This institutional system of adoption assumes a particular family structure: two heterosexuals, a male and a female, in a state-sanctioned marriage. It assumes a model of parentage in which fathers are males and mothers are females. Thus, it is not surprising that the social workers charged (by California's Department of Social Services) with conducting investigations of adopting parents have relied on a normative conception of parenthood that requires heterosexuality, a man/woman pairing. Indeed, all prospective adoptive parents are *at risk* of evaluation and judgment by social workers in relation to those gendered conceptions. Through their encounters with prospective adoptive parents, institutional gendering is accomplished. Three examples follow.

POLICIES AND PROCEDURES WITHIN CALIFORNIA'S DEPARTMENT OF SOCIAL SERVICES PRIOR TO 1986[7]

BLACKWELL'S FIRST ADOPTION

Social workers from California's Department of Social Services encountered their first openly lesbian couple seeking to adopt a child in November of 1982, when a San Francisco attorney, Norma Blackwell, applied to adopt a child.[8] The child's birth mother had already placed this child with Ms. Blackwell and her partner, declaring, "[I] could not provide for [my] daughter a better home than with Norma."[9] Soon after welcoming the child into her home Ms. Blackwell filed an adoption petition, which initiated her interactions with the CDSS. Recognizing that they might run into insurmountable legal hurdles attempting to adopt the child together, she and her partner decided that Ms. Blackwell would file for adoption as a single adult.

From the beginning, Ms. Blackwell and her partner made their sexual orientation (lesbian) and family structure (two unmarried adults of the same sex and a child) known to the CDSS social worker assigned to their case. Prior to completing her evaluation of the Blackwell home, the social worker asked her supervisor for advice: "She informed me that . . . Blackwell had said she was a lesbian (and) that there was another woman living in the home. [She] wanted to know was there any problem with approving this case" (CDSS deposition 1987). Unsure about how to respond, the supervisor passed the decision to *her* immediate supervisor, the bureau chief. After considering the matter, the bureau chief advised the supervisor to proceed with the case by categorizing Ms. Blackwell as a single adult seeking a single-parent adoption.[10]

We can surmise that the bureau chief elected to officially ignore the presumably clear gender normative violations within the Blackwell's household. In effect, he intervened to exempt Ms. Blackwell from what could be perceived as the "normal" exercise of institutional accountability. Following the bureau chief's instructions, the social worker returned to Blackwell's home, completed her investigation of the family, and filed a court report recommending that the adoption be granted. Soon thereafter, the adoption was approved.

BLACKWELL'S SECOND ADOPTION

In 1985, Ms. Blackwell applied with her partner for the joint adoption of a second child. This time both women sought to become legal parents. The same social worker was assigned to the case, and again, she faced the dilemma of what to do. Recognizing this challenge as more significant than the first, the social worker again requested guidance from her supervisor, who, in turn, sought clarification from the bureau chief. Realizing, perhaps,

DOING GENDER, DOING DIFFERENCE

that he could not simply sweep this norm violation under the institutional carpet, the bureau chief turned to *his* supervisor, the branch chief, for advice.

Blackwell's second adoption petition presented CDSS administrators with a forced choice. They could accept the Blackwell family's assertion that the heterosexual pairing of parents is not fundamental to the legal definition of the two-parent family and thus significantly modify the normative standards by which future judgments would be rendered. Alternatively, they could decide that the heterosexual pairing of partners is fundamental to the definition of the two-parent family, and then invoke that normative conception to deny Ms. Blackwell and her partner further access to legal adoption. In this case, the social worker was instructed to proceed with the home study and to evaluate the family on its merits, an instruction that set aside the agency's heterosexual imperative.

While in the case of Blackwell's first adoption, the bureau chief chose to simply ignore Blackwell's "deviant" status, in the case of the second, the branch chief clearly *decided* to accept Blackwell's alternative interpretation of "family." In both cases the accomplishment of gender is clear: Ms. Blackwell's household was held accountable to a heterosexist conception of family. Yet, in the second case, and clearly contingent on the outcome of the first, institutional actors chose to depart from normal practice, thereby broadening the institution's normative conceptions of two-parent families, at least momentarily.

However, this reconceptualization had not yet been institutionalized. For example, decisions regarding Blackwell and her partner's first and second adoption petitions were made on a case-by-case basis. If a lesbian couple in San Diego filed a joint petition, the individual choice to pass the decision up the administrative hierarchy would still have to be made; there is no indication that the decisions for the Blackwell family were viewed as precedents within the CDSS. Since the accountability of would-be parents to a heterosexist conception of family remained intact, any one individual along the chain of command could halt progression of a case simply by reaffirming the existing normative conception. Without institutionalization, change would still depend on the exercise of discretion by individual employees.

Moreover, at this stage change might not be lasting without codification. Even if word were to spread throughout the agency of an apparent shift in policy, employees would remain relatively free to ignore it if they didn't agree with it. The lack of codification would keep this apparent change in policy extremely vulnerable to outside forces; institutional actors might reverse course and even deny that any change was under way. In fact, this is what happened to Blackwell and her partner when they filed their third adoption petition.

Immediately following the completion of the second adoption, Blackwell's partner filed an adoption petition attempting legally to secure the relationship between herself and the child first adopted by Ms. Blackwell.[11] This third petition presented no *new* challenges to the CDSS's normative standards regarding two-parent families. With the successful completion of the second adoption, Ms. Blackwell and her partner had already achieved "co-parent" status, a status CDSS administrators assisted them in obtaining. With the third adoption petition, the two women were merely seeking the legal recognition of a parent-child relationship—between Ms. Blackwell's partner and the child first adopted by Ms. Blackwell—that agency administrators not only knew existed but helped establish.[12]

The same social worker, by now thoroughly familiar with the family and well aware of the departure that previous decisions represented, began her third investigation of the Blackwell household—this time without seeking additional consultation with her supervisors. Once again she concluded that Ms. Blackwell and her partner were exemplary parents, and she began preparing the court report.

The case took an unexpected turn in late June of 1986. CDSS administrators intervened, ordering the social worker to supply them with an interim report and to postpone her final court report indefinitely. The bureau chief later explained that the case caught the interest of administrators because it was "different than what was normally the norm"; he explained this difference by noting that "usually all petitioners . . . are married" (deposition 1987). The case remained on hold until December of 1986, when administrators, citing a new policy (ACL 87–80) that required negative recommendations on *all* adoption petitions filed by lesbian or gay couples, ordered the social worker to close the case by recommending against the adoption.[13] The memo sent to the social worker by the deputy director of the adoption division explained, "The recommendation to deny is based on the opinion that the child is not in need of an additional parent. The child already has a parent" (deposition 1987). Fully aware that this decision contradicted the recommendation filed in Blackwell's adoption, with her partner, of a second child, CDSS administrators included a note at bottom of the family's court report stating, "We recognize that in the past the Department has made some individual exceptions to this policy and one of these involved this petitioner. However, the Department now believes it was an error to make such an exception" (Trial brief, exhibit H).

The development and implementation of policy ACL 87–80 explicitly reinscribed a normative standard that included a heterosexual requirement for all two-parent families. Essentially, CDSS administrators directed their social workers to respond positively to heterosexual pairings but negatively to homosexual pairings. Had lesbian would-be parents simply accepted this new policy statement as unassailable, this might be the end of the story. Instead many lesbian couples decided to file adoption petitions, thereby calling into question the institutional standards evident in social workers' evaluations.

The first lesbian couple to challenge ACL 87–80 was Ms. Blackwell and her partner. They responded to the negative recommendation attached to their third adoption petition by filing suit against the agency. This allowed them to depose agency administrators, whose depositions revealed that neither the negative recommendation in their case nor the reimplementation of the more restrictive normative standard was based on the particulars of their third adoption.

When asked about his decision-making processes, the deputy director of the adoption division, the administrator directly responsible for both decisions, responded, "The circumstances were such that brought into question, at least in my mind, as to, you know, gee whiz, should we be approving those kinds of situations, the issues as to whether it is appropriate for lesbian and gay couples" (deposition 1987). When asked if he was aware of the particulars of the Blackwell case or the conclusions the social worker had reached regarding the family, he admitted that he was not.

Instead, the decisions to deny the couple a positive recommendation on their third adoption petition and to enact policy ACL 87–80 seem to reflect an attempt by the deputy director to protect the agency from outside criticism over the apparent change in policy. Shortly after Blackwell and her partner filed their third adoption petition, two gay men murdered a child who had been placed in their home for adoption. This murder gained considerable media attention and resulted in extensive criticism of the CDSS's policies and procedures (for a discussion of these events, see Ricketts and Achtenberg 1990). Armed with the information that the CDSS' recommendation was not based on the particulars of their case, Blackwell and her partner obtained a court hearing in which a judge set aside the CDSS's negative recommendation and approved the adoption.

LESBIAN MOTHERS AND SOCIAL WORKERS UNITE: GENDER AND INSTITUTIONAL CHANGE

As word of Blackwell and her partner's success trickled out, primarily through a network of lesbian attorneys in the San Francisco/Bay Area, other lesbian couples began filing adoption petitions. Each couple's plan was relatively simple: File the adoption petition, allow the CDSS to recommend negatively, and then take the case to court making the argument that the negative recommendation—because it was based on policy and not the particulars of a case—should be set aside.

Administrators at the CDSS responded to this obvious attempt to undermine their institutional authority by ordering social workers to deny home studies to lesbian and gay couples. Denial of a home study would in theory stop the cases dead in their tracks, preventing them from proceeding to court hearings. When asked about the administrators' intent to deny lesbian couples access to the agency's services, the supervisor explained that a home study is conducted to assess the suitability of an adoption placement: "Because we're not looking at suitability, [there] seems no point in writing about the suitability of the Petitioners if you're going to deny, anyhow" (deposition 1987).

Lesbians seeking adoptions (with considerable help from their attorneys) responded to this denial of services by requesting court hearings in which they persuaded judges to order the CDSS to perform the necessary home studies.[14] Faced with the prospect of being repeatedly called before judges (already irritated by overburdened calendars), the CDSS soon capitulated and returned social workers to the practice of conducting thorough investigations of all petitioners.[15]

As word continued to spread through lesbian and gay communities that the CDSS's policy of issuing negative recommendations might be overcome within the courts, an increasing number of couples filed adoption petitions. The increase in the number of filings had a cumulative effect on the CDSS. It brought an increasing number of social workers into direct contact with lesbians while simultaneously increasing the number of would-be parents with whom any one social worker was likely to interact. For the most part, these women were both well educated and well versed in the various discourses used to challenge the traditional conceptions reflected in CDSS practices.[16]

THE CHANGING ROLE OF THE SOCIAL WORKER

With the implementation of policy ACL 87–80, CDSS social workers were put in the unenviable position of having to investigate lesbian (and, to a far lesser but slowly increasing extent, gay male) adoption petitioners, and then, often in direct contradiction with their own professional judgment, having to recommend against their adoption requests.[17] One of the effects of the policy was that agency social workers were forced to categorize lesbian and gay couples as distinctly different per se from heterosexual couples. One of the more obvious assumptions underlying the policy was that heterosexual couples make better parents than do homosexual ones. When asked about these assumed differences, however, most of the social workers replied that differences either didn't exist or that the few that did exist (such as needing to consciously provide role models of the "missing sex") were well managed by the parents and thus didn't constitute a meaningful difference. One social worker had this to say:

Well, the only difference is that they have to go out of their way to make sure the child has relationships with a person of the opposite sex. You know, that . . . role model that might be missing in, uh, in the picture.[18]

She concluded:

I don't see it as a difference. Yeah, as long as they are going to allow them to have exposure to people of the opposite sex. . . . They're making allowance for that you know. That would be the difference.[19]

A few social workers did report noticing differences between lesbian/gay and heterosexual couples. But all of these social workers noted that differences ran in the opposite direction than the one assumed by CDSS administrators. As one social worker put it,

I think they [lesbian- and gay-headed families] are different in that . . . I see them to be more conscientious about being good parents, or better parents, and providing the child as much information as they need in order to be responsible individuals. You know, even though I see heterosexual couples doing a lot of family activities, I think the homosexual . . . couples . . . tend to basically surround their life 99 percent of the time, when they can, in doing family activities because they are so excited that they can be a same-sex couple and have children. They just really want to be, you know, parents to them. And it shows.

Another responded,

I guess because there (are) . . . no accidental pregnancies with gay and lesbian families that they put much more, much more thought and planning into being parents than heterosexual couples. I find that the lesbian families that I see overwhelmingly adjust their work hours to meet the needs of their kids as opposed to having their kids adjust their needs to their work hours. I just admire families, lesbian families, because they put so much more thought into their plan to raise children than most, even adoptive families who spent seven years in fertility [treatment].

A third social worker noted,

As an example of the difference between a heterosexual couple and a lesbian couple, is when I go there they have to sign, like, a release of information. And when I ask the mother—if she's holding the baby—to sign this, she will say to her husband, "Here, take the baby for me for a minute while I sign this." In a lesbian family the other person who's not holding the baby just goes and takes the baby. You know what I'm saying? So there's a lot more of anticipatory things that women just do for women. You know they'll go into the kitchen and not just bring back one cup of coffee, they'll bring back two cups of coffee. Or the baby needs to be changed and if the nursing biological mother has just been nursing and the kid, [her] partner goes in and whisks the kid and says, you know, "I'll go change her." Not even, again, not so much verbally, they just, they're in sync with each other.

These findings indicate that lesbian and gay parents have been successful in their attempts to undermine the normative standards employed by CDSS administrators, at least as far as the social workers are concerned. These parents' success, however, forced the social workers into a professional quandary. On the one hand, the social workers' job is to investigate adoption petitioners and then use their professional judgment to advise the courts. On the other hand, CDSS policy requires that they advise against *all* lesbian- or gay-headed two-parent families, even when their professional opinion of these families would predict otherwise.[20]

When asked what they thought about policy ACL 87–80, all but one of the social workers—who declined to comment on the issue—expressed disapproval. Many complained about a policy that flatly contradicted their professional judgment. As one explained,

It's a really uncomfortable situation for us . . . to tell these couples who are the same sex, "We like you, we think you're great parents, you've been doing wonderful; however, we need to deny you." We can't explain it. There is no logic. It's just the law.

Others felt that the policy undermined them as professionals. One supervisor explained the feelings of many of the social workers by noting,

Well, you know, they feel that the state is not allowing them to do their job as a professional. They're not able to . . . [report] their true assessments and recommendations to the court; that their assessments are not honored as professionals who have been working in this field and who know, you know, what is a good home for a child.

Some expressed frustration and anger, as did the social worker who said, "I think it looks a little ridiculous. I think it makes the state look ridiculous. It just shows they don't know what's going on or [are] playing politics, of course."

These statements make clear that many of the adoption social workers employed by the CDSS (and all of those interviewed noted that this understanding of lesbian- and gay-headed families was by far the dominant view among social workers in the agency) no longer subscribe to the normative standards embedded within the agency's institutional policies and procedures. Many said that they felt extremely uncomfortable issuing negative recommendations to lesbian and gay parents.

Social workers, faced with explicit instructions to recommend against all adoption petitions filed by lesbian or gay couples, were given the exact language to use in their reports. They finessed their predicament through the creation of a dual reporting system. They divided the home study report into two distinct sections: the narrative and the recommendation. Instead of the usual report, in which the narrative is used to lay out the evidence supporting the final recommendation, social workers writing for lesbians or gays used the narrative to discuss in elaborate detail their conclusions regarding the positive features of the adopting parent(s). Through these means, they communicated to the judge their favorable professional opinions regarding the adoption request. Their elaborate descriptions were then followed with a formulaic "policy denial" that contradicted the content and tone of the body of the narrative. As one social worker explained,

> The home studies for the assessments that are done on these [lesbian or gay] couples, most of them are glowing studies, and it is written into the report. It is only the final last page where it says "recommendation"—that's the only place where we're required to put that negative statement saying, "However, besides all the great information that we've learned on this couple, according to the policy, we cannot approve this family."

This dual reporting system provided social workers with a method of actively undermining the normative standard insisted upon by CDSS administrators in favor of a standard that is broader and more inclusive of lesbians and gays as parents. Additionally, the social workers refused to defend the state's official denial in court. Although it is common practice for social workers to attend hearings and strenuously argue the state's case when there is a denial for cause, social workers working with lesbian or gay parents either attended the court hearings but declined to verbally support the state's position or simply skipped the court hearings altogether, thereby providing judges latitude to disregard the state's objections.[21]

MOVING FROM THE INTERACTION TO THE INSTITUTION

In December of 1995, there was an explicit test of the extent to which challenges to the normative standards employed by the CDSS had changed its institutional structure. By this time, the deputy director who had ordered the development and implementation of policy ACL 87–80 had left the agency. One of the new deputy director's early acts was to issue directive ACL 94–104, aimed at rescinding ACL 87–80. In her accompanying letter the new deputy director stated,

> The Department has concluded that the policy is not appropriate and should be discontinued. The child's best interest is served by providing for his or her health, safety, and emotional well-being through placement in a stable and permanent home. That home may best be one in which there are two parents with the support, both emotional and financial, that they can provide regardless of their marital status.[22]

This change in policy, it turned out, was relatively short-lived. Within three months, then Governor Pete Wilson—in the process of launching a bid for the Republican presidential nomination—ordered the reinstatement of the original policy with the proviso that it be upgraded from a departmental policy to an official regulation.[23] Pursuant to the governor's order, CDSS administrators convened a series of hearings during which agency employees and other interested individuals were invited to express their concerns about the original policy as well as the governor's intent to codify it in regulation form.

Of the 1,243 responses received by the CDSS, the overwhelming majority (1,206) expressed the opinion that policy ACL 87–80 treated lesbian and gay couples unfairly, worked against the best interests of children, and should be abolished. These responses came from seven adoption social workers, 21 adoption agencies, five DSS county offices, two chapters of the National Association of Social Workers, the Association of County Welfare Directors, and the Bay Area Social Services Consortium. Those identifying themselves as working in the field of adoptions or any other social services agency expressed no support for the policy.

Following this public comment period, CDSS administrators had approximately 10 months to complete the paperwork required to change the policy into an official regulation.[24] Interestingly, CDSS administrators allowed this deadline to quietly pass without completing the necessary filings. Shortly thereafter, social workers resumed their use of the dual reporting/recommendation system. In 1999, Gray Davis replaced Pete Wilson as governor of California. Under his stewardship, policy ACL 87–80 was officially rescinded, and CDSS administrators moved to officially broaden the agency's normative standards in ways that were inclusive of prospective lesbian and gay parents.[25]

CONCLUSION

This analysis clearly demonstrates a reciprocal relationship between interpersonal interactions and institutional structures. On the one hand, institutional structures influence the form and content of interpersonal interactions that occur within institutional settings. Individuals interacting within institutional settings frequently accomplish gender—through face-to-face interactions—in accordance with normative conceptions that are embedded within the institution's history, policies, and practice. When individuals act in accord with accepted institutional practice, they also reaffirm particular normative standards against which they evaluate and respond to the behaviors of those with whom they interact.[26] Institutions, after all, cast a powerful cultural context over all interactions within it. At the same time, some face-to-face interactions ultimately may promote change in the normative standards employed by institutions. When those who violate standards are successful in persuading institutional representatives to subvert institutionally supported practices, they plant the seeds of institutional change. If circumstances and repeated practices allow, actions that were once "subversive" can later be taken as "only natural." What we are suggesting here is all models of institutional change—change resulting from the frequent and regular contestation of institutionally embedded normative standards—are interactional in character. These findings support West and Fenstermaker's (1995a) assertion that interactional practices and the institutional auspices invoked in those practices are all of an interactional piece; indeed they are two aspects of the same social dynamic. Individuals participating within these interactions always have the potential to challenge the normative constructions being invoked and applied and by doing so may change the institution.

As Friedland and Alford (1991) suggest, effective challenges to institutionally maintained normative standards may rely heavily upon the existence of "contradictory logics" (i.e., competing interpretations of the contested behavior that have gained acceptance in other institutional settings). In the data presented here the effectiveness of lesbian challenges to the normative conceptions of gender insisted upon by CDSS administrators was bolstered considerably by the availability of psychological, anthropological, and psychiatric studies—all of which offered competing normative conceptualizations of gender.

This analysis also suggests that, while it may be possible for aggrieved individuals to successfully challenge institutionally embedded normative constructions of gender on a case-by-case basis (i.e., to successfully argue that a normative standard should be temporarily suspended in their case), their behavior does not necessarily lead to lasting change in the institutional structure. Instead our findings strongly suggest that institutional change requires a more sustained effort, one that takes place over an extended period of time and is the outcome of many face-to-face interactions. Ultimately, however, and no matter how we carve up the social world into "micro" or "macro" bits, institutional structures draw their justification, rationale, and power from the accumulated meanings of interactions. Over time, each enables the other and makes possible both stasis and change.

NOTES

1. Vermont and Massachusetts recently expanded their adoption systems, through Supreme Court decisions or new legislation, to specifically include same-sex parenting couples. In some additional states, including Illinois, New Jersey, New York, and the District of Columbia, appellate courts have interpreted the state's adoption laws as applicable to same-sex parents. In a number of other states, including California, some trial court judges have applied existing adoption laws to same-sex parenting couples, although these decisions hold no precedent and thus may vary widely from county to county (Dalton 2001).

2. While California courts generally support this statute (as they did in *Dawn D. v. Jerry K.*, 1998), some recent decisions may have begun to erode the standard (see *Buzzanca v. Buzzanca*, 1998).

3. In California, the state investigation includes a brief meeting between a social worker from the Department of Social Services and the child's custodial and adopting parents. Additionally, a sexual abuse registry check must be completed for the adopting parent (Dalton 2001).

4. If adopting adults are married, they must adopt children jointly with their spouse.

5. In California, the investigation for an independent adoption includes a visual inspection of the home and an investigation of the adopting adult's medical history, employment and financial standing, past drug or alcohol abuse, disciplinary and child rearing philosophies and practices, prior intimate relationships, past and current relationships with existing family members, religious and philosophical beliefs, and current marriage (if one exists). It also includes a criminal records check, a sexual abuse registry check for the adopting adult(s), and an investigation of anyone else living in the home. This generally occurs over a four- to eight-month period and includes a minimum of two two-hour visits to the adopting parent's home (Dalton 2001).

6. Judges who have applied the independent adoption statutes to same-sex couples have done so by expanding the meaning of the parental relinquishment requirement to include a partial relinquishment of parent rights under which the legal parent relinquishes only his or her right to sole parenthood (Dalton 2001).

7. The data used in this section were obtained from three sources. Depositions taken by attorney Roberta Achtenberg from personnel within California's Department of Social Services were obtained from the archives at the National Center for Lesbian Rights. Information regarding Ms. Blackwell's adoption of children was obtained through an in-depth interview with Norma Blackwell. Some details regarding these adoptions are also available in the archives of the University of California Berkeley's Bancroft library in conjunction with the case the *Guardianship of the Children of Lisa W.* Finally, a complete set of files documenting the CDSS's development of policy ACL 87–80 as obtained directly from the CDSS using the Freedom of Information Act.

8. The name Norma Blackwell is a pseudonym.

9. This quote was taken from the adoption files of Blackwell and her partner obtained from the National Center for Lesbian Rights in San Francisco.

10. In a case note written by the social worker, she states that the "supervisor of the Berkeley

District Office informed me on this day [January 22, 1986] that the Department of Social Services has no objections to this adoption of a minor child by a lesbian couple" (CDSS files).

11. Recall that in the case of the first adoption, Ms. Blackwell adopted as a single parent, which created a legal parent-child relationship only between the child and her.

12. The agency helped establish this parent-child relationship by initially approving the adoption of the child by Ms. Blackwell knowing full well that her partner lived in the home and was also establishing a parental relationship with the child.

13. For a detailed discussion of the social forces driving this decision (primarily an unrelated murder of a young child by a gay male couple) see Ricketts and Achtenberg 1990.

14. This was a fairly easy argument to make since adoption decisions ultimately rest with judges rather than CDSS administrators. When CDSS ordered the cessation of home study investigations in all cases involving lesbian and gay couples, its administrators were effectively assuming that decision-making authority, a move to which many judges strongly objected. (This information was gathered through interviews conducted by Dalton with a number of attorneys and judges in the San Francisco/Bay Area.)

15. One social worker who had been called before a judge to explain the CDSS's policy reported that the judge made it crystal clear that he did not wish to repeat the experience each time a lesbian couple filed an adoption petition.

16. In interviews attorneys and parents said that reports of scientific studies are commonly distributed to social workers who are suspected of being either unfamiliar or uncomfortable with lesbian- or gay-headed families. For examples of this sort of material see Kirkpatrick, Smith, and Roy 1981; Kurdek 1993; Patterson 1992, 1994, 1995; and Weston 1991.

17. For a discussion of why parents seeking second-parent adoptions are overwhelmingly lesbians and not gay men see Dalton 2001.

18. Note the underlying assumption that children *need* their parents to actively provide them with both "male" and "female" role models. By employing the language of sex assignment, social workers continue to employ a normative notion of heterosexuality as "natural."

19. This statement appears to invoke the stereotype of lesbians and gays as people who dislike or feel uncomfortable with the opposite sex. Providing an opposite-sex role model appears to allay these fears.

20. This policy has recently been changed, and this change is discussed below.

21. All but one of the judges who worked in geographic locations where second-parent adoptions have become routinely available reported that they understand exactly what the social workers are doing and generally support their efforts. The judge who disagreed reported that he understood the social workers' position but did not believe that second-parent adoptions are legal under the present statutes.

22. Throughout the administrative discussions regarding policy ACL 87–80, marital status is used as a code word for sexual orientation because administrators feared that explicit targeting of lesbian and parents would open the door for a legal challenge to policy. While the California courts have generally been unwilling to uphold policy that uses the terms *lesbian* or *gay* on the grounds that it is unlawfully discriminatory, they have been much more accepting of the use of "unmarried couple" even when it is clear that the latter is simply a stand-in for the former.

23. Changing the practice from a policy to a regulation would have theoretically made it harder to ignore and more difficult to overturn.

24. Under state law, the administrators were required to solicit public comment but not required to follow it. Thus, they could have implemented the regulation despite the overwhelming opposition to it.

25. The California legislature recently passed a law that will move lesbian and gay second-parent adoptions under the existing stepparent adoption rubric. This law took effect on January 1, 2002, and made the entire second-parent adoption procedure obsolete.

26. See Cassell (1996), S. Murray (1996), Rospenda, Richman, and Nawyn (1998), Schacht (1996), and Yoder and Aniakudo (1997).

Section III   **THEORETICAL**

ELABORATIONS

CHAPTER TEN

Performance and Accomplishment:
Reconciling Feminist Conceptions of Gender

MOLLY MOLONEY AND SARAH FENSTERMAKER

Women's studies, gender studies, and feminist studies are all rightly celebrated as "multi," "cross," or "inter" disciplinary endeavors, born of a critique
of traditional disciplinary practice, arbitrary divisions, and territorial displays (e.g., Bowles et al. 1980).[1] The location of an interdisciplinary feminist studies within a traditionally organized academy has brought with it a
tension between a true blurring of disciplinary boundaries and a retreat to
more familiar divisions among ideas, points of view, and epistemological
terrain. Nowhere is this felt more strongly than between the work of gender scholars in the humanities and the social sciences. Even as the feminist
scholarship on gender theory has exploded in both the humanities (e.g.,
Alcoff and Potter 1992; De Lauretis 1989; Flax 1991; Sandoval 2000; Scott
1999; Spivak 1988) and the social sciences (e.g., Baca Zinn 1999; Collins
1990; Feree 1998; Lorber 1994; Smith 1994; Thorne 1993) there is a
notable reinscription of conventional academic distinctions and a singular
lack of communication across the divide. One of the challenges presented
by this state of affairs is to articulate the differences, at least so that their
implications are not overdrawn and their parallels not overlooked.

When some humanities scholars draw on very early scholarship on sex
roles to represent "sociological" perspectives on gender, they overlook
decades of feminist sociological work that followed. Such work has radically
transformed our understandings of what gender is and what gender does.
Likewise, when some social science scholars assume that feminist work
based in the humanities simply reduces everything to text or discourse, they
ignore fundamentally important contributions to social analyses of gender.
At the same time, however, we should not thoughtlessly pick and choose

from these various approaches to gender, ignoring potentially serious departures in underlying assumptions about the social, the cultural, the material and the relations among them.

Here we ask: do foundational concepts—such as gender—differ fundamentally in meaning and use across the disciplines of feminist studies? Might not apparent differences mask more deep-rooted similarities? Or, might the obverse be true, that concepts that look alike harbor consequential contradictions? As an initial move to address these questions, we will examine two key formulations of gender: Judith Butler's (1990) theory of gender performativity and Candace West and Don Zimmerman's (1987) concept of "doing gender" or Sarah Fenstermaker's (1985) application of gender as situated accomplishment.[2] Both concepts have gained substantial currency in feminist scholarship and have effectively challenged earlier conceptualizations of how gender operates in social life. Moreover, both have encouraged other scholars' elaborations and applications. Butler's work has had its primary impact in literary criticism and the humanities (e.g., Bordo 1993; Case 1996; Cornell 1998; Parker and Sedgwick 1994; Sedgwick 1993), whereas West and Fenstermaker's contributions have been most widely recognized in the social sciences, particularly in feminist sociology (e.g., Bird 1996; DeVault 1991; Leidner 1993; Lorber 1996; Martin and Jurik 1996).

In this chapter we will offer a first pass at the convergence and divergence of the two conceptions of gender and will explore some of the implications of those similarities and differences for feminist theory. As an initial attempt, we will not do much more than map a set of questions for further thought and, we hope, further dialogue. We begin by describing the broad outlines of the two formulations under discussion.

Drawing from the insights of Erving Goffman (1977, 1979) and Harold Garfinkel (1967), Candace West and Don Zimmerman (1987) developed the concept of gender as "an accomplishment, an achieved property of situated conduct." Instead of casting gender as an attribute of individuals, West and Zimmerman conceived it to be "an emergent property of social situations: both an outcome of and a rationale for . . . justifying one of the most fundamental divisions of society" (9). Prior to the publication of West and Zimmerman's "Doing Gender," Sarah Fenstermaker (1985) applied their concept in her analysis of the division of household labor and argued that "neither traditional sociological nor economic explanations of the division of household and market labor make it easy to give formal attention to the two realities of choice and constraint" (200). She found, instead, "It is this [new] maximization process, with its complicated agendas involving work and gender—the material and the symbolic—that effectively guarantees the asymmetric patterns found so often in the studies of the division of household labor. And ultimately, it is within these two inter-woven structures that household members make their choices and get the business of living done" (117).

West and Fenstermaker went on to elaborate the "doing gender" for-mulation to include its institutional parallels, its viability as a theory of inequality, its counterpart in the accomplishment of race and class, and the role of accountability as the motivating system underlying the ubiquitous accomplishment of sex categorical membership (West and Fenstermaker, chapter 8, in this volume). In so doing, they hoped to provide a framework for understanding *how* social categories are accomplished and operate to produce well-documented outcomes of inequality.

Butler, in her formulation of gender performativity, adapts work in speech act theory and poststructuralism, drawing on Derrida (1977), Foucault (1979; 1984), and others. Additionally, her work is rooted in French psychoanalysis, particularly Lacan and feminist critiques and appro-priations of Lacan. Butler's *Gender Trouble* (1990) sought to question and critique the presumed foundation of feminism—the category "woman"—arguing against essentialism, overly stable and naturalized conceptualiza-tions of subjectivity, and understandings of agency and identity as existing outside of or prior to discourse. Gender, subjectivity, and identity, she argues, are constituted in and performatively produced (and reproduced) through discourse. "The view that gender is performative sought to show that what we take to be an internal essence of gender is manufactured through a sustained set of acts, posited through the gendered stylization of the body" (xv).

Butler further elaborates her analytic framework of gender performa-tivity in later works. In *Bodies That Matter* (1993) she extends her analysis of the construction and constitution of gender to the cultural and discursive constitution of sex, materiality, and "the body." She also clarifies her con-ceptualization of gender performativity, as it relates to feminist politics, structure, and agency, in her dialogue with Benhabib, Cornell, and Fraser (Benhabib et al. 1995). Butler argues that not only is performativity not antithetical to agency and resistance, but she also maintains that agency is an important part of her theory. In addition, she clarifies the linguistic sense in which she uses the idea of gender performativity. Much of Butler's more recent work does not center primarily on gender but offers more detailed discussion of theories underpinning her work on performativity. For exam-ple, Butler's understanding of performativity in relationship to speech acts is productively elaborated in *Excitable Speech* (1997), which examines the relationship between "speech" and "conduct" in contemporary debates about hate speech, pornography, and the "don't ask, don't tell" policy of the U.S. military. In *The Psychic Life of Power* (1997), she further addresses the relationship between a Foucauldian understanding of power and a psychoanalytic understanding of subjectivity (both of which inform *Gender Trouble*), arguing that it will be necessary to draw on both of these seemingly disparate traditions in bridging our understandings of the social and the psychic. In this piece, she examines the ideas of Foucault, Freud, Nietzsche, Hegel, and Althusser, reading them against one another and focusing on "how might the formation of the subject involve the regulatory formation of the psyche, including how we might rejoin the discourse of power with the discourse of psychoanalysis" (18).

On the surface, the work of Butler and the work of West, Zimmerman, and Fenstermaker seem quite different from one another. Butler explicitly distinguishes her conceptualization of gender identity from one she understands to be sociological: a set of roles and social functions (1990, 16). West and Zimmerman (1987) describe their initial formulation as "distinctively sociological" (126) as it conceives of gender as departing from fixed social functions. Certainly the two approaches draw on quite different theoretical traditions. While Butler's work is rooted in (French) poststructuralism and psychoanalysis, West and Fenstermaker rest upon symbolic interactionism, ethnomethodology, and social constructionism. Yet at the same time, there seems to be a notable overlap between Butler and West, Fenstermaker, and Zimmerman, in their critique of previous gender theories as well as in their understanding of gender as a workable concept.

Both formulations are similarly critical of the conventional distinction between sex and gender. For example, Butler's (1990) argument that "the presumption of a binary gender system implicitly retains the belief in a mimetic relation of gender to sex whereby gender mirrors sex or is otherwise restricted by it" (7) is recapitulated by West and Fenstermaker's (1993) argument that the "bifurcation of gender into femininity and masculinity effectively reduces gender to sex" (155). This gender/sex distinction has been crucial to refuting the idea that "biology is destiny" in matters of gender. Additionally, however, the authors point out that there are also important limitations to this formulation—from ignoring the cultural/social constructedness of biological sex to reifying gender by tying it too closely to sex.

Butler and West and Fenstermaker find fault with some previous approaches to gender on similar grounds. Butler's (1990) critiques of humanist feminism, "which understands gender as an *attribute* of a person who is characterized essentially as a pregenderd substance or 'core' called the person" (10), operate with some of the same logic that lies behind West and Fenstermaker's critiques of the concepts of sex roles and gender displays— namely that these cannot account for the omnirelevance or the situated adaptability of gender. West and Fenstermaker (1993) argue, "Doing gender is so central to the organization of human conduct that it should not be conceptualized as an intrusion on—or 'intervening variable' in—such conduct (as approaches predicated on sex differences often imply). Indeed, in the case of some social arrangements, gender's achievement may be the central work accomplished" (158). Gender is no mere variable for West and Fenstermaker or for Butler. Thus, both treatments critique and depart from a perspective that Butler (1990) describes as "sociological"[3] (16); this in and of itself points to a misapprehension between humanities and social science scholars as to what *contemporary* feminist sociological conceptions of gender look like.

PERFORMING AND DOING

West and Zimmerman (1987) present an "understanding of gender as an *accomplishment:* an emergent feature of social situations that is both an outcome of and a rationale for the most fundamental division of society." Gender, they argue, is a situated doing, an accomplishment of members' conduct locally managed in reference to powerful normative conceptions, relevant to particular sex categories, female or male. Similarly, Butler (1990) argues that

> gender is not a noun, but neither is it a set of free-floating attributes, for we have seen that the substantive effect of gender is performatively produced and compelled by the regulatory practices of gender coherence . . . gender proves to be performative—that is constituting the identity it is purported to be. (25)

Butler particularly examines these regulatory practices in relationship to a system of compulsory heterosexuality, about which, she argues, a naturalized gender binary both serves and is dependent upon. Similarly, the concept of "accountability" is crucial to West and Fenstermaker's understanding of the normative, regulatory order at the heart of the accomplishment of gender. Given Butler's and West and Fenstermaker's shared vision of a social world that actively regulates and creates both our "private" and "social" selves, is "doing" gender the same as "performing" gender? On this point, the formulations appear to diverge.

Central to Butler's arguments is a critique of the pre-discursive subject as traditionally presented in liberal political theory. The subject does not precede discourse, she argues, but is produced in and through it. Speaking in terms of gender, she argues that "gender is always a doing, though not a doing by a subject who might be said to pre-exist the deed" (1990, 25). There is no subjectivity, Butler explains, that is prior to gendering, that exists and then becomes gendered; rather, part of what makes one an intelligible subject is being and becoming gendered. She argues that gendering, as with subjectivation more generally, occurs through, and is structured by, discourse. Individuals do not simply use, but are constituted by language—a language that precedes them historically and temporally. Butler (1999) argues, however, that this is not a completely determinist approach: "I am not outside the language that structures me, but neither am I determined by the language that makes this 'I' possible" (xxiv). She also stresses that to say that neither gender nor subjectivity can exist outside of discourse is not to utterly reduce everything to discourse (Butler 1993, 15). This conceptualization—of gender specifically and subjectivity more generally—is something that stands in contrast to the assumptions of liberal political theory, demanding that there be a stable, coherent subject in order for there to be political action or agency. The issues explicitly raised by Butler's critiques of liberal humanism regarding the relationships among identity, subjectivity, and discourse in subject constitution are not issues that are explicitly addressed by West and Fenstermaker; they engage with other theoretical traditions and position their argument differently. Indeed, they would maintain (as would ethnomethodologists more generally) that like the idea of norms abstracted from their use, or the concept of the individual apart from the social group, the "pre-discursive" subject is a theoretical contrivance. But, of course, this theoretical contrivance is precisely what Butler is arguing against. Here, the two theories seem not so much opposed as speaking past one another.

In both conceptualizations, gender is not an attribute but an activity. That they both articulate gender as a "doing" is quite striking.[4] So perhaps the most important question for comparing the two is: Do they understand this "doing" similarly? In Butler's theory, gender is *discursively* constituted; gender is "performed" through discourse, broadly defined. In West and Fenstermaker, gender is *interactionally* produced; gender is "done" in interactions, broadly defined. While discursivity may not be synonymous with interaction, Butler uses a very broad model of discourse, while West and Fenstermaker have expanded our notions of interaction. Neither Butler's nor West and Fenstermaker's works are particularly clear on the limits of these respective concepts, and greater theoretical precision would doubtless clarify further convergences and contradiction. For some insight, however, we can turn to others' criticisms of Butler's and West and Fenstermaker's frameworks, which converge on two major issues.

SOCIAL STRUCTURE, ACCOUNTABILITY, AND THE NORMATIVE ORDER

Both frameworks have drawn criticism for the treatment of macro-institutional and structural forces. For instance, it has been argued of both frameworks that they seem preoccupied with the "micro" level and neglect the so-called "macro" issues of social structure and its normative power. Fraser (1995), for instance, maintains that "Butler's approach is good for theorizing the micro level, the intrasubjective, and the historicity of gender relations. It is not useful, in contrast, for the macro level, the intersubjective, and the normative" (164). Similarly, Maldonado (1995) faults West and Fenstermaker for not granting sufficient attention to "the constraints imposed by these macro level forces in the social environment" (495). In response to West and Fenstermaker's (1995) "Doing Difference," Weber (1995) charges that "because of its exclusive attention on face-to-face interaction, macro social structural processes . . . are rendered invisible" (500).[5]

Somewhat paradoxically, other critics contend that these two frameworks are overly deterministic and do not allow enough room for agency or resistance. Benhabib (1995) asks of Butler, "How can one be constituted by discourse without being determined by it? A speech-act theory of performative gender constitution cannot give us a sufficiently thick and rich account of gender formation that would also explain the capacities of human agents for self-determination" (110). Along the same lines, Thorne (1995) chides West and Fenstermaker for overly "emphasizing the maintenance and reproduction of normative conceptions, but neglecting countervailing processes of resistance, challenge, conflict, and change" (498).[6] Butler and West and Fenstermaker do not respond to these criticisms in the same manner. Indeed it is a notable place where they diverge.

To understand West and Fenstermaker's response to these issues it is helpful to start with the concept of "accountability," the key concept within their formulation. In the original formulation, West and Zimmerman (1987) argue that "to 'do' gender is not always to live up to normative conceptions of femininity or masculinity; it is to engage in behavior *at the risk of assessment*" (137). It is this risk of assessment—accountability—that shapes and drives the production of gender, whether in conformity or deviance, and however it is defined in the situation. It is through this concept of accountability that both the normative character of doing difference and the power of social structural forces *as* complex sets of situated interactions can be appreciated. West and Fenstermaker (1995a) later argue, "While individuals are the ones who do gender, the process of rendering something accountable is both interactional and institutional in character: it is a feature of social relationships, and its idiom derives from the institutional arena in which those relationships come to life" (21). The accomplishment of gender, along with race, class, and other categorical differences, driven by accountability, is a crucial part of the very reproduction of the social structure (21). Thus, the implications of West and Fenstermaker's model go well beyond the so-called micro level within which its critics locate it. Indeed, as West and Fenstermaker (1995a, 24) argue, the dichotomy between micro and macro is a misleading and reifying bifurcation because the two are utterly reciprocal and produced simultaneously. Further explication of this simultaneous and reciprocal relationship between structures of power and the interactions that comprise and create them is obviously indicated.

While there is no such concept as accountability, explicitly theorized, within Butler's model, she does make some statements that seem congruent with its workings. For instance, she proposes that "as a strategy of survival within compulsory systems, gender is a performance with clearly punitive consequences" (1990, 139). But this idea is just hinted at (though implicit throughout) in *Gender Trouble*. Without some articulation of how compulsory systems operate, gender performativity can seem overly conscious and voluntaristic.[7] Butler could perhaps prevent charges of voluntarism by more explicitly addressing this issue; West and Fenstermaker's use of the idea of accountability (Heritage 1984) may be helpful in achieving this.

Butler does address this criticism of her approach in later works (e.g., Butler 1993), refuting the characterization of performativity as overly voluntaristic. She examines the idea that gender performativity might mean that she "thought that one woke in the morning [and] perused the closet or some more open space for the gender of choice." Such a characterization, though, she points out, "such a willful and instrumental subject, one who decides *on* its gender . . . would restore a figure of a choosing subject—humanist—at the center of a project whose emphasis on construction seems to be quite opposed to such a notion" (1993, x). It is precisely this notion of the subject that *Gender Trouble* (and to some degree all of her works that follow) seeks to criticize. Therefore, Butler (1993) argues that "the reading of 'performativity' as willful and arbitrary choice misses the point that the historicity of discourse and, in particular, the historicity of norms (the chains of iterations invoked and dissimulated in the imperative utterance) constitute the power of discourse to enact what it names" (188). Indeed, she argues, "These are for the most part compulsory performances, ones which none of us choose, but which each of us is forced to negotiate. I write 'forced to negotiate' because the compulsory character of these norms does not always make them efficacious" (237). Yet Butler's work is frequently read as comprising a volitional model of gender; the reasons for this are very much bound up with questions about the meaning of "performance" and "performativity" within Butler's theory, to which we will now turn.

The opposite critique—that the possibility for individual agency is at most denied and at least neglected—has been directed at West and Fenstermaker's work as well as Butler's. To address it returns us to essentially common elements in both frameworks. Butler's anti-essentialist, non-humanistic conceptions of identity and subjectivity are said to be fully deterministic, allowing scant room for resistance and change. Benhabib (1995), for instance, examines Butler's concept of gender performativity, in particular Butler's statement that "there is no gender identity behind the expression of gender; that identity is performatively constituted by the very expressions that are said to be its results." Benhabib then asks: "If this view of the self is adopted, is there any possibility of changing these 'expressions' which constitute us?" (21) and concludes: no, there is not. And yet, as Butler observes both in *Gender Trouble* and in her later response to Benhabib (Butler 1995), her theory of gender performativity does explicitly address issues of agency. In fact, Butler argues, it is this constitution of the subject that is the prerequisite for and site of agency. "Paradoxically, the reconceptualization of identity as an *effect*, that is, as *produced* or *generated*, opens up possibilities of 'agency' that are insidiously foreclosed by positions that take identity categories as foundational and fixed. . . . Construction is not opposed to agency; it is the necessary scene of agency, the very terms in which agency is articulated and becomes culturally intelligible" (1990, 147). To appreciate this, it is necessary to understand the particular use of performativity that Butler takes from speech-act theory—from linguistic philosopher J. L. Austin read through Derrida.

PERFORMANCE AND PERFORMATIVITY

One of the most common misreadings of Judith Butler's work is interpreting "performativity" solely in theatrical or dramaturgical terms.[8] Butler (1993) distinguishes performativity from "performance as bounded 'act,'" arguing that performativity "consists of a reiteration of norms which precede, constrain, and exceed the performer and in that sense cannot be taken as the fabrication of the performer's 'will' or choice" (234). Therefore, she argues, "the reduction of performativity to performance would be a mistake" (234). Some of the confusion over this matter, though, is attributable to some ambiguities within Butler's work itself. As she notes in her preface to a new edition of *Gender Trouble* (1999), her "theory waffles between understanding performativity as linguistic and casting it as theatrical. I have come to think that the two are invariably related" (xxv). It should be noted that even when invoking the theatrical or dramaturgical connotations of performativity, she does so in a specific manner, which is not identical to their sociological connotation. For instance, she argues that "theatricality need not be conflated with self-display or self creation" (1993, 233) and that theatricality is not "fully intentional" or fully "voluntary or deliberate" (283). Additionally, she explicitly distinguishes her understanding of performativity from the dramaturgical project of Goffman (1995, 134). Though Butler at times uses the concept of "performativity" in this manner, suggesting a performance analogous to acting and evoking a dramaturgical metaphor, often she uses the term in a different manner: linguistically, with reference to speech-act theory.

In this linguistic context, "a performative is that discursive practice that brings into being or enacts that which it names and so marks the constitutive or productive power of discourse" (Butler 1995, 134). In the classic example, from Austin, a judge's statement "I now pronounce you man and wife" not only describes or leads to an action, but is a (performative) action in and of itself; it brings the marriage into existence. This speech act succeeds (and Butler argues that success is always provisional) because "that action echoes prior actions and *accumulates the force of authority through repetition or citation of a prior and authoritative set of practices*" (Butler 1997a, 51; emphasis in the original).

Speaking of gender, "The doctor who receives the child and pronounces—'It's a girl'—begins that long string of interpellations by which the girl is transitively girled: Gender is ritualistically repeated, whereby the repetition occasions both the risk of failure and the congealed effect of sedimentation" (Butler 1997a, 49). The power of the performative, then, comes from continual re-iteration, re-citation, and re-signification. Performativity, Butler (1993) argues, "must be understood not as a singular or deliberate "act" but, rather, as the reiterative and citational practice by which discourse produces the effects that it names" (2). Here, loosed from the limitation imposed by the dramaturgical, Butler's "performative act" may find its parallel in the ethnomethodologist's "constitutive act" (Heritage 1984). Where Butler speaks of the authority conferred on the moment by past practice, West and Fenstermaker (1995b) speak of "the accomplishment of gender, race, and class [which] rest on and are situated in history, institutional practices, and social structure, rather than disembodied from people's lives. . . . By viewing these as accomplishments, we can see how situated social action contributes to the reproduction of social structure at any particular sociological moment" (509).

For Butler, reiteration and constant resignification enable the possibility for agency, resistance, and change. She argues that contrary to the idea that there is no room for change within the model of gender performativity, "change and alteration is part of the very process of performativity" (Butler 1995, 134). This is because "to be constituted by language is to be produced within a given network of power/discourse which is open to resignification, redeployment, subversive citation from within, interruption and inadvertent convergences with other such networks. 'Agency' is to be found precisely at such junctures where the discourse is renewed" (135). Because the success of a performative—of the performativity of gender—is always provisional and deferred, because it must constantly be renewed, there lies the possibility for agency, for transforming and subverting the gender system, according to Butler. This is not by escaping the citations of gender or the production of subjectivity and gender in discourse, but by changing what exactly it is that is being iterated and reiterated. If subjectivity were coherent and stable, as Benhabib assumes it must be in order for there to be agency, this form of change would not be possible, Butler explains. "If a subject were constituted once and for all, there would be no possibility of a reiteration of those constituting conventions or norms" (1995, 135).

West and Fenstermaker's conception of gender as interactional accomplishment is likewise open to charges that it does not sufficiently account for possibilities of agency or social change. They argue that the accomplishment of gender is ubiquitous and omnirelevant and that even when we wish otherwise, we cannot avoid the risk of being held accountable and subject to the particular prevailing relevant normative order. However, and like Butler, they argue (1995b) that the possibility for agency or resistance is not therefore foreclosed, but is inherent in interaction. "Since difference is 'done,' there is both activity (including resistance) and agency at its foundation. Indeed, it is likely that resistance is as ubiquitous a feature of the shaping of inequality as is the doing of difference itself" (510). Resistance within the context of accountability and accomplishment is not necessarily futile because

> the accomplishment of gender is what gives existing social arrangements that are predicated on sex category their legitimacy (i.e., as "only natural" ways of organizing social life). So, even as we as individuals may be held accountable (in relation to our character and motives) for our failure to live up to normative conceptions of gender, the accountability of *particular* conduct to sex category may thereby be weakened. What is more, collective social movements may, by calling into question *particular* institutional practices based on sex category, promote alternatives to those practices. (West and Fenstermaker 1993, 170–1)

Thus, West and Fenstermaker offer no simple voluntarisitic conceptualization of agency, but, like Butler, do assert a deep-seated logic of resistance and agency, through situated creation, reaffirmation, and transformation of past practice.

Though both Butler and West and Fenstermaker offer important theoretical explanations of the centrality of agency and resistance in their conceptualizations of gender, more work is needed to compare these theories in an applied, grounded fashion. For instance, Butler's framework does not translate fully this very abstract concept of reiteration and resignfication as agency into more concrete terms. Her analysis of drag is often cited as paradigmatic of her model for subverting gender. She argues that "in imitating gender, drag implicitly reveals the imitative structure of gender itself—as well as its contingency" (1990, 137), which potentially destabilizes the naturalization of gender as essential and inherent to an individual. In later work, though, she stresses that drag "is not precisely *an example* of subversion. It would be a mistake to take it as the paradigm of subversive action or, indeed, as a model for political agency" (1999, xxii). Instead, she explains, "[t]he purpose of the example is to expose the tenuousness of gender 'reality' in order to counter the violence performed by gender norms" (xxiii).

It is not clear whether gender nonconformity and subversive cultural production are the only forms of efficacious agency and resistance authorized by her analysis of gender performativity, or if they allow room for forms of collective social resistance, social movements, or political action aimed at material inequalities. West and Fenstermaker, on the other hand, do address collective social movements and the potential for a variety of forms of social change with regard to the accomplishment of gender (West and Zimmerman 1987; West and Fenstermaker 1993). However, more work is needed to connect their articulation of the theoretical relationships among accountability, the accomplishment of gender, and social change, and to empirical and historical analyses of these in a more grounded fashion.

MULTIPLICITIES OF DIFFERENCE

Perhaps the most obvious difference between Butler and West and Fenstermaker is how they explain the doing of gender in relation to other social categories. With the publication of "Doing Difference" (1995), West and Fenstermaker broadened their focus on gender as an accomplishment and began to develop a more fully elaborated perspective on the accomplishment of difference and the confluence of gender, race, and class. They argue that "while gender, race, and class—what people come to experience as organizing categories of social difference—exhibit vastly different descriptive characteristics and outcomes, they are, nonetheless, comparable as mechanisms for producing social inequality" (9). In this approach, they seek neither to conflate nor "to separate gender, race, and class as social categories, but to build a coherent argument for understanding how they work simultaneously" (19) and operate together to shape relations of domination and inequality. We have focused on the doing of gender (West and Zimmerman 1987; West and Fenstermaker 1993) in this chapter, but we note that for West and Fenstermaker, the doing of gender is simultaneously confluent with the accomplishment of race, class, and other important categories of social identity.

Butler has not centrally explored these issues in her work, although they are not missing entirely. Her examination of Nella Larsen's story "Passing," for instance, analyzes race, racialization, and "the convergent modalities of power by which sexual difference is articulated and assumed" (1993, 167). Here, she argues *against* feminist psychoanalytic theories (e.g., Irigaray 1984) that privilege gender or sexual difference as more foundational than other types of difference. She argues that "though there are clearly good historical reasons for keeping 'race' and 'sexuality' and 'sexual difference' as separate analytic spheres, there are also quite pressing and significant historical reasons for asking how and where we might read not only their convergence, but the sites at which the one cannot be constituted save through the other" (1993, 168). In looking back at the first edition of *Gender Trouble*, Butler (1999) comments that if she were writing the book today, she would "also include a discussion on racialized sexuality and, in particular, how taboos against miscegenation (and the romanticization of cross-racial sexual exchange) are essential to the naturalized and denaturalized forms that gender takes" (xxvi). In this piece she also argues that

> racial presumptions invariably underwrite the discourse on gender in ways that need to be made explicit, but [also] that race and gender ought not to be treated as simple analogies. I would therefore suggest that the question to ask is not whether the theory of performativity is transposable onto race, but what happens to the theory when it tries to come to grips with race . . . the sexualization of racial gender norms calls to be read through multiple lenses at once and the analysis surely illuminates the limits of gender as an exclusive category of analysis. (xvi)

It is not clear whether this provisional statement of Butler's contradicts West and Fenstermaker's (1995) view. The notion of "multiple lenses" or of race "underwriting the discourse on gender" can suggest a kind of additive approach to illuminating the workings of such things as "racial gender norms." If this reading is fair, West and Fenstermaker would obviously take issue with Butler's approach. In "Doing Difference" they explicitly state that people experience their identities as simultaneous, indivisible aspects of themselves. Separating these into "lenses" or "intersections," no matter how theoretically convenient, is distorting (West and Fenstermaker 1995a, 1995b). Butler's further exploration of these issues may be necessary in order to determine just where she and West and Fenstermaker converge and diverge in their conceptualizations of race/class/gender.

Butler has given much extended analysis to sexuality and its relationship to gender, something that West and Fenstermaker have not yet fully explicated. Indeed, Butler has had at least as much, and probably more, influence on the fields of sexuality studies and queer theory as she has in gender studies and feminist scholarship. Throughout her work, she argues that "the category of woman achieves stability and coherence only in the context of the heterosexual matrix" (Butler 1990, 5); this is a theme that continually emerges through her works. Gender performances, for Butler, are always shaped by and seen in relation to an understanding of (hetero)sexuality. Butler elaborates on this claim in the new edition of *Gender Trouble* (1999) by explaining that the initial motivation for writing the earlier edition was to respond to the pervasive heteronormative assumptions found throughout the literature on gender. Thus, challenging such assumptions was one of her central tasks—examining how the regulation and performance of gender are essential to a reciprocal system of compulsory heterosexuality. For Butler (1999), key questions are: "To what extent does gender hierarchy serve a more or less compulsory heterosexuality and how often are gender norms policed precisely in the service of shoring up heterosexual hegemony" (xii). Though she argues against reducing gender to sexuality or sexuality to gender, she also argues that the two cannot be understood in isolation from one another. West and Fenstermaker, on the other hand, do not treat sexuality as a separate category of doing difference within their analysis. They would argue that in its idealized forms, gender draws much of its meaning and content from a hegemonic model of compulsory heterosexuality. In its situated form, the accomplishment of gender variably requires heteronormative content. Beyond that, the particulars of sexuality remain unaddressed within their framework.

CONCLUSION

There are no simple answers to questions about where and whether Butler's gender performativity and West and Fenstermaker's gender as interactional accomplishment converge and diverge. They appear to intersect rather strikingly in some areas and not at all in others. At the beginning of the chapter, we noted the radically different theoretical traditions from which Butler's and West and Fenstermaker's ideas emerge. This difference in the foundations of the two theories is a source of continued misgiving about the potential for truly reconciling Butler's work with that of West and Fenstermaker. Can a theory that draws so fundamentally on psychoanalysis and poststructuralist language theory be truly compatible with West and Fenstermaker's sociological approach to gender?

In comparing the conclusions that the two frameworks draw about what gender is and how it operates, the general results of their analyses, and the overall arguments about gender that they provide, we are left with remarkably similar answers. Both perspectives are grounded in similar critiques of the dichotomy between sex and gender and of the idea that gender is simply a variable. Both frameworks regard gender as an activity rather than an attribute. This activity, in both perspectives, is neither utterly deterministic nor completely voluntaristic. Both postulate the ubiquity of the production of gender, yet both also point to the ever-present possibilities for resistance and transgression. There is a complicating of the "micro" and the "macro" in both of the frameworks, and the two theories speak to both of these levels (while problematizing the very distinction implied in the terms). And, certainly, there is need for further elaboration and more precise articulation in both of these theories of the boundaries of "discourse" (for Butler) and "interaction" (for West and Fenstermaker). And both require further consideration of the actual doing of gender and the transgression that is potentially a part of it, as well as the relationship of gender with race, class, and sexuality.

One continuing source of potential divergence between Butler and West and Fenstermaker comes from the dual meaning of performativity for Butler—its theatrical and linguistic uses in her work. Though it would be a serious misreading to reduce Butler's conception of gender solely to the theatrical sense of performativity or to treat it as simply a dramaturgical exercise, it remains unclear as to what the present status of performativity vis-à-vis performance is in her framework. Without question, for West and Fenstermaker, doing difference is *not* a set of performances, or a series of "displays" (cf. Goffman 1976). These authors not only do not embrace this model, they actively reject it. It is sometimes difficult to discern, however, where Butler's gender performativity falls on this issue. "Performativity" is a messy concept. One the one hand, this messiness is a strength, as it lends itself to a rich and complex theoretical framework. On the other hand, the potential for performativity to slide into nothing more than performance represents a significant obstacle to reconciling the two formulations.

It is pointless, however, to make some final determination about whether Butler's theories completely agree with West and Fenstermaker's. Instead, the implications of the convergences and divergences between these two feminist conceptualizations of gender may be more important with respect to the potential for opening up theoretical boundaries within the humanities and social sciences. Would it make sense for a scholar using the concept of gender performativity to also turn to work on the accomplishment of gender and doing difference? Should sociologists working on doing gender and doing difference incorporate the concept of gender performativity into their research?

There are no easy or final answers to these questions. In light of our examination, we recommend that the two frameworks should not be used interchangeably or treated as synonymous with one another. Important divergences and potential divergences—regarding questions of intentionality and performance, social structure and social change, the relationship between the doing, accomplishment, or performance of gender and other categories of difference—should not be simply glossed over. Yet neither should the two feminist projects develop in isolation from one another. Research and criticism drawing on the framework of performativity may have much to gain by attending to questions of accountability, as elaborated in West and Fenstermaker's model of doing difference, for instance. Likewise, research on the accomplishment of difference may be much strengthened by working with Butler's arguments about the relationship among gender, sex, and (hetero)sexuality as well as her more general contributions to queer theory.

Both models—Butler's gender performativity and West and Fenstermaker's accomplishment of difference—are in need of further expansion and refinement through empirical analysis and application. Further work can ground these theories in lived experience and complex historical (and contemporary) examples to resolve questions of institutional dynamics, their relationship to agency, resistance, and social change, as well as to the complexities of the simultaneity of gender, race, class, and sexuality. Only through grounded empirical work can the utility of these theoretical frameworks, on their own and in relationship to one another, be discerned.

NOTES

1. This chapter was drawn in part from a paper presented at the annual meeting of the American Sociological Association, Washington D.C., August 2000.

2. We can safely assume that none of the principal authors discussed in this paper was sufficiently conversant with—or even aware of—the others' work to have any direct influence on one another.

3. Foster (1999) points out that common to much of the "sexual difference theory" perspective located in the humanities is a misreading of contemporary feminist gender theory, purported to reify a sex/gender dichotomy and overemphasize the material. Sexual difference theory neglects most contemporary feminist sociological analyses of gender, including that of West and Fenstermaker. Foster argues that Butler, though connected in some ways to sexual difference theorists (e.g., Bradiotti 1994; Cornell 1994), is best categorized apart from them. However, Butler does seem to share with them an outdated notion of the sociology of gender.

4. In addition to sometimes referring to gender as a "doing," Butler also, at times, speaks of the "accomplishment" of gender. "Accomplishment" is the central claim in West and Fenstermaker's conceptualization of doing gender and doing difference (e.g., 1991, 1993, 1995a; West and Zimmerman 1987). For example, in a critique of Freud, Butler (1997b) writes: "To accept this view we must begin by presupposing that masculine and feminine are not dispositions, as Freud sometimes argues, but indeed *accomplishments*, ones which emerge in tandem with the achievement of heterosexuality" (135).

5. Curiously, Fraser's praises for Butler's framework in its usefulness in theorizing both the "micro" level and the "historicity" of gender relations can be contrasted with critiques of West and Fenstermaker's framework that its focus on the "micro" level renders it "ahistorical" (e.g., Weber 1995).

6. Interestingly, Thorne (1995) explicitly contrasts Butler's focus on gender transgression with that of West and Fenstermaker.

7. More akin, it would seem, to Goffman's (1976) "gender displays" or Garfinkel's (1967) analysis of Agnes's exhibitions of being "120 percent Female."

8. A common reading of Butler; see, e.g., Thorne 1995; Benhabib 1995.

CHAPTER ELEVEN

"Doing Difference" Revisited:
Problems, Prospects, and the Dialogue in Feminist Theory

SARAH FENSTERMAKER AND CANDACE WEST

When Western academics socialize neophytes to their profession, they often liken books, journal articles, and research presentations to an unseen but powerful intellectual "dialogue"—an exchange among all those engaged with a particular scholarly field.[1] The products of intellectual work become the vehicles by which ideas are circulated, responded to, modified, sharpened, and enhanced. The image intentionally invoked for newcomers to the profession is one of eager engagement with ideas: ideas to which each participant has access, and ideas that thrive in a time-honored, unfettered, and faithful exchange. The rather quaint notion of inevitable intellectual "progress" is not far behind, where, with each iteration of the dialogue, sociological theory improves and advances in linear fashion. From that vantage point, the process seems not only productive, but also downright sentimental. The image, of course, is an idealized one; those who have participated in such "dialogues" know that real-life intellectual exchange and debate proceed slowly, are often at cross-purposes or based on divergent interpretations, and are sometimes even rancorous or self-serving.

In the last decade, we have tried to articulate an ethnomethodological perspective on the simultaneous workings of gender, race, and class as these produce the ubiquitous manifestations of social inequality, repression, and domination seen in Western societies. In this chapter we revisit our formulation to clarify and extend what remains a work in progress, and one dependent upon the very best aspects of a feminist dialogue among sociologists. This chapter, then, provides the occasion for revisiting papers we have published elsewhere, and our commenting briefly on our work as the focus of scholarly attention and debate—as the object of "the dialogue."

"DIFFERENCE" AS AN ONGOING INTERACTIONAL
ACCOMPLISHMENT

In 1995, we observed a peculiar trend in feminist scholarship, namely, a tendency to use mathematical metaphors in descriptions of relationships among gender, race, and class (West and Fenstermaker 1995a). In some cases, scholarship seemed to draw on addition, summing up the effects of each "variable" in order to characterize the whole. In other cases, analyses invoked multiplication, using expressions such as "double negative" and "triple disadvantage" to describe their compound effects. Even geometry came into play, in turns of phrase like "intersecting systems" and "interlocking categories" describing relationships among gender, race, and class. We noted that the very existence of these distinctive metaphors seemed premonitory of the problems scholars were experiencing in coming to terms with the topic. . . .

We began "Doing Difference" (West and Fenstermaker 1995a) by asking how feminist scholarship came to draw on mathematical metaphors in the first place. One reason for these metaphors, we suggested, was the white middle-class preoccupation of much feminist thought. But we also proposed that existing conceptualizations of gender contributed to the problem by offering no alternatives but those mathematical metaphors. What was lacking, we contended, was a way of thinking about gender that provided for understanding how gender, race, and class operate *simultaneously* with one another. This would allow us to see how the importance of these socially relevant, organizing experiences might differ across interactional contexts. Moreover, this would give us a way to address the mechanisms that produce power and inequality in social life. We proposed a conceptual mechanism, the "doing" of difference, to illuminate "the relations between individual and institutional practice, and among forms of domination" (1995a, 19).

With the publication of "Doing Difference" (West and Fenstermaker 1995a), we completed a trilogy of papers advancing our proposition that class-, race-, and gender-based inequalities result from the ongoing interactional accomplishments of class, race, and gender (see also Fenstermaker, West, and Zimmerman 1991; West and Fenstermaker 1993, 1995a). We have asserted that whatever the inequality they produce, these accomplishments are seemingly infinitely adaptable to specific social circumstances. Although their relative standing in any given interaction may vary, they are nonetheless governed by the same underlying interactional mechanisms. We have argued that each of us, specifically located in groups, institutions, relationships, and human activities, is held accountable—in varying ways and to differing degrees—to particular "classed," "raced," and "gendered" expectations. These expectations are informed by the past outcomes of interactions, which, in turn, resulted in historical and institutional practices. Through these means, we not only produce "natural" differences among human beings, but also reaffirm inequality based on such differences as an "only natural" state of affairs. Class, race, and gender are related to one another *as accomplishments*: dynamic, adaptable, mutable, and deriving their particular meaning through social interaction.

By way of summary: People "do" difference by creating invidious distinctions among themselves—for example, as members of different sex categories, different race categories, and different class categories—differences that are hardly "natural." These far-from-"natural" distinctions are then brought forward to affirm and reaffirm the "essentially different natures" of different category members and institutional arrangements based on these. The accomplishment of class, race, and gender makes social arrangements based on category membership understandable as normal and natural (i.e., as *legitimate*) modes of social organization. Thus, distinctions that are generated through this process are seen as basic and enduring dispositions of persons. In the end, patriarchy, racism, and class oppression are seen as *responses* to those dispositions—as if the social order were merely a rational accommodation to "natural differences" among social beings.

Each of the *theoretical* assertions in the foregoing summary rightfully garnered comments and criticisms, and we organize this article around the ones that are consequential for further theory development. Yet it also bears mention that, in each of our three more recent attempts to advance our formulation, we called for concerted attention to the *empirical* manifestations of the dynamics of gender, race, and class. We made clear that for us the utility of the theoretical formulation would be realized only if it facilitated understanding of the empirical actualities of social inequality. For example, we concluded "Doing Difference" (1995a) by urging that "empirical evidence must be brought to bear on the question of variation in the salience of categorical memberships, while still allowing for the simultaneous influence of these memberships on interaction" (33). Since the original formulation of "Doing Gender" (West and Zimmerman 1987), and the extensions that followed (Fenstermaker, West, and Zimmerman 1991; West and Fenstermaker 1993), scores of empirical analyses have employed the formulation in one way or another—usually as a device to make post hoc theoretical sense of empirical findings.[2]

Despite the apparent attraction of the formulation among researchers, the 1995 publication of "Doing Difference" stirred a good deal of controversy, primarily among feminist sociologists of race and gender. A symposium in the feminist sociology journal *Gender & Society* only added to the number of comments we had already received from colleagues in response to the work. In the symposium, other scholars raised a number of issues central to our framework, and we briefly responded to them. In this article we return to our response and the central doubts raised about "Doing Difference," and we employ the text of the others' commentary in a way that grounds our comments in the original feminist dialogue. In so doing we hope both to clarify our position and to point to issues yet unresolved.

We hope that this contribution to the ongoing debate will dispel several common misapprehensions surrounding the notion that social inequality is the outcome of ongoing interactional doings. People—*we*—function in interaction not only as individuals, but also as purveyors of institutional action and as defenders of the sensibilities of and rationales for past action. One great achievement of social science has been the detailed description and systematic measurement of the outcomes of social domination and oppression. We proceed on the premise that a clear sense of the ways in which such outcomes actually happen—how they are brought into being and made material through interaction—would greatly enhance our understanding of power, inequality, and social change.

COMMON MISAPPREHENSIONS

We have found that in any discussion of the "doing" of race, class, or gender, we must first turn to the inevitable confusion between process and outcome, and restate our interest in unearthing the mechanisms *by which inequality outcomes obtain.* Yet no number of italicized words, phrases, or sentences appears to do the trick. Our work is often interpreted as suggesting that the inequalities surrounding race, class, and gender oppression are equivalent. Perhaps this stems from sociology's historical (and often rightful) preoccupation with the compelling details of race, class, and gender domination. What we argue, however, is that the *accomplishment* of race, class, and gender is what lies at the heart of social inequality and what allows us to understand how forms of oppression intersect and overlap (West and Fenstermaker 1995b). . . .

The likelihood of this misapprehension coloring readers' more general understanding of our formulation has had the unfortunate effect of preoccupying us with repeated discussions of the nature of gender, race, and class. We have been rightly criticized (Schwalbe 2000) in this regard. Schwalbe argues that sociology is fixated on the reifications of gender, race, and class as *things*—characteristics, attributes, discrete "variables"—rather than pursuing these as active social accomplishments. In regard to our work, he argues that even we are sometimes seduced into such language, generating little forward motion in articulating the processes we assert. Perhaps so: The common confusion of the results of inequality with the workings of it has surely taken its toll on the productive elaboration of our theoretical framework.

Another misapprehension that follows from a misreading of our original theorizing about gender (West and Zimmerman 1987; Fenstermaker et al. 1991)—and perhaps, from a broader confusion over social constructionism—is that we are proposing a social science version of Judith Butler's theory of gender performativity (Butler 1990, 1993): a kind of "inequality as performance" theory. For us, the doing of difference is certainly not a set of performances nor a simple combination of gender, race, and class displays. However, the very notion of accomplishment allows for attention to the performative aspects of communicating difference and complying with (or defying) normative expectations for members of particular race, class, and sex categories.[3]

From this conflation of our work and Butler's springs another misreading: a view of our formulation as a kind of poststructural erasure of differences that are consequential to people's lives. Patricia Hill Collins (1995) has put this charge most forcefully:

> Recasting racism, patriarchy, and class exploitation solely in social constructionist terms reduces race, class, and gender to performances, interactions between people embedded in a never ending string of equivalent relations, all containing race, class, and gender in some form, but a chain of equivalences devoid of power relations. (493)

We could never provide an adequate response to this charge, since the ideas within it so obviously conflict with our argument: the idea that social construction necessarily implies the reduction of raced, classed, and gendered social dynamics to performances; the idea that the doing of difference is confined to face-to-face interactions; the idea that interactions appear in never ending strings of "equivalent relations"; and the idea that the interactions we speak of are even conceivable when "devoid of power relations." . . .

But within Collins's criticism lie extremely productive questions about the nature of social accomplishment, the nature of difference, and how we are conceptualizing such processes. First is the notion that the "doing" of gender, race, and class are phenomena best confined to face-to-face interaction. Second (and immediately related to the first) are time-worn questions concerning the relationship of social structure and the individual (sometimes packaged as the "micro/macro" problem that seems to plague so many sociologists). Obviously related to these questions is how historically repeated patterns of inequality bequeath their legacy to present-day processes. Thus, a crucial third question is how, within this formulation, resistance might operate and social change might occur. To clarify both critique and response, we will briefly return to these three concerns.

THE DYNAMICS OF DOING DIFFERENCE

In her recent attempt to offer an integrative framework for the concepts of racial and gender formation Evelyn Nakano Glenn (1999) proposes that scholars focus on the processes of racialization and gendering rather than the reified and static categories of race and gender. She asserts that *both* social structure and expressions of cultural representation are implicated in what we would call the "doing" of race, class, and gender. She argues that "these processes take place at multiple levels, including *representation . . . micro-interaction . . . and social structure"* (9). Other scholars have also reconsidered the distinction between micro and macro phenomena and some have begun to adapt Anthony Giddens's (1984) earlier model of structuration to social processes. For example, Harvey Molotch, William Freudenburg, and Krista Paulsen (2000) argue:

> In their structure-making actions, humans draw, per force, from existing conditions—that is, from structures resulting from their prior actions. Thus, as people take actions they make structures, and every action is both enabled and constrained by the prior structures. (793)

Likewise, and long ago, Philip Abrams (1972) called for a greater sensitivity to the ambiguities of such multiple levels in a "sociology of process," wherein "society must be understood as a process constructed historically by individuals who are constructed historically by society" (227). If we allow for the logic of individual agency *in interaction* with the accumulated decisions of history, the patterned practices of individuals as institutional actors, and the legacies of prior individual decisions, the "doing" of social inequality can take on far more meaningful proportions than Collins (1995) described, or those that Lynn Weber (1995) reduced to "a few unremarkable actors in everyday interactions" (501). Indeed, we would argue that those "few unremarkable actors in everyday interactions" are responsible for the force of history, the exercise of institutional power, and enduring social structures.[4]

Sociologists may also draw on Dorothy Smith's (1987) work to make greater sense of the ways in which these multiple levels may be apprehended. We would argue that viewing the "micro/macro" problem as a useful and accurate depiction of the world is only a variation on the theme of a "bifurcated consciousness," where multiple standpoints are kept systematically from official view. If we allow for the constant confluence of what we have called "situated social action" and social structure, how race, class, and gender are done is informed both by past practice and by a response to the normative order of the moment. As we said in the symposium on "Doing Difference" (West and Fenstermaker 1995b),

Our focus on ever-changing, variously situated social relationships as the sites for the doing of difference does not denude those relationships of the powerful contexts in which they unfold. We argue only that the impact of the forces of social structure and history is realized *in the unfolding of those relationships*. (509)

This claim, that individual action and social structure are only different aspects of the daily—and often unremarkable—social accomplishment of race, class, and gender, raises the question of how we might conceive of resistance and opposition to those structures daily brought into being, reaffirmed, and reproduced. How might those structures be changed?

In their groundbreaking book on racial formation, Michael Omi and Howard Winant (1994) criticize perspectives that derive from a primary focus on ethnic group, class, or nation for neglecting "the specificity of race as an autonomous field of social conflict, political organization, and cultural/ideological meaning"(48). In their design of a formulation that calls for attention to processes of racialization, Omi and Winant release race from its portrayal as a static, unchanging "variable." Describing racial formation as occurring through "a linkage between structure and representation," they build into their concept of racial projects a constant reinterpretation, representation, and motive for the redistribution of resources—material or symbolic—along racial lines (56). We find great intellectual resonance here, since the everyday "doing" of race (which we argue is done simultaneously with class and gender) also allows us to discern the accumulated workings of what Omi and Winant refer to as a "racialized social structure." Presumably, the situated social conduct surrounding race interacts with the preexisting (likewise situated) normative structures to which interaction is subject—including race and class—and the result is a racialized, classed, and gendered social structure.

Winant takes some issue, however, with the ability of the "doing difference" framework to allow for the possibility of change.[5] In his critique of "Doing Difference" (Winant 1995, 505) he writes: "If race consists of 'situated conduct' through which actual human subjects *necessarily reproduce their subordination*, how can large-scale sociopolitical change *ever* occur on racial lines?" (italics added) Here, we would argue, Winant makes the assumption that situated conduct is tantamount to *determined* conduct. Situatedness allows for the seizing of opportunity for subversion, resistance, or even conscious and consequential opposition to systems of domination. Indeed, the degree of variability in prevailing expectations, responses to transgression, and opportunities for opposition, all accommodate hegemonic forms that contain the seeds of change. Both intentional and inadvertent resistance to existing expectations is what makes for change first, last, and always. Further, we contend that only by conceiving of social inequality as the product of *ongoing interactional accomplishments* can we understand how social change occurs. Thus, we see the notion of social process itself as the source of both change and the inevitability of it. In short, we share Winant's (1995) view of social structure within racial (and class and gender) formation,

> In my view, social structure must be understood as dynamic and reciprocal; it is not only a *product* of accreted and repeated subjective action but also *produces* subjects. (504)

Moreover, we agree wholeheartedly with his conclusion that "the permanence of difference, situated and structured, but above all oppositional, still points toward freedom" (505).

We turn now to a brief elaboration of the central and most neglected feature of our formulation as a way to reconcile some of the critical questions posed thus far.

ACCOUNTABILITY AND DIFFERENCE

To reiterate, accomplishing gender, race, and class means managing conduct for members of particular race categories, sex categories, and class categories (West and Fenstermaker 1995a). Our argument relies on Heritage's (1984, 136–7) formulation of accountability, which leads people to manage conduct in anticipation of how others might describe it on a particular occasion. Thus, the doing of gender, race, and class requires situated conduct (including feelings, aspirations, and self-assessments) that is locally managed *with reference to and in light of* normative conceptions of what constitutes appropriate behavior for members of particular sex, race, and class categories.

This, we believe, is the most neglected aspect of our formulation. Few of those who have used our approach have recognized the essential contribution that accountability makes to it, and this does not surprise us. The operation of accountability in human affairs is a theoretical assertion that can only be inferred in the empirical manifestations of class, gender, and race accomplishment. In an effort to empirically demonstrate its workings, we undertook an analysis of deliberations in a University of California Regents meeting (see chapter 8), where the university's existing affirmative action policies were questioned (and ultimately dismantled). Our analysis of speakers' presentations to the Regents led us to conclude:

> Self-categorizations invoke those normative conceptions to which "someone like me" should be held accountable, and other-categoriza-

tions invoke those to which "someone like you" should be held accountable. In both instances, normative conceptions impose structure on the proceedings as much as any set of rules regarding who may speak, about what, and for how long. Such structure ratifies notions of difference, dominance, and entitlement. (36)

Thus, accountability presents to each of us the ever-present possibility of consequential evaluation with respect to our "essential nature." Accordingly, we align our beliefs, our behavior, and ourselves to the possibility of that evaluation.

In work cited earlier, Michael Schwalbe (2000) has elaborated on the concept of accountability and how it might operate. He proposes "nets of accountability" to more adequately convey the extent to which structures of accountability are multiple and interdependent—just like interactions and their consequences. Extending our formulation, he argues that nets of accountability are the engines driving the consequential reaffirmation of categorical "otherness"—and allowing for the material and symbolic allocation of resources based on compliance with prevailing normative expectations. Schwalbe (2000) writes,

> We see that accountability depends on Othering, since categories must exist and people must be identified as belonging to them before they can be held accountable. The holding of people accountable in turn reinforces the social reality, and the consequentiality of the categories. (781)

With a firmer grasp on structures of accountability that motivate the accomplishment of class, race, and gender, we can shed further light on some of the prior questions about the "doing difference" framework. First, it is clear that the particular meanings attached to class-, race-, or gender-appropriate actions can derive only from the contexts in which all normative orders acquire their power: historically specific institutional and collective practices in the "natural" (and thus "rightful") allocation of material and symbolic resources. As Schwalbe (2000, 781) helps us see, the interest here is in the "patterning of joint actions that constitute othering and exploitation." So, far from being confined to face-to-face interaction, or disembodied from history or institutional practice, the doing of difference draws its meaning and its power from historically specific institutional and collective contexts. In the accomplishment of difference, accountability is the driving motivator; the specifics of the normative order provide the content, with social interaction the medium. The result is the exercise of power and various manifestations of social inequality.

The possibilities of resistance, opposition, and change also reside in these dynamics. As Schwalbe would no doubt argue, when we move from a description of the reified *categories* of race or class or gender to a framework that reveals *joint action* in *specific situations*, we can see how the doing of difference actually happens, and how it might change. The great variability in systems of inequality alone tells us that change is an inevitable product of the accomplishment. But how the possibility of change obtains within the structure of accountability is a matter for empirical investigation. As Schwalbe (2000) concludes,

> From a perspective that focuses on doing, joint action, and process, many of the theoretical problems arising out of Sociology's tangle of reifications either dissolve or transform into empirical ones. (781)

THE LIMITS OF THEORIZING

There are, of course, theoretical quandaries that still dog our formulation and which continue to trouble us. A sampling of these would include: greater clarity in our articulation of the relationship *between* the individual and the social structure in the workings of accountability; theoretical clarification of accountability in the workings of heteronormative expectations as part of the accomplishment of gender; and the exciting theoretical implications of sex- and race-categorical "blurring" suggested by the increasing presence of multiracial and transgender experience as intellectual and social concerns.[6] Ultimately, however, there is a limited usefulness to theorizing a formulation that depends so completely on empirical referents. At any moment the doing of difference varies in the salience of its particular aspects (e.g., sex category, race category, class category). The situatedness of place-to-place, time-to-time, and member-to-member imposes variation not only in how the process actually unfolds, but also in the particular result. Opposition, resistance, and change in inequality outcomes are embedded in the actualities of those particular "doings." In short, however productive the theoretical dialogue, the answers to most of the important questions lie in the empirical world. The recent work of Julie Bettie serves as an exemplar of what is needed.

Bettie's work "Women without Class: *Chicas, Cholas*, Trash, and the Presence/Absence of Class Identity" (2000) was a product of her ethnographic study of Mexican-American and white working-class high school seniors in California's Central Valley. By exploring how these young women make sense of the class differences that pervade their everyday lives, Bettie demonstrates the subtle and dynamic interplay in the accomplishment of categorical identities. One of her findings illustrates how race and gender promote the social invisibility of class:

In fact, it was the essentialized conceptualizations of race and gender that helped to keep the difference of class invisible. . . . Accusations of "acting white" obscured class at the same time that they provided a way of talking about class difference between white middle-class preps and working-class Mexican Americans, as well as among Mexican-American students themselves. Likewise, the distinction between "good girls" and "bad girls" was wrongly perceived as about sexual morality, yet at the same time school-sanctioned femininity and dissident femininity were read as symbolic markers of class and race difference. (28)

Bettie's research illuminates the conjoint actions involved in doing class, race, and gender in a specific historical, regional, and institutional context. It both provides new directions to further theoretical work and illustrates the rightful dependence that our formulation has on empirical insight. Here we see that class, race, and gender are not only accomplished together (varying in their standing in any given set of interactions) but can at once enable and eclipse one another with unanticipated results. Moreover, and as we have argued previously (West and Fenstermaker 1995a), Bettie's work shows us once again that the doing of difference—the creation and reaffirmation of categorical identities—does not happen (as she says) "evenly" but draws its meaning and character from the specifics of interaction.

Bettie's (2000) work is only one convincing confirmation that any theoretical description of such a complex and dynamic set of practices must depend for further development upon analyses of the empirical world. In the end, the dialogue in feminist theory is dependent not only on the iterations of new theoretical formulations such as ours, but on a meaningful application of those ideas to a world where gender, class, and race are symbolic and material realities.

NOTES

1. The original version of this chapter appeared in *Kolner Zeitschrift fur Soziologie und Sozialpsychologie,* ed. Bettina Heintz., 2002.

2. Even an inexhaustive and haphazard collection of empirical pieces employing the framework covers a wide variety of topics (e.g., men's and women's prisons, women surgeons, rock music, the Internet, crime and violence, coal mines, and firehouses). (For a few examples of the varied use of the "accomplishment" formulation in empirical work, see Bettie 2000; Bird 1996; Britton 1997; Cassell 1997; Clawson 1999; Cook and Stambaugh 1997; Dryden 1999; Gilgun and McLeod 1999; S. Martin and Jurik 1996; Messerschmidt 1997; Pike 1996; Tallichet 1995; Uchida 1997; Yoder and Aniakudo 1997).

3. Butler's theories cannot be reduced to the dramaturgical either. Elsewhere in this volume (chapter 10) we explore the convergences and divergences between the two theoretical formulations.

4. Joan Acker's work (e.g., 1992a, 1992b) demonstrates that the presence of gender in work organizations is certainly ubiquitous and takes on a variety of aspects. The operational mechanisms

behind these manifestations, we would argue, point directly to the accomplishment of difference as an everyday yet powerful feature of organizations.

5. Interestingly, others have implied that our formulation casts structures as wholly underdetermined, where the world of organizational reality becomes just a matter of interpretation (e.g., Britton 1997; Maldonado 1995).

6. The conception of change as ever present in racial formation has led Daniel (forthcoming 2002) to argue:

> The pattern of racial meanings and identities, the racial dimensions of social inequality, and the degree of political mobilization based upon race, therefore, all display instability and flexibility. Consequently, the logic of race is multiply determined at any given historical moment. (viii)

(See also Roediger 1991 for a compelling, historically situated analysis of race and the white working class in all its only apparent permanence.)

CONCLUSION

Central Problematics: An Agenda for Feminist Sociology

SARAH FENSTERMAKER AND CANDACE WEST

In her foreword to this book, Dorothy Smith characterized the aim of ethnomethodology as "discovering just how people go about producing what we can recognize as just this or just that everyday event, occasion, setting, act, or person." This collection promotes the discovery of just how people go about producing what we can recognize as gender, as race, and as class. That being said, our concern with "doing gender" and "doing difference" is not only in the myriad instances in which people make gender, race, and class notable agendas within social life, however remarkable that process. Our interest is not some ethnomethodological equivalent of John James Audubon's determination to capture as much of the wondrous diversity of the bird kingdom as possible. To be sure, such a mission may enhance every subsequent effort to make larger sense of such thoroughgoing specificity. After all, Audubon's meticulously crafted drawings of birds provided the detail necessary to gain new insights into the mechanics of flight. Nevertheless, our interest is not just in knowing that gender—or difference—is ubiquitously *done*, or that it is done in fascinating variety, but how it is done systematically and with social consequence.

The questions that remain rightly turn on that overarching goal: to understand the accomplishment of gender, race, and class as outcomes of, and rationales for, rendering social inequality legitimate. Indeed, the dramatic historical and cultural variegation in which "doing difference" reveals itself are *at the same time* multiple manifestations of enduring relations of patriarchy, racism, and class oppression. Here, we reiterate our interest as explicating the conjoint reality of human conduct that momentarily produces power relations, but does that only *in the situated context* of particular institutions, their histories, and the profound weight of their taken-for-granted character.

Many questions remain, we hope, for others to tackle, and the pieces within this collection outline an important subset of them. We don't need to belabor this closing by revisiting those discussions. Three general problems demand some final mention, however, and each is worthy of concerted research effort. We believe that together they not only set an agenda for future sociological research on our little formulation, but speak directly to the vaster feminist project that continues to inspire: to articulate the workings of dominance as it simultaneously structures women's choices and provides signposts en route to liberation.

The first item on this agenda is to speak—both theoretically and empirically—to the division of the social world into "micro and "macro": to explore what it hinders, and what it may enable. Thus far, and for us, the distinction is not a distinction; it is a relationship between the realities of social structure as it limits choices for what members may say, may do, and may be, and the real autonomy of individuals to shape their interactions in seemingly unbounded ways. We have taken the position repeatedly that the bifurcation of "micro"/"macro" reduces to one of "little" versus "big," or "trivial" versus "consequential," or "unstructured" versus "structured" and precludes a vision of the bridges across the divide. Nevertheless, we await the work that makes the other case—or a third—convincingly.

Second, much more thought is needed to bring the simultaneous doing of gender, race, and class into sharper focus. To resolve many questions about the nature of such concurrent accomplishments, we would suggest future work at the interstices of assignment and categorization practices (on the one hand), and the accomplishment of difference (on the other hand). For example, we have noted that in Western societies, the process of initial sex assignment depends on clinicians' abilities to sort newborns into one or the other of two mutually exclusive classes. Clinicians, in turn, rely on *socially agreed upon* biological criteria for classifying persons as females or males. But with the notable exception of Suzanne Kessler (1998), no one we know of has devoted sustained empirical attention to how clinicians make sense of what they do in the case of intersexed infants, whose anatomical, hormonal, and/or chromosomal features defy mutually exclusive and exhaustive classification. In addition, a new wave of research that has sought to reconceptualize transsexual and multiracial identities as topics in their own right (e.g., Bolin 1988; Daniel 2002; Denny 1998; Devor 1997; Kessler 1998; Kich 1996; T. Powell 1999; R. Young 1995) holds great promise for continued research. This raises again the question we have posed before but have not sufficiently resolved. What is there beyond the powerful heteronormative dynamics likely to be inherent the doing of gender? What might we mean when we talk about "doing" sexuality—conduct managed in reference to situated normative conceptions of what is appropriate? Any answer to that question must be made *in light of* the compulsory heterosexuality that marks the doing of gender.

In part, our formulation depends upon members' conduct oriented to a constructed *stability* in practices surrounding assignment, categorization, and the accomplishment of meaningful difference. When categorization, and categories, become fundamentally destabilized—when the transsexual, transgender, and multiracial terrains shift into *new* categories and the practices that emerge from them—we can learn more about the adaptable, ultimately changeable nature of accomplished inequality. The process by which new inputs into existing categorical distinctions are apprehended and made "natural" holds great promise for our formulation. In addition, historian Leila Rupp and sociologist Verta Taylor's (forthcoming) research on gay male drag queens holds some provocative insights into the effects of destabilized gender relations. Their work suggests that drag shows, intentionally crafted to disrupt the "natural" status of sex category, gender, and the binaries of sexual practice, may have profound effects on individual patrons and the neighborhood cultures in which the shows are performed.

Third, we are reminded of Howard Winant's comments in response to "Doing Difference": He asks if our conception of social structure is more than something "constantly reproduced from moment to moment"; if it is, in fact, "engraved in time and space" (Winant 1995, this volume). His queries prompt us to peer again across the "micro"/"macro" divide to ask what *is* the "weight" of social structure as it is created, reproduced, and brought to bear on interaction? For us, this question implies another: Is ours a theory that can sustain its own political vision? With that question, we are engaged in more than theoretical parlor games, however entertaining they may be; such questions and the research suggested by them are necessary to any meaningful consideration of social change. We believe we have made a strong case that within the dynamic nature of the accomplishment of categorical difference reside the seeds of inevitable change. But how does change occur, and what is its nature? Certainly the "doing" of any categorical difference, with such a locally produced, situated character, could present the possibility for lots of changes—spasmodic, fitful, sporadic—but what of lasting change? We think that Dalton and Fenstermaker have taken us some of the way there with their finding that face-to-face interactions can interact with existing and particular institutional histories and conditions to facilitate change in the normative standards employed by them. Obviously, many more instances for analysis are indicated.

This entire collection was presented originally and in this partial redux, as Dull and Westsaid in chapter 7, "in a spirit of invitation—with the hope of simulating among sociologists a broader range of interest in the topic." It is an invitation not only to grapple theoretically with these ideas but to explore them empirically. Each of the abiding problems we have identified in this chapter or throughout the collection (e.g., the "micro"/"macro" relationship; the simultaneous accomplishment of categorical differences; how particular settings eclipse doing some differences and not others; the nature of "transgression" in accomplishment; the workings of accountability structures in particular settings) is best understood and developed as a result of empirical work. Moreover, just as we were uncomfortable years ago with the confinement of the accomplishment of categorical difference solely to gender, so too are we increasingly anxious for empirical researchers to share their importation of our formulation beyond the industrialized West.

None are more cognizant than we that within this formulation, the number of unanswered questions overwhelm settled ones. A feminist research agenda that includes the puzzles with which our formulation grapples could begin from many different points, yet converge on a destination of great value. We encourage our colleagues to embark on such a journey.

REFERENCES

Abrams, P. 1972. *Historical sociology*. Ithaca, NY: Cornell University Press.

Acker, Joan. 1992a. Gendered institutions: From sex roles to gendered institutions. *Contemporary Sociology* 21: 565–9.

———. 1992b. Gendering organizational theory. In *Gendering organizational theory*, edited by Albert J. Mills and Peta Tancred. London: Sage.

Adams, J. 1984. Women at West Point: A three-year perspective. *Sex Roles* 11: 525–41.

Aguirre, A. 1979. Intelligence testing and Chicanos: A quality of life issue. *Social Problems* 27: 186–95.

Aisenberg, N. and M. Harrington. 1988. *Women of academe: Outsiders in the sacred grove*. Amherst: University of Massachusetts Press.

Alcoff, L. and E. Potter. 1992. *Feminist epistemologies*. New York: Routledge.

Almquist, E. 1989. The experiences of minority women in the United States: Intersections of race, gender, and class. In *Women: A feminist perspective*, edited by Jo Freeman. Mountain View, CA: Mayfield.

Alvarado, D. 1995. Scientist: Race not defined by genes. *San Jose Mercury News*, 20 February, pp. A1ff.

American Society of Plastic and Reconstructive Surgeons. 1988. Press release. Estimated number of cosmetic procedures performed by ASPRS members. Arlington Heights, IL: Department of Communications.

Amsden, A. H., ed. 1980. *The economics of women and work*. New York: St. Martin's.

Anderson, M. L. and P. H. Collins, eds., 1994. *Race, class and gender: An anthology*, 2nd edition. Belmot, CA: Wadsworth.

Andersen, M. L. and P. H. Collins. 1992. Preface to *Race, class, and gender*, edited by Margaret L. Andersen and Patricia Hill Collins. Belmont, CA: Wadsworth.

Aptheker, B. 1989. *Tapestries of life: Women's work, women's consciousness, and the meaning of daily experience*. Amherst: University of Massachusetts Press.

As smart as they look. 1993. *Mirabella*, June: pp. 100–11.

Atkinson, J. M. 1985. Refusing invited applause: Preliminary observations from a case study of charismatic oratory. In *Handbook of discourse analysis*, vol. 3: *Discourse and dialogue*, edited by Teun A. van Dijk. New York: Academic Press.

Austin, J. L. 1962. *How to do things with words*. Cambridge, MA: Harvard University Press.

Baca Zinn, M. 1999. *Gender through the prism of difference*. New York: Allyn and Bacon.

Baca Zinn, M. and B. T. Dill. 1994. *Women of color in U.S. society*. Philadelphia: Temple University Press.

Bahr, S. 1974. Effects on power and division of labor. In *Working mothers*, edited by L. Hoffman and F. I. Nye. San Francisco: Jossey-Bass.

Bartholet, E. 1993. *Family bonds: Adoption and the politics of parenting*. Boston: Houghton Mifflin.

Bartlett, K. T. 1984. Rethinking parenthood as an exclusive status: The need for legal alternatives when the premise of the nuclear family has failed. *Virginia Law Review* 70: 879–963.

Baxter, J. Forthcoming. Competing discourses in the classroom: A post-structuralist discourse analysis of girls' and boys' speech in public contexts. *Discourse & Society*.

Beale, F. 1970. Double jeopardy: To be Black and female. In *The Black woman: An anthology*, edited by Toni Cade. New York: Signet.

Becker, G. S. 1981. *A treatise on the family*. Cambridge, MA: Harvard University Press.

Beer, W. R. 1983. *Househusbands: Men and housework in American families*. New York: Praeger.

Begley, S. 1995. Three is not enough: Surprising new lessons from the controversial science of race. *Newsweek*, 13 February, pp. 67–9.

Bem, S. L. 1983. Gender schema theory and its implications for child development: Raising gender-aschematic children in a gender-schematic society. *Signs: Journal of Women in Culture and Society* 8: 598–616.

Beneria, L. and C. R. Stimpson, eds. 1987. *Women, households, and the economy*. New Brunswick, NJ: Rutgers University Press.

Benhabib, S. 1995. Feminism and postmodernism. In *Feminist contentions: A philosophical exchange*, edited by Benhabib et al. New York: Routledge.

Benhabib, S., J. Butler, D. Cornell, and N. Fraser. 1995. *Feminist contentions: A philosophical exchange*. New York: Routledge.

Berger, J., B. P. Cohen, and M. Zelditch, Jr. 1972. Status characteristics and social interaction. *American Sociological Review* 37: 241–55.

Berger, J., T. L. Conner, and M. H. Fisek, eds. 1974. *Expectation states theory: A theoretical research program*. Cambridge: Winthrop.

Berger, J., M. H. Fisek, R. Z. Norman, and M. Zelditch, Jr. 1977. *Status characteristics and social interaction: An expectation states approach*. New York: Elsevier.

Berheide, C. W., S. F. Berk, and R.A. Berk. 1976. Household work in the suburbs: The job and its participants. *Pacific Sociological Review* 14: 491–517.

Berk, R. A. and S. F. Berk. 1979. *Labor and leisure at home: Content and organization of the household day*. Beverly Hills, CA: Sage.

Berk, S. F. 1985. *The gender factory: The apportionment of work in American households*. New York: Plenum.

Bernstein, R. 1986. France jails 2 in odd case of espionage. *New York Times* 11 May.

Bettie, J. 2000. Women without class: *Chicas, cholas*, trash, and the presence/absence of class identity. *Signs: Journal of Women in Culture and Society* 26: 1–36.

Bhavani, K. 1994. Talking racism and the editing of women's studies. In *Introducing women's studies*, edited by Diane Richardson and Vicki Robinson. New York: Macmillan.

Billig, M. 1999a. Conversation analysis and the claims of naivity. *Discourse and Analysis* 10: 572–6.

———. 1999b. Whose terms? Whose ordinariness? Rhetoric and ideology in conversation analysis. *Discourse & Society* 10: 543–82.

Bird, S. 1996. Welcome to the men's club: Homosociality and the maintenance of hegemonic masculinity. *Gender & Society* 10: 120–32.

Blackwood, E. 1984. Sexuality and gender in certain Native American tribes: The case of cross-gender females. *Signs: Journal of Women in Culture and Society* 10: 27–42.

Blau, F. D. and M. A. Ferber. 1985. Women in the labor market: The last twenty years. In *Women and work: An annual review*, 1, edited by L. Larwood, A. H. Stromberg, and B. A. Gutek. Beverly Hills, CA: Sage.

Blumberg, R. L. 1978. *Stratification: Socioeconomic and sexual inequality*. Dubuque, IA: William C. Brown.

————. 1984. A general theory of gender stratification. In *Sociological theory*, edited by Randall Collins. San Francisco: Jossey-Bass.

Bolin, A. 1988. *In search of Eve: Transsexual rites of passage*. South Hadley, MA: Bergin and Garvey.

Bordo, S. 1993. *Unbearable weight: Feminism, Western culture, and the body*. Berkeley: University of California Press.

Bourdieu, P. 1977. *Outline of a theory of practice*. Cambridge: Cambridge University Press.

Bourne, P. G. and N. J. Wikler. 1978. Commitment and the cultural mandate: Women in medicine. *Social Problems* 25: 430–40.

Bowles, G. and R. Duelli-Klein, eds. 1980. *Theories of women's studies*. Berkeley: University of California Press.

Bradiotti, R. 1994. *Nomadic subjects*. New York: Columbia University Press.

Bridenthal, R. 1981. The family tree: Contemporary patterns in the United States. In *Household and kin*, edited by Amy Swerdlow, Renate Bridenthal, Joan Kelly, and Phyllis Vine. Old Westbury, NY: Feminist Press.

Britton, D. 1997. Gendered organizational logic: Policy and practice in men's and women's prisons. *Gender & Society* 11: 796–818.

Butler, J. 1990. *Gender trouble: Feminism and the subversion of identity*. New York: Routledge.

————. 1993. *Bodies that matter: On the discursive limits of "sex."* New York: Routledge.

————. 1995. Contingent foundations. In *Feminist contentions*, edited by Benhabib et al. New York: Routledge.

————. 1997a. *Excitable speech: A politics of the performative*. New York: Routledge.

————. 1997b. *The psychic life of power: Theories in subjection*. Stanford, CA: Stanford University Press.

————. 1999. Preface (1999). *Gender trouble: Feminism and the subversion of identity* (10th anniversary edition). New York: Routledge.

Cahill, S. E. 1982. Becoming boys and girls. Ph.D. dissertation, University of California Santa Barbara Department of Sociology.

————. 1986a. Childhood socialization as recruitment process: Some lessons from the study of gender development. In *Sociological studies of child development*, edited by Patricia Adler and Peter Adler. Greenwich, CT: JAI Press.

————. 1986b. Language practices and self-definition: The case of gender identity acquisition. *Sociological Quarterly* 27: 295–311.

Carby, H. 1995. *Reconstructing womanhood: The emergence of the Afro-American woman novelist*. Oxford: Oxford University Press.

Case, S. 1996. *The domain-matrix: Performing lesbian at the end of print culture*. Bloomington: Indiana University Press.

Cassell, J. 1997. Doing gender, doing surgery: Women surgeons in a man's profession. *Human Organization* 56: 47–52.

Chafetz, J. S. 1984. *Sex and advantage: A comparative, macro-structural theory of sex stratification*. Totowa, NJ: Rowman & Allanheld.

Chase, J. 2001. Misleading comparison (a letter to the editor). *San Jose Mercury News*, 22 August, p. B7.

Chodorow, N. 1978. *The reproduction of mothering: Psychoanalysis and the sociology of gender*. Los Angeles: University of California Press.

Clawson, M. 1999. When women play the bass: Instrument specialization and gender interpretation in alternative rock music. *Gender & Society* 13: 193–210.

Clayman, S. E. 1991. Booing: The anatomy of a disaffiliative response. *American Sociological Review* 58: 110–30.

Colen, S. 1986. "With respect and feelings": Voices of West Indian child care and domestic workers in New York City. In *American women*, edited by Johnetta B. Cole. New York: Free Press.

Collins, P. H. 1990. *Black feminist thought: Knowledge, consciousness, and the politics of empowerment*. New York: Routledge.

———. 1995. Symposium: On West and Fenstermaker's "Doing difference." *Gender & Society* 9: 491–4.

Coltrane, S. 1989. Household labor and the routine production of gender. *Social Problems* 36: 473–91.

Connell, R. W. 1983. *Which way is up? Essays on sex, class, and culture.* London: Allen & Unwin.

———. 1985. Theorizing gender. *Sociology* 19: 260–72.

———. 1987a. The body and social practice. In *Gender and power: Society, the person and sexual politics.* Stanford, CA: Stanford University Press.

———. 1987b. *Gender and power: Society, the person and sexual politics.* Stanford, CA: Stanford University Press.

Conrad, P. 1976. *Identifying hyperactive children: The medicalization of deviant behavior.* Lexington, MA: Lexington Books.

Conrad, P. and J. W. Schneider. 1980. *Deviance and medicalization: From badness to sickness.* St. Louis, MO: Mosby.

Cook, K. J. and P. M. Stambaugh. 1997. Tuna memos and pissing contexts: Doing gender and male dominance on the internet. In *Everyday sexism in the third millennium,* edited by Carol R. Ronai, Barbara Zsembik, and Joe R. Feagin. New York: Routledge.

Cornell, D. 1994. *Transformations: Recollective imagination and sexual difference.* New York: Routledge.

———. 1998. *At the heart of freedom: Feminism, sex, and equality.* Princeton, NJ: Princeton University Press.

Cucchiari, S. 1981. The gender revolution and the transition from bisexual horde to patrilocal band: The origins of gender hierarchy. In *Sexual meanings: The cultural construction of gender and sexuality,* edited by S. B. Ortner and H. Whitehead. New York: Cambridge University Press.

Dalton, S. E. 2001. Protecting our parent-child relationships: Understanding the strengths and weaknesses of the second parent adoptions. In *Queer families, queer politics: Challenging culture and the state,* edited by Mary Bernstein and Renate Reimann. New York: Columbia University Press.

Dandavati, A. 2001 Exploitation must stop (letter to the editor). *San Jose Mercury News,* 22 August, p. B7.

Daniel, G. R. 2002. *Black no more or more than Black: Multiracial identity and the new racial order.* Philadelphia: Temple University Press.

Daniels, A. K. 1986. *Invisible careers: Women civic leaders in the volunteer world.* Chicago: University of Chicago Press.

Davis, A. 1971. The Black woman's role in the community of slaves. *Black Scholar* 3: 3–15.

———. 1981. *Women, race, and class.* New York: Random House.

Davis, P. 1980. *The social context of dentistry.* London: Croom Helm.

de Beauvoir, S. 1953. *The second sex.* New York: Knopf.

De Lauretis, T. 1989. *Technologies of gender: Essays on theory, film, and fiction.* Bloomington: Indiana University Press.

DeMott, B. 1990. *The imperial middle: Why Americans can't think straight about class.* New Haven, CT: Yale University Press.

Denny, D. 1998. *Current concepts in transgender identity.* New York: Garland.

Derrida, J. 1977. *Limited Inc.* Evanston, IL: Northwestern University Press.

DeVault, M. 1991. *Feeding the family: The social construction of caring as gendered work.* Chicago: University of Chicago Press.

Devor, H. 1997. *FTM: Female-to-male transsexuals in society.* Bloomington: Indiana University Press.

Dill, B. T. 1988. Our mothers' grief: Racial ethnic women and the maintenance of families. *Journal of Family History* 13: 415–31.

DiMaggio, P. J. and W. W. Powell. 1991. Introduction. In *The new institutionalism in organizational analysis,* edited by Walter W. Powell and Paul J. DiMaggio. Chicago: University of Chicago Press.

Dolgin, J. L. 1993. Just a gene: Judicial assumptions about parenthood. *UCLA Law Review* 40: 637–94.

———. 1997. *Defining the family: Law, technology, and reproduction in an uneasy age.* New York: New York University Press.

Dryden, C. 1999. *Being married, doing gender: A critical analysis of gender relationships in marriage.* New York: Routledge.

Du Bois, W. E. B. [1903] 1989. *The souls of Black folk.* New York: Penguin.

Eisenstein, Z. 1981. *The radical future of liberal feminism.* New York: Longman.

Emirbayer, M. and A. Mische. 1998. What is agency? *American Journal of Sociology* 103: 962–1023.

Epstein, C. F. 1973. Positive effects of the double negative: Explaining the success of Black professional women. In *Changing women in a changing society,* edited by Joan Huber. Chicago: University of Chicago Press.

———. 1981. *Women in law.* New York: Basic Books.

Epstein, S. 1994. A queer encounter: Sociology and the study of sexuality. *Sociological Theory* 12: 188–202.

Essed, P. 1991. *Understanding everyday racism: An interdisciplinary theory.* Newbury Park, CA: Sage.

Farkas, G. 1976. Education, wage rates, and the division of labor between husband and wife. *Journal of Marriage and the Family* 38: 473–83.

Feldberg, R. L. and E. N. Glenn. 1979. Job versus gender models in the sociology of work. *Social Problems* 25: 524–38.

Fenstermaker, S., C. West, and D. H. Zimmerman. 1991. Gender inequality: New conceptual terrain. In *Gender, family and economy: The triple overlap,* edited by Rae Lesser Blumberg. Newbury Park, CA: Sage.

Fernandez-Kelly, M. P. 1983. *For we are sold, I and my people: Women and industry in Mexico's frontier.* Albany: State University of New York Press.

Ferree, M. M., J. Lorber, and B. B. Hess. 1998. *Revisioning gender.* Thousand Oaks, CA: Sage.

Fineman, H. (with G. Beals and B. Turque). 1995. The rollback begins: California—killing affirmative action in time for '96. *Newsweek,* 31 July, p. 30.

Firestone, S. 1970. *The dialectic of sex: The case for feminist revolution.* New York: William Morrow.

Fishman, P. 1978. Interaction: The work women do. *Social Problems* 25: 397–406.

Flax, J. 1991. *Thinking fragments: Psychoanalysis, feminism, and postmodernism in the contemporary West.* New York: Routledge.

Floge, L. and D. M. Merrill. 1985. Tokenism reconsidered: Male nurses and female physicians in a hospital setting. *Social Forces* 64: 925–47.

Foster, J. 1999. An invitation to dialogue: Clarifying the position of feminist gender theory in relation to sexual difference theory. *Gender & Society* 13: 431–56.

Foucault, M. 1965. *Madness and civilization: A history of insanity in the age of reason.* New York: Vintage.

———. 1977. *Discipline and punish.* Translated by A. Sheridan. New York: Vintage.

———. 1978. *The history of sexuality, Volume 1: An introduction.* New York: Vintage.

———. 1984. *History of sexuality, an introduction.* New York: Vintage.

Frankenberg, R. 1993. *The social construction of whiteness: White women, race matters.* Minneapolis: University of Minnesota Press.

Fraser, N. 1995. Pragmatism, feminism, and the linguistic turn. In *Feminist contentions,* edited by Benhabib et al. New York: Routledge.

Freedman, R. 1986. *Beauty bound.* Lexington, MA: D.C. Heath.

French, H. W. 2001. China warns Japanese leader not to visit war memorial. *San Jose Mercury News,* 26 July, p. A6.

Friedan, B. 1963. *The feminine mystique.* New York: Dell.

Friedland, R. and R. R. Alford. 1991. Bringing society back in: Symbols, practices, and institutional contradictions. In *The new institutionalism in organizational analysis,* edited by Walter W. Powell and Paul J. DiMaggio. Chicago: University of Chicago Press.

Frye, M. 1983. *The politics of reality: Essays in feminist theory.* Trumansburg, NY: Crossing Press.

Garfinkel, H. 1967. *Studies in ethnomethodology.* Englewood Cliffs, NJ: Prentice-Hall.

Gates, H. 1987. *Chinese working-class lives: Getting by in Taiwan.* Ithaca, NY: Cornell University Press.

Gerson, J. M. 1986. The variability and salience of gender: Issues of conceptualization and measurement. Paper presented at the annual meeting of the American Sociological Association, Washington, D.C.

Gerson, J. M. and K. Peiss. 1985. Boundaries, negotiation, consciousness: Reconceptualizing gender relations. *Social Problems* 32: 317–31.

Gerstel, N. and H. E. Gross, eds. 1987. *Families and work.* Philadelphia: Temple University Press.

Giddens, A. 1984. *The constitution of society.* Berkeley: University of California Press.

Giddings, P. 1984. *When and where I enter: The impact of Black women on race and sex in America.* New York: Bantam.

Gilgun, J. F. and L. McLeod. 1999. Gendering violence. *Studies in Symbolic Interaction* 22: 167–93.

Gilkes, C. 1980. "Holding back the ocean with a broom": Black women and community work. In *The Black woman,* edited by La Francis Rodgers-Rose. Beverly Hills, CA: Sage.

Gilman, C. P. 1979. *Herland.* New York: Pantheon.

Glaser, B. and A. Strauss. 1967. *The discovery of grounded theory.* Chicago: Aldine.

Glazer, N. 1977. A sociological perspective: Introduction. In *Woman in a man-made world,* edited by Nona Glazer and Helen Youngelson Waehrer. Chicago: Rand McNally.

Glenn, E. N. 1985. Racial ethnic women's labor: The intersection of race, gender, and class oppression. *Review of Radical Political Economics* 17: 86–108.

———. 1992. From servitude to service work: Historical continuities in the racial division of paid reproductive labor. *Signs: Journal of Women in Culture and Society* 18: 1–43.

———. 1999. The social construction and institutionalization of gender and race: An integrative framework. In *Revisioning gender,* edited by Myra Marx Ferree, Judith Lorber, and Beth B. Hess. Thousand Oaks, CA: Sage.

Goffman, E. 1961. *Encounters.* Indianapolis, IN: Bobbs-Merrill.

———. 1967 (1956). The nature of deference and demeanor. In *Interaction ritual.* New York: Anchor/Doubleday.

———. 1976. Gender display. *Studies in the Anthropology of Visual Communication* 3: 69–77.

———. 1977. The arrangement between the sexes. *Theory and Society* 4: 301–31.

———. 1979. *Gender advertisements.* New York: Harper & Row.

Goode, W. J. 1982. Why men resist. In *Rethinking the family,* edited by B. Thorne and M. Yalom. New York: Longman.

Gossett, T. 1965. *Race: The history of an idea in America.* New York: Schocken.

Gramsci, A. 1971. *Selections from the prison notebooks.* Edited by Quintin Hoare and Geoffrey Nowell-Smith. New York: International Publishers.

Grosz, E. 1994. *Volatile bodies: Toward a corporeal feminism.* Bloomington: Indiana University Press.

Guillemin, J. H. and L. L. Holmstrom. 1986. *Mixed blessings: Intensive care for newborns.* New York: Oxford University Press.

Hacker, H. M. 1951. Women as a minority group. *Social Forces* 30: 60–9.

Hall, S. 1980. Race, articulation, and societies structured in dominance. In *Sociological theories: Race and colonialism.* Paris: UNESCO.

———. 1992. What is this "Black" in Black popular culture? In *Black popular culture,* edited by G. Dent and M. Wallace. Seattle: Bay Press.

Haraway, D. J. 1991. Situated knowledges: The science question in feminism and the privilege of partial perspective. In *Simians, cyborgs, and women: The reinvention of nature,* edited by D. J. Haraway. New York: Routledge.

Hartmann, H. I. 1987. Changes in women's economic and family roles in post–World War II United States. In *Women, households, and the economy,* edited by L. Beneria and C. R. Stimpson. New Brunswick, NJ: Rutgers University Press.

Henley, N. M. 1977. *Body politics: Sex and nonverbal communication.* Englewood Cliffs, N.J.: Prentice-Hall.

———. 1985. Psychology and gender. *Signs: Journal of Women in Culture and Society* 11: 101–19.

Heritage, J. 1984. *Garfinkel and ethnomethodology.* Cambridge: Polity.

Herrnstein, R. 1994. *The bell curve: Intelligence and class structure in American life.* New York: Free Press.

Hertz, R. 1986. *More equal than others: Women and men in dual-career marriages.* Berkeley: University of California Press.

Hill, W. W. 1935. The status of the hermaphrodite and transvestite in Navaho culture. *American Anthropologist* 37: 273–79.

Hochschild, A. R. 1973. A review of sex roles research. *American Journal of Sociology* 78: 1011–29.

———. 1983a. *The managed heart: Commercialization of human feeling.* Berkeley: University of California Press.

———. 1983b. Smile wars: Counting the casualties of emotional labor. *Mother Jones,* December, pp. 35–43.

———. 1989. *The second shift: Working parents and the revolution at home.* New York: Viking.

Hollinger, J. H. 1996. *Adoption and law practice.* New York: Mathew Bender.

hooks, bell. 1981. *Ain't I a woman: Black women and feminism.* Boston: South End.

———. 1984. *From margin to center.* Boston: South End.

Howe, L. K. 1977. *Pink collar workers: Inside the world of women's work.* New York: G. P. Putnam.

Hughes, E. C. 1945. Dilemmas and contradictions of status. *American Journal of Sociology* 50: 353–9.

———. 1958. *Men and their work.* Glencoe, IL: Free Press.

Hull, G. T., P. B. Scott, and B. Smith, eds. 1982. *All the women are white, all the Blacks are men, but some of us are brave.* Old Westbury, NY: Feminist Press.

Humphreys, P. and J. Berger. 1981. Theoretical consequences of the status characteristics formulation. *American Journal of Sociology* 86: 953–83.

Hurtado, A. 1989. Relating to privilege: Seduction and rejection in the subordination of white women and women of color. *Signs: Women in Culture and Society* 14: 833–55.

———. 1992. The politics of sexuality in the gender subordination of Chicanas. Unpublished manuscript. Psychology Board: University of California, Santa Cruz.

Irigaray, L. 1993. *An ethics of sexual difference.* Translated by C. Burke. Ithaca, NY: Cornell University Press.

Jaggar, A. M. 1983. *Feminist politics and human nature.* Totowa, NJ: Rowman & Allanheld.

Jefferson, G. 1973. A case of precision timing in ordinary conversation: Overlapped tag-positioned address terms in closing sequences. *Semiotics* 9: 47–96.

Jepperson, R. L. 1991. Institutions, institutional effects, and institutionalism. In *The new institutionalism in organizational analysis,* edited by Walter W. Powell and Paul J. DiMaggio. Chicago: Chicago University Press.

Jordan, J. 1985. Report from the Bahamas. In *On call: Political essays.* Boston: South End.

Joseph, G. I. 1981. White promotion, Black survival. In *Common differences: Conflicts in Black and White feminist perspectives,* edited by Gloria I. Joseph and Jill Lewis. Garden City, NY: Anchor/Doubleday.

Joseph, G. I. and J. Lewis, eds. 1981. *Common differences: Conflicts in Black and White feminist perspectives.* Garden City, NY: Anchor/Doubleday.

Kahn-Hut, R., A. K. Daniels, and R. Colvard, eds. 1982. *Women and work.* New York: Oxford University Press.

Kaminer, W. 1984. *Women volunteering: The pleasure, pain, and politics of unpaid work from 1830 to the present.* Garden City, NY: Anchor.

Kanter, R. M. 1977. *Men and women of the corporation.* New York: Basic Books.

Keller, E. F. 1985. *Reflections on gender and science.* New York: Yale University Press.

Kelly, R. D. G. 1994. *Race rebels: Culture, politics, and the Black working class.* New York: Free Press.

Kessler, S., D. J. Ashendon, R. W. Connell, and G. W. Dowsett. 1985. Gender relations in secondary schooling. *Sociology of Education* 58: 34–48.

Kessler, S. J. 1998. *Lessons from the intersexed*. New Brunswick, N.J.: Rutgers University Press.

Kessler, S. J. and W. McKenna. 1978. *Gender: An ethnomethodological approach*. New York: Wiley.

Kich, G. K. 1996. In the margins of sex and race: Difference, marginality, and flexibility. In *The multiracial experience: Racial borders as the new frontier*, edited by Maria P. P. Root. Thousand Oaks, CA: Sage.

King, D. 1993. *The transvestite and the transsexual: Public categories and private identities*. Aldershot, England: Avebury.

King, Martin Luther, Jr. 1994. I have a dream. In *I have a dream: Writings and speeches that changed the world.*, edited by James Melvin Washington, Martin Luther King, Jr., and Coretta Scott King. New York: St. Martin's Press.

Kirkpatrick, M., C. Smith, and R. Roy. 1981. Lesbian mothers and their children: A comparative survey. *American Journal of Orthopsychiatry* 51: 345–551.

Kollock, P., P. Blumstein, and P. Schwartz. 1985. Sex and power in interaction. *American Sociological Review* 50: 34–46.

Komarovsky, M. 1946. Cultural contradictions and sex roles. *American Journal of Sociology* 52: 184–9.

———. 1950. Functional analysis of sex roles. *American Sociological Review* 15: 508–16.

———. 1992. The concept of social role revisited. *Gender & Society* 6: 301–12.

Kurdek, L. 1993. The allocation of household labor in homosexual and heterosexual cohabiting couples. *Journal of Social Issues* 49: 127–39.

Kurtzman, L. 1995. Regents' vote cuts deep among Asian-Americans. *San Jose Mercury News*, 29 July.

Kurtzman, L. and S. Thurm. 1995. UC regents bring an end to race, gender rules: Wilson's victory likely to be felt across U.S. *San Jose Mercury News*, 21 July.

Langston, D. 1991. Tired of playing monopoly? In *Changing our power: An introduction to women's studies*. 2nd ed., edited by Jo Whitehorse Cochran, Donna Langston, and Carol Woodward. Dubuque, IA: Kendall-Hunt.

Laqueur, T. 1990. *Making sex: Body and gender from the Greeks to Freud*. Cambridge, MA: Harvard University Press.

Laws, J. L. 1975. The psychology of tokenism: An analysis. *Sex Roles* 1: 51–67.

Leidner, R. 1993. *Fast food, fast talk: Service work and the routinization of everyday life*. Berkeley: University of California Press.

Lewis, M. 1994. Melting pot ingredients: Oil and water? *San Jose Mercury News*,14 July, pp. A1ff.

Linton, R. 1936. *The study of man*. New York: Appleton-Century.

Lopata, H. Z. and B. Thorne. 1978. On the term "sex roles." *Signs: Journal of Women in Culture and Society* 3: 718–21.

Lorber, J. 1975a. Good patients and problem patients: Conformity and deviance in a general hospital. *Journal of Health and Social Behavior* 6: 213–25.

———. 1975b. Women and medical sociology: Invisible professionals and ubiquitous patients. In *Another voice: Feminist perspectives on social life and social science*, edited by Marcia Millman and Rosabeth Moss Kanter. Garden City, NY: Anchor/Doubleday.

———. 1984. *Women physicians: Careers, status and power*. New York: Tavistock.

———. 1986. Dismantling Noah's ark. *Sex Roles* 14: 567–80.

———. 1994. *Paradoxes of gender*. New Haven, CT: Yale University Press.

———. 1996. Beyond the binaries: Depolarizing the categories of sex, sexuality, and gender. *Sociological Inquiry* 66: 143–59.

Lorde, A. 1984. *Sister outsider*. Trumansburg, NY: Crossing Press.

Maldonado, L. A. 1995. Symposium: On West and Fenstermaker's "Doing difference." *Gender & Society* 9: 494–6.

Mann, M. 1993. *The sources of social power—Vol. II*. New York: Cambridge University Press.

Marini, M. M. 1988. Sociology of gender. In *The future of sociology*, edited by E. F. Borgatta and K. S. Cook. Newbury Park, CA: Sage.

Martin, M. K. and B. Voorheis. 1975. *Female of the species*. New York: Columbia University Press.

Martin, S. 1980. *Breaking and entering: Policewomen on patrol.* Berkeley: University of California Press.

Martin, S. E. and N. C. Jurik. 1996. *Doing justice, doing gender.* Thousand Oaks, CA: Sage.

Mathews, R. C. O. 1986. The economics of institutions and the sources of growth. *Economic Journal* 96: 903–18.

Maynard, D. W. and D. H. Zimmerman. 1984. Topical talk, ritual, and the social organization of relationships. *Social Psychology Quarterly* 47: 301–16.

Mead, M. 1963. *Sex and temperament.* New York: Dell.

———. 1968. *Male and female.* New York: Dell.

Meissner, M., E. W. Humphreys, S. M. Meis, and J. W. Sheu. 1975. No exit for wives: Sexual division of labor and the cumulation of household demands. *Canadian Review of Sociology and Anthropology* 12: 424–39.

Messerschmidt, J. W. 1997. *Crime as structured action: Gender, race, class, and crime in the making.* Thousand Oaks, CA: Sage.

Mishler, E. G. 1984. *The discourse of medicine: Dialectics of medical interviews.* Norwood, NJ: Ablex.

Mitchell, A. 2001. Letter to the editor. *San Jose Mercury News,* 22 August, p. B7.

Mitchell, J. 1966. Women: The longest revolution. *New Left Review* 40: 11–37.

Mithers, C. L. 1982. My life as a man. *The Village Voice,* 5 October.

Moloney, M. and S. Fenstermaker. 2000. Performance and accomplishment: Reconciling feminist conceptions of gender. Paper presented at the annual meeting of the American Sociological Association, Washington, D.C.

Molotch, H., W. Freudenburg, and K. E. Paulsen. 2000. History repeats itself, but how? City character, urban tradition, and the accomplishment of place. *American Sociological Review* 65: 791–823.

Money, J. 1968. *Sex errors of the body.* Baltimore: Johns Hopkins University Press.

———. 1974. Prenatal hormones and postnatal sexualization in gender identity differentiation. In *Nebraska symposium on motivation,* Vol. 21, edited by J. K. Cole and R. Dienstbier. Lincoln: University of Nebraska Press.

Money, J. and J. G. Brennan. 1968. Sexual dimorphism in the psychology of female transsexuals. *Journal of Nervous and Mental Disease* 147: 487–99.

Money, J. and A. A. Ehrhardt. 1972. *Man and woman/boy and girl.* Baltimore: John Hopkins University Press.

Money, J. and C. Ogunro. 1974. Behavioral sexology: Ten cases of genetic male intersexuality with impaired prenatal and pubertal androgenization. *Archives of Sexual Behavior* 3: 181–206.

Money, J. and P. Tucker. 1975. *Sexual signatures.* Boston: Little, Brown.

Montagu, A., ed. 1975. *Race and IQ.* London: Oxford University Press.

Moraga, C. 1981. La guerra. In *This bridge called my back: Radical Writing by Radical women of color,* edited by Cherrie Moraga and Gloria Anzaldua. New York: Kitchen Table Press.

Moraga, C. and G. Anzaldua, eds. 1981. *This bridge called my back: Writings by radical women of color.* Watertown, MA: Persephone.

Morganthau, T. with S. Miller, G. Beals, and R. Elam. 1995. What color is Black? *Newsweek,* 13 February, pp. 63–5.

Morris, J. 1974. *Conundrum.* New York: Harcourt Brace Jovanovich.

Morrison, T., ed. 1992. *Race-ing justice, engender-ing power: Essays on Anita Hill, Clarence Thomas, and the construction of social reality.* New York: Pantheon.

Murray, B. and B. Duffy. 1998. Jefferson's secret life. *U.S. News & World Report,* 9 November, pp. 59–63.

Murray S. B. 1996. "We all love Charles": Men in child care and the social construction of gender. *Gender & Society* 10: 368–85.

Nieva, V. F. 1985. Work and family linkages. In *Women and work: An annual review,* edited by L. Larwood, A. H. Stromberg, and B. A. Gutek. Beverly Hills, CA: Sage.

Nussbaum, M. 1999. The professor of parody. *The New Republic,* 2 February, pp. 37–45.

Oakley, A. 1974. *The sociology of housework.* New York: Pantheon.

Omi, M. and H. Winant. 1986. *Racial formation in the United States from the 1960s to the 1980s.* New York: Routledge and Kegan Paul.

———. 1994. *Racial formation from the 1960s to the 1980s.* Revised edition. New York: Routledge.

Parade Magazine. 1990. Cosmetic surgery curbed. 26 August, p. 14.

Parker, A. and E. Sedgwick, eds. 1994. *Performance and performativity: Essays from the English institute.* New York: Routledge.

Parsons, T. 1951. *The social system.* New York: Free Press.

Parsons. T. and R. F. Bales. 1955. *Family, socialization, and interaction process.* New York: Free Press.

Patterson, C. J. 1992. Children of lesbian and gay parents. *Child Development* 63: 1025–42.

———. 1994. Children of the baby boom: Behavioral adjustment, self-concepts, and sex role identity. In *Lesbian and gay psychology: Theory, research, and clinical applications*, edited by B. Greene and G. M. Herek. Newbury Park, CA: Sage.

———. 1995. Families of the lesbian baby boom: Parents' division of labor and children's adjustment. *Developmental Psychology* 31: 115–23.

Pettigrew, T. F. 1964. *A profile of the Negro American.* Princeton, NJ: Van Nostrand.

Pike, K. D. 1996. Class-based masculinities: The interdependence of gender, class, and interpersonal power. *Gender & Society* 10: 527–49.

Pleck, J. H. 1977. The work-family role system. *Social Problems* 24: 417–27.

———. 1985. *Working wives/working husbands.* Beverly Hills, CA: Sage.

Powell, T., ed. 1999. *Beyond the binary: Reconstructing cultural identity in a multicultural context.* New Brunswick, NJ: Rutgers University Press.

Powell, W. W. and P. J. DiMaggio. 1991. *The new institutionalism in organizational analysis.* Chicago: University of Chicago Press.

Rafter, N. H. 1992. Claims-making and sociocultural context in the first U.S. eugenics campaign. *Social Problems* 39: 17–34.

Raymond, J. G. 1979. *The transsexual empire.* Boston: Beacon.

Rich, A. 1979. Disloyal to civilization: Feminism, racism, gynephobia. In *On lies, secrets, and silence.* New York: Norton.

———. 1980. Compulsory heterosexuality and lesbian existence. *Signs: Journal of Women in Culture and Society* 5: 631–60.

Richards, R. with J. Ames. 1983. *Second serve: The Renee Richards story.* New York: Stein and Day.

Ricketts, W. and R. Achtenberg. 1990. Adoption and foster parenting for lesbians and gay men: Creating new traditions in family. In *Homosexuality and family relations*, edited by Frederick W. Bozett and Marvin B. Sussman. New York: Harrington Park Press.

Rocha, E. 2001. Emphasis on SAT II tests does not favor minorities (letter to the editor). *San Jose Mercury News*, 22 July, p. B7.

Roediger, D. R. 1991. The wages of whiteness: Race and the making of the American working class. London: Verso.

Roget's International Thesaurus. 1977. 4th ed. Revised by Robert L. Chapman. New York: Thomas Y. Crowell.

Rospenda, K. M., J. A. Richman, and S. J. Nawyn. 1998. Doing power: The confluence of gender, race, and class in contrapower sexual harrassment. *Gender & Society* 12: 40–60.

Rossi, A. 1984. Gender and parenthood. *American Sociological Review* 49: 1–19.

Roth, A. 1995. Who makes the news? Descriptions of television news interviewees' public personae. Paper presented at the annual meeting of the American Sociological Association, Washington, D.C.

Rubin, G. 1975. The traffic in women: Notes on the "political economy" of sex. In *Toward an anthropology of women*, edited by R. Reiter. New York: Monthly Review Press.

Rupp, L. and V. Taylor. forthcoming. *What makes a man a man: Drag queens at the 801 Cabaret.* Chicago: University of Chicago Press.

Sacks, H. 1972. On the analyzability of stories by children. In *Directions in sociolinguistics*, edited by J. J. Gumperz and D. Hymes. New York: Holt, Rinehart, & Winston.

Sacks, K. B. and D. Remy, eds. 1984. *My troubles are going to have troubles with me: Everyday triumphs of women workers.* New Brunswick, NJ: Rutgers University Press.

Sanchez, G. 1993. *Becoming Mexican American: Ethnicity, culture, and identity in Chicano Los Angeles, 1900–1945.* New York: Oxford University Press.

Sandoval, C. 2000. *Methodology of the oppressed.* Minneapolis: University of Minnesota Press.

Schacht, S. P. 1996. Misogyny on and off the "pitch": The gendered world of male rugby players. *Gender & Society* 10: 550–65.

Schafer, R. B. and P. M. Keith. 1981. Equity in marital roles across the family life cycle. *Journal of Marriage and the Family* 43: 359–67.

Schegloff, E. 1991. Reflections on talk and social structure. In *Talk and social structure*, edited by Deirdre Boden and Don H. Zimmerman. Berkeley: University of California Press.

———. 1997. Whose text? Whose context? *Discourse & Society* 8: 165–87.

———. 1999a. Naivete vs. sophistication or discipline vs. self-indulgence: A rejoinder to Billig. *Discourse & Society* 10: 577–82.

———. 1999b. "Schegloff's text" as "Billig's data": A critical reply. *Discourse & Society* 10: 558–72.

Schroedel, J. R. 1985. *Alone in a crowd: Women in the trades tell their stories.* Philadelphia: Temple University Press.

Schutz, A. 1943. The problem of rationality in the social world. *Economics* 10: 130–49.

Schwalbe, M. 2000. Charting futures for sociology: Inequality mechanisms, intersections and global change. *Contemporary Sociology* 29: 275–81.

Schwartz, W. B. and D. N. Mendelson. 1989. Physicians who have lost their malpractice insurance. Their demographic characteristics and the surplus-lines companies that insure them. *Journal of the American Medical Association* 262: 1335–41.

Scott, J. 1999. *Gender and the politics of history.* New York: Columbia University Press.

Scull, A. 1993. *The most solitary afflictions: Madness and society in Britain, 1700–1900.* New Haven, CT: Yale University Press.

Scully, D. 1980. *Men who control women's health: The miseducation of obstetrician-gynecologists.* Boston: Houghton Mifflin.

Sedgwick, E. K. 1993. Queer performativity: Henry James's The Art of the Novel. *GLQ: A Journal of Lesbian and Gay Studies* 1: 1–15.

Segura, D. A. 1992. Chicanas in white-collar jobs: "You have to prove yourself more." *Sociological Perspectives* 35: 163–82.

Sewell, W. H., Jr. 1992. A theory of structure: Duality, agency, and transformation. *American Journal of Sociology* 98: 1–29.

Smith, D. E. 1987. *The everyday world as problematic: A feminist sociology.* Boston: Northeastern University Press.

———. 1994. *Texts, facts, and femininity: Exploring the relations of ruling.* New York: Routledge.

Spelman, E. V. 1988. *Inessential woman: Problems of exclusion in feminist thought.* Boston: Beacon.

Spivak, G. C. 1988. *In other worlds: Essays in cultural politics.* New York: Routledge Kegan Paul.

Stacey, J. 1983. *Patriarchy and socialist revolution in China.* Berkeley: University of California Press.

Stacey, J. and B. Thorne. 1985. The missing feminist revolution in sociology. *Social Problems* 32: 301–16.

Stack, C. B. 1974. *All our kin: Strategies for survival in a Black community.* New York: Harper & Row.

Stephans, N. 1982. *The idea of race in science.* Hamden, CT: Archon.

Stromberg, A. H. and S. Harkess. 1988. *Women working: Theories and facts in perspective.* Mountain View, CA: Mayfield.

Symposium on West and Fenstermaker's "Doing difference." 1995. Edited by Margaret Andersen. *Gender & Society* 9: 491–513.

Tallichet, S. E. 1995. Gendered relations in the mines and the division of labor underground. *Gender & Society* 9: 697–711.

Takagi, D. 1995. Symposium: On West and Fenstermaker's "Doing Difference." *Gender & Society* 9: 496–497.

Taylor, C. 1992. *The ethics of authenticity.* Cambridge, MA: Harvard University Press.

Taylor, V. and N. Whittier. 1992. Collective identities and social movement communities: Lesbian feminist motivation. In *Frontiers in social movements theory*, edited by Aldon D. Morris and Carol McClung Mueller. New Haven, CT: Yale University Press.

Thorne, B. 1973. Professional education in medicine. In *Education for the professions of medicine, law, theology and social welfare (a report for the Carnegie Commission on higher education)*, by Everett C. Hughes, Barrie Thorne, Agostino M. DeBaggis, Arnold Gurin, and David Williams. New York: McGraw-Hill.

———. 1976. Is our field misnamed? Towards a rethinking of the concept "sex roles." American Sociological Association *Newsletter* 4: 4–5.

———. 1980. *Gender . . . How is it best conceptualized?* Unpublished manuscript. Michigan State University Department of Sociology, East Lansing.

———. 1986. Girls and boys together . . . but mostly apart: Gender arrangements in elementary schools. In *Relationships and development*, edited by W. Hartup and Z. Rubin. Hillsdale, NJ: Lawrence Erlbaum.

———. 1993. *Gender play: Girls and boys in school.* New Brunswick, NJ: Rutgers University Press.

———. 1995. Symposium: On West and Fenstermaker's "Doing Difference." *Gender & Society* 9: 497–9.

Thorne, B. and Z. Luria. 1986. Sexuality and gender in children's daily worlds. *Social Problems* 33: 176–90.

Tresemer, D. 1975. Assumptions made about gender roles. In *Another voice: Feminist perspectives on social life and social science*, edited by M. Millman and R. M. Kanter. New York: Anchor/Doubleday.

Uchida, A. 1997. Doing gender and building culture: Toward a model of women's intercultural communication. *Howard Journal of Communications* 8: 41–76.

U.S. National Center for Health Statistics. 1987. *Detailed diagnoses and surgical procedures.* Washington, D.C.: U.S. Government Printing Office.

Walshok, M. L. 1981. *Blue-collar women: Pioneers on the male frontier.* Garden City, NY: Anchor.

Walster E. G., W. Walster, and S. Traupman. 1978. *Equity theory and research.* Boston: Allyn and Bacon.

Weber, L. 1995. Symposium: On West and Fenstermaker's "Doing Difference." *Gender & Society* 9: 499–503.

Webster M., Jr., and J. E. Driskell, Jr. 1985. *Status, rewards, and influence: How expectations organize behavior.* San Francisco: Jossey-Bass.

West, C. 1982. Why can't a woman be more like a man. *Work and Occupations* 9: 5–29.

———. 1984. When the doctor is a "lady": Power, status, and gender in physician-patient encounters. *Symbolic Interaction* 7: 87–106.

West, C. and S. Fenstermaker. 1993. Power, inequality, and the accomplishment of gender: An ethnomethdological view. In *Theory on Gender/Feminism on Theory*, edited by Paula England. New York: Aldine de Gruyter.

———. 1995a. Doing difference. *Gender & Society* 9: 8–37.

———. 1995b. (Re)Doing difference: A reply. *Gender & Society* 9: 506–13.

———. 1996. Accountability in action: The accomplishment of gender, race, and class in a meeting of the University of California Board of Regents. Paper presented at the annual meeting of the American Sociological Association, New York.

West, C. and A. Garcia. 1988. Conversational shift work: A study of topical transitions between women and men. *Social Problems* 35: 551–75.

West, C. and B. Iritani. 1985. Gender politics in mate selection: The male-older norm. Paper presented at the annual meeting of the American Sociological Association, Washington, D.C.

West, C. and D. H. Zimmerman. 1983. Small insults: A study of interruptions in conversations between unacquainted persons. In *Language, gender and society*, edited by B. Thorne, C. Kramarae, and N. Henley. Rowley, MA: Newbury House.

———. 1984. *Doing gender.* University of California Santa Cruz, unpublished manuscript.

———. 1987. Doing gender. *Gender & Society* 1:125–51.

Weston, K. 1991. *Families we choose: Lesbian, gays, kinship.* New York: Columbia University Press.

Wetherell, M. 1998. Positioning and interpretive repertoires: Conversation analysis and post-structuralism in dialogue. *Discourse & Society* 9: 387–412.

Wieder, D. L. 1974. *Language and social reality: The case of telling the convict code*. The Hague: Mouton.

Williams, P. 1991. *The alchemy of race and rights*. Cambridge, MA: Harvard University Press.

Williams, W. L. 1986. *The Spirit and the flesh: Sexual diversity in American Indian culture*. Boston: Beacon.

Wilson, E. W. 1987 Gender and identity. In *Adorned in dreams: Fashion and modernity*. Berkeley: University of California Press.

Wilson, T. P. 1970. Conceptions of interaction and forms of sociological explanation. *American Sociological Review* 35: 697–710.

Winant, H. 1995. Symposium: On West and Fenstermaker's "Doing difference." *Gender & Society* 9: 503–6.

Yoder, J. D. 1984. An academic woman as a token: A case study. *Journal of Social Issues* 41: 61–72.

Yoder, J. D. and P. Aniakudo. 1997. "Outsiders" within the firehouse: Subordination and difference in the social interactions of African American women firefighters. *Gender & Society* 3: 324–41.

Young, I. M. 1990. Impartiality and the civic public. In *Throwing like a girl and other essays in feminist philosophy*. Bloomington: Indiana University Press.

Young, M. and P. Wilmott. 1973. *The symmetrical family*. London: Routledge Kegan Paul.

Young, R. J. C. 1995. *Colonial desire: Hybridity in theory, culture, and race*. New York: Routledge.

Zavella, P. 1987. *Women's work and Chicano families: Cannery workers of the Santa Clara Valley*. Ithaca, NY: Cornell University Press.

Zimmer, L. 1986. *Women guarding men*. Chicago: University of Chicago Press.

———. 1988. Tokenism and women in the workplace: The limits of gender-neutral theory. *Social Problems* 35: 64–77.

Zimmerman, D. H. 1978. Ethnomethodology. *American Sociologist* 13: 6–15.

Zimmerman, D. H. and D. L. Wieder. 1970. Ethnomethodology and the problem of order: Comment on Denzin. In *Understanding everyday life*, edited by J. Denzin. Chicago: Aldine.

Zinn, M. B. 1980. Employment and education of Mexican-American women: The interplay of modernity and ethnicity in eight families. *Harvard Educational Review* 50: 47–62.

———. 1990. Family, feminism and race in America. *Gender & Society* 4: 68–82.

Zinn, M. B., L. W. Cannon, E. Higginbotham, and B. T. Dill. 1986. The costs of exclusionary practices in women's studies. *Signs: Journal of Women in Culture and Society* 11: 290–303.

Zola, I. K. 1972. Medicine as an institution of social control. *Sociological Review* 2: 487–504.

Zucker, L. G. 1983. The role of institutionalization in cultural persistence. In *Research in organizational behavior*, edited by S. B. Bacharach. Greenwich, CT: JAI Press.

———. 1986. Production of trust: Institutional sources of economic structure, 1840–1920. In *Research in organizational behavior*, edited by Barry M. Staw and L. L. Cummings. Greenwich, CT: JAI Press.

———. 1991. The role of institutionalization in cultural persistence. In *The new institutionalism in organizational analysis*, edited by Walter W. Powell and Paul J. DiMaggio. Chicago: University of Chicago Press.

PERMISSIONS

"Doing Gender" is reprinted by permission of Sage Publications, Inc. from West, C. & Zimmerman, D., *Gender & Society* (1, 2), pp. 125–151.

"Gender Inequality: New Conceptual Terrain" is reprinted by permission of Sage Publications, Inc. from *Gender, Family, and Economy: The Triple Overlap*, pp. 289–307.

"Power, Inequality and the Accomplishment of Gender: An Ethnomethodological View" is republished with permission from Paula England, Editor, from *Theory on Gender: Feminism on Theory*, Copyright © 1993 Walter de Gruyter, Inc., New York.

"Doing Difference" is reprinted by permission of Sage Publications, Inc. from West, C. & Fenstermaker, S., *Gender & Society* (9, 1), pp. 8–37.

"*Gender & Society* Symposium on 'Doing Difference'" is reprinted by permission of Sage Publications, Inc. from *Gender & Society* (9, 1), pp. 419–506.

"Reply—(Re)Doing Difference" is reprinted by permission of Sage Publications, Inc. from West, C. & Fenstermaker, S., *Gender & Society* (9, 1), pp. 506–513.

"'Conclusion' to *The Gender Factory* is reprinted by permission of Kluwer Academic/Plenum Publishers from Fenstermaker, S. 1985. "Conclusions: Work and Gender", *The Gender Factory*, New York: Plenum, pp. 185–211.

"Accounting for Cosmetic Surgery: The Accomplishment of Gender" is reprinted by permission of The University of California Press from West, C. & Dull, D. *Social Problems*, (38, 1), Copyright © 1991 by The Society for the Study of Social Problems

"'Doing Gender' Revisited" is reprinted by permission of Westdeutscher Verlag, in Wiesbaden, from Fenstermaker, Sarah, and West, Candace. 2001. "'Doing Difference' Revisited. Probleme, Aussichten und der Dialog in der Geschlechterforschung." [in English: Problems, Prospects and the Dialogue in Feminist Theory] Geschlechtersoziologie, Kölner Zeitschrift für Soziologie und Sozialpsychologie 41:236–249.

INDEX

Abrams, P., 210
accomplishment
    of class, race, and gender, xvi,
        xvii, 49–51, 66, 68–69, 74–75,
        75–78, 79n., 89, 92, 96, 98, 100,
        142–143, 144, 147, 153, 163,
        164–165, 191, 195, 198, 200,
        201, 203, 206, 207, 208, 209,
        210, 211, 212, 213, 214–215,
        216n., 217, 218, 219, 220.
    See also class,accomplishmment
        of; gender, accomplishment of;
        race, accomplishment of
accountability, xvi, 12–13, 20, 26,
        29–32, 37, 38, 38–39n., 41, 43,
        47–49, 53, 54, 65, 67, 68–69,
        79n., 96–97, 98, 99, 111,
        134–137, 138, 139n., 141–142,
        147, 153, 164–165, 191, 193,
        195, 196, 200, 206, 212, 213,
        214, 220
Achtenberg, R., 185n.
Acker, J., 62–63, 215n.
Adams, J., 27
adoption
    by lesbian couples, 174–185

independent adoption, 173
statutes in California, 172–174,
    185n.
stepparent adoption, 173
summary adoption, 172–173
affirmative action
    policies at the University of
        California, 141, 142, 145, 148,
        153, 164, 165n., 212
agency
    and accountability, 199, 203, 210
    of discourse, 191, 293–194, 195,
        196, 197, 198
Agnes
    Garfinkel's case study of, 8–12,
        17, 204n.
Aguirre, A., 143
Aisenberg, N., 35
Alcoff, L., 189
Alford, R. R., 171, 193
Almquist, E., 59
Alvarado, D., 99
American Society of Plastic and
    Reconstructive Surgeons, 120
Amsden, A. H., 25
Andersen, M. L., 59, 60, 70, 91